Food & Everyday Life in the Postsocialist World

Food & Everyday Life in the Postsocialist World

EDITED BY

MELISSA L. CALDWELL

FOREWORD BY

MARION NESTLE

AFTERWORD BY

ELIZABETH CULLEN DUNN

INDIANA UNIVERSITY PRESS

Bloomington & Indianapolis

This book is a publication of

Indiana University Press
601 North Morton Street
Bloomington, IN 47404-3797 USA

www.iupress.indiana.edu

Telephone orders   800-842-6796
Fax orders   812-855-7931
Orders by e-mail   iuporder@indiana.edu

♾ The paper used in this publication
meets the minimum requirements of
the American National Standard for Information Sciences—Permanence of Paper
for Printed Library Materials, ANSI
Z39.48-1992.

Manufactured in the United States of
America

Library of Congress Cataloging-in-
Publication Data

Food and everyday life in the postsocialist
world / edited by Melissa L. Caldwell,
foreword by Marion Nestle, afterword by
Elizabeth Cullen Dunn.
p. cm.
Includes bibliographical references and
index.
ISBN 978-0-253-35384-9 (cloth : alk. paper)
— ISBN 978-0-253-22139-1 (pbk. : alk.
paper)
1. Food habits—Europe, Eastern. 2. Food
habits—Russia (Federation) 3. Food
supply—Europe, Eastern. 4. Food supply—
Russia (Federation) 5. Food consumption
—Europe, Eastern. 6. Food consumption—
Russia (Federation) 7. Post-communism—
Europe, Eastern. 8. Post-communism—
Russia (Federation) I. Caldwell,
Melissa L., date II. Dunn, Elizabeth C.,
date III. Nestle, Marion.
GT2853.E85F66 2009
394.1'20947—dc22
2009017098

1 2 3 4 5 14 13 12 11 10 09

For our informants

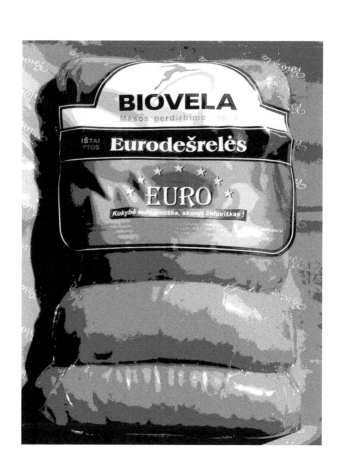

CONTENTS

FOREWORD

When Melissa Caldwell invited me to write the foreword to *Food and Everyday Life in the Postsocialist World,* I could not have been more pleased. I knew this would be the perfect opportunity to learn about the daily life of people living through the post-Soviet transition in Eastern Europe. From reading newspapers, I was aware of the political and economic changes under way in that part of the world, and in recent years I had seen some of the results of those changes on brief visits to Berlin and Budapest.

But most of my personal observations of life in Eastern Europe took place so long ago that they preceded the construction of the Berlin Wall. As I recall those pre-Wall Eastern European travels, the countries were still recovering from the destruction of World War II. West Berlin was undergoing rapid reconstruction, but East Berlin was not. I knew this because one could easily go back and forth between West and East Berlin by subway without presenting identification papers or travel documents. This was a huge relief, as American passports of that era were not valid for travel in Soviet-controlled areas.

The ease of travel between East and West made the differences between the sectors especially stark. Food—or the lack thereof—was the most obvious difference. Finding food in Eastern Europe was a problem. Even in the larger cities of the former Soviet Union, Czechoslovakia, and East Germany, it was hard to find decent food. The food one stumbled upon was barely edible, and I lost a good deal of weight on that trip. But West Berlin was an exception. In that isolated island in the midst of East

Germany, food was gloriously abundant. Airlifted in, the food was familiar, clean, and varied—just like at home—and also subsidized.

Even at that time, long before the field of Food Studies had evolved into a lively academic discipline, food was obviously a potent index of the larger political, economic, and social environment. The contrast between the availability and quality of the food in the East and West—and the reasons for that contrast—explained much about the Cold War era and its effects on the daily lives of ordinary citizens. To understand how the food culture and food system worked in the East and West was to understand immediately how those societies functioned in many other important ways.

I was eager to read the essays in this book, confident that I would learn what is really going on in Eastern Europe and how its societies have changed in the years since my first and later visits. Scholarly examinations of food and food practices would surely illuminate current events in post-Soviet societies and bring those events to life. And that is exactly what these essays do.

That accomplishment, of course, is precisely the point of Food Studies. As someone deeply involved in this field, I am often asked to explain what Food Studies is and does. As my colleagues and I like to explain, Food Studies uses food as a central organizing principle to illustrate, analyze, and explain the most important and interesting issues facing modern societies. In this sense food becomes the part that stands for the whole— what I think of as the perfect example of synecdoche (one of those wonderful words one rarely gets to use) in action.

Examine, as this book does, how women sell raw milk in Lithuania, and you will gain enormous insight into the role of women in a rapidly changing postsocialist economy. Observe how Hungarian paprika, an iconic food in that country, is becoming "contaminated" with peppers from Brazil, and you will immediately grasp the complications of globalization. Study how consumers in modern Lithuania react to sausages with the brand names "Soviet" or "Euro," and the pitfalls of that country's headlong plunge into a free-market economy become clear. Describe women's use of vodka in rural Siberia, and you will know why alcohol is such a problem in these areas and also much about women's roles in post-Soviet Russia.

But food is more than a symbol. When you study food, you get to the heart (the stomach, really) of the Europeanization of former Soviet-bloc countries. You understand the events of that transition at a level well beyond abstract concepts of globalization and free-market economics. Food makes abstractions real. Food makes the political personal. Simply because everyone eats, food makes issues accessible, vivid, and tangible. Food makes it easier to relate to the daily experiences of people in distant countries as their societies transform around them. To what extent are the transformations successful? Discover what is happening with food and you will have your answer.

The case studies in this volume provide especially illustrative examples of food as synecdoche. The contributors are all academic researchers classically trained in field anthropology or sociology. They use the classic tools of ethnography—total immersion in a society, participation in daily activities, careful observations, pointed interviews, data collection, and analysis and synthesis—to discover how food practices are responding to the postsocialist transition.

The authors locate their work in Bulgaria, Hungary, Lithuania, and present-day Russia, both urban (Moscow) and rural (Siberia). In observing the production and consumption of raw milk, paprika, vodka, canned food, and sausages, and the functioning of cooking schools and coffee houses, they deal with personal questions of gender and identity, and with political questions of societal transformation. In examining the ways in which Europeanization has affected these countries' food cultures and food systems, the essays deal with issues of food quality, food safety, the transition from small to large agriculture, the standardization of food products, pressures to produce cheap goods, the undermining of local food production, and the erosion and disappearance of national food identity.

Most striking about these essays is how well they reveal the complexity of these particular social upheavals. Food under the repressive Soviet regimes may have been scarce, but at least some survivors of the earlier regime considered it delicious, natural, and healthful. In contrast, although the new Europeanized food may be abundant, many find it artificial and tasteless. As food systems become more globalized, and an increasing number of developing countries undergo food transitions, the issues discussed in this book become even more widely applicable. The

Europeanization of post-Soviet states especially fascinates because the changes are so profound and are occurring so quickly that we can hardly keep up with them.

Today much of the world is experiencing political, economic, and social transitions. I can think of no better or more enjoyable way to understand these changes than by studying how present-day societies provide food to their citizens and how these citizens grow, sell, cook, and eat this food. This book does all that, and more.

Marion Nestle
New York
October 2008

ACKNOWLEDGMENTS

This volume has been a long time in the making, and many people helped in seeing it come to fruition. The idea for the book first emerged in the 1990s during conversations with Woody Watson, Maris Gillette, and Fuji Lozada, as we discussed why food seemed to be such a popular topic for postsocialist ethnography, not just in formerly Soviet countries but also in China.

During the late 1990s and early 2000s, a small group of anthropologists and sociologists working in the former Soviet Union and Eastern Europe turned their attention to serious consideration of food topics. Julianna Acheson, Elizabeth Dunn, Zsuzsa Gille, Neringa Klumbytė, Diana Mincyte, and Yuson Jung were all members of this group. Not only have we shared many conversations about food topics, but we have also read, commented on, and learned from one another's work on numerous occasions. We were joined later by Stas Shectman and Katherine Metzo. Thus this collection represents the culmination of many years of conversations as we have worked through ideas, challenged one another's hypotheses, and sharpened one another's conclusions. In the end, the book is very much a collaborative venture, and I am indebted to my wonderfully generous and brilliant colleague-interlocutors both for their hard work and for the richness of their research.

Several other individuals deserve special recognition for their assistance and encouragement along the way. Becky Tolen and Janet Rabinowitch at Indiana University Press have supported this project since its inception. Becky has offered just the right encouragement and just the right critical suggestions at all the necessary moments, and this volume is definitely stronger because of her advice. Laura MacLeod has worked behind the scenes to pull various details together. Working with them has been a pleasure. I also thank Rita Bernhard for her careful editing. For allowing us to reproduce their photographs, I am grateful to A. G. Baker (p. xvi) and Fuji Lozada (cover).

Finally, I thank Andy Baker for his continued good humor with yet another food project in our house.

Food & Everyday Life
in the Postsocialist
World

Introduction

Food and Everyday Life after State Socialism

MELISSA L. CALDWELL

Across the Soviet Union and Eastern Europe during the socialist period, food emerged as a practical symbol and medium for articulating both the successes and failures of socialist ideals of progress, equality, and modernity. On the one hand, social engineers concerned with enhancing the productivity of socialist workers introduced measures such as communal kitchens and public canteens that liberated citizens, especially women, from the drudgery of shopping, cooking, and cleaning up, and supported futurist food sciences and technologies that promised to provide healthy, tasty, and affordable foods. On the other hand, recurring food shortages caused by inefficiencies in socialist production and distribution systems threatened both the well-being of socialist citizens and the utopian visions of progress and egalitarianism. Bread lines and other queues for scarce goods became internationally recognizable symbols for the shortcomings of state socialist systems.

By the late 1980s the climate of political change that swept across the socialist world was symbolically realized with the arrival of McDonald's "behind the Iron Curtain." McDonald's first appeared in Eastern Europe with the 1988 opening of a restaurant in Yugoslavia, followed less than two years later by the arrival of the Golden Arches in the Soviet Union in January 1990. Not quite two decades later, the effects of these arrivals are evident in the spread of foreign food corporations across the postsocialist world and their integration in local communities.[1] The diverse food products, food technologies, and food cultures spawned by these interactions with global capitalism include new kitchen architectures (Fehérváry 2002) and appliances (Shevchenko 2002); new types of foods and food experiences, ranging from sushi and cappuccino to Western-style grocery stores and discount cards; and new political, religious, and social orientations to both foreign and domestic foods (Caldwell 2002; Harper 1999; Lankauskas 2002; Patico 2002). Professional and popular interests in food are represented in an ever expanding variety of food programs and channels on television, cooking magazines, cooking schools, and cooking implements. Glitzy food shops selling expensive imported foods occupy prime real estate along central avenues in big cities and small towns alike.

Perhaps the example that best captures the profoundness, and frequent ironies, of these changes is a restaurant that appeared in the late 1990s in downtown Moscow. Located in a historic shopping district next to the Lubyanka, the infamous building that was the headquarters of the KGB (now renamed the FSB, or Federal Security Bureau), this restaurant belonged to the latest craze in Moscow's forever changing food fashions: the sports bar. The sidewalk entrance leading downstairs to the sports bar was covered by a red and yellow awning advertising cheap beer, big-screen televisions, and continuous sports coverage. Flanking the awning and staircase was the bar's name and signature decoration: a set of books, with the title written in large letters on the spine: Karl Marx's classic text *Das Kapital.*

As these examples show, food offers perhaps the most fascinating and compelling lens for tracking and measuring the diverse, unexpected, curious, and often paradoxical trajectories and consequences of the dramatic transformations that have spread across the former Soviet Union and Eastern Europe over the past century. Throughout the twentieth century and continuing into the twenty-first, food has been central to both socialist and postsocialist reformist projects as social engineers have used food to promote new societies based on modernity, progress, and culturedness (see, especially, Glants and Toomre 1997). The explicit attention that social engineers—and their analysts—have consistently paid to the types of foods that citizens eat, the places where food is produced and consumed, the social relationships that can be fostered through food practices, and even the cultural values that can be inculcated through food and eating reveals the tremendous impact that food has had on practically every aspect of daily life in the presocialist, socialist, and now postsocialist countries of this region. Food is a particularly conducive channel for enacting and understanding social change, both because its materiality makes it a concrete marker of transformation and because the sensual qualities of food evoke visceral responses that transform external, anonymous social processes into intimate, immediate, and personal experiences. Not only does food make the political personal, but it also makes the world accessible to ordinary people in ways that other things do not.

This volume takes food seriously as a starting point for exploring the political, economic, social, and cultural transformations that have taken place across the formerly socialist worlds of the former Soviet Union and Eastern Europe. The authors in this volume grapple with the legacies of state socialism and the consequences of global capitalism as each shapes the lives of the residents of this region. Through careful, critical studies based on fine-grained, ethnographically informed research, the authors probe fundamental and enduring questions: In what ways have the social worlds of socialist and now postsocialist systems changed over the past two decades? What changed, what did not, and how do formerly socialist consumers make sense of these processes? How do people living in postsocialist societies understand these transformations and the world around them? And, finally, what do these shifting food habits reveal about the nature of postsocialist social systems and the expectations of those inhabiting them and, perhaps more important, about the significance of postsocialist societies for the field of food studies itself?

A key objective of this volume is to unsettle the idea, often presented in both scholarly and popular accounts of this region, that a "postsocialist" cultural form is somehow distinctive and definitive. The social world of state socialism in Eastern Europe and the former Soviet Union has too often been presented as a monolithic, singular cultural phenomenon so that only the similarities across the region are acknowledged. This is partly a consequence of the homogenizing and standardizing practices among state socialist leaders, most notably Soviet leaders, where "culture" was invented at the center (i.e., Moscow) and distributed outward. Further, the particular institutions and structures of state socialism—economic, political, and religious, among others—cultivated a unique *habitus* that produced similar cultural forms in different contexts. At the same time a persistent tendency in state socialism discourses is to treat the entire Eurasian mass as a socially and culturally homogeneous entity. Soviet experiences—and, more specifically, Russian or Moscow experiences—are typically represented as emblematic of life throughout the Soviet Union and Eastern Europe. This penchant for homogenizing and, more explicitly, substituting urban Russian cultural forms for the totality of state socialism, obscures the tremendous diversity of social life across the region, thereby preventing careful attention to similarities *and* differences in the ways in which inhabitants have experienced and managed state socialist systems. For their part, consumers in this region of the world have embraced these changes in different ways—or, in some cases, not at all. It is therefore risky, and intellectually shortsighted, to presume a universal postsocialist experience. This warning is especially relevant given that European expansion has offered countries like Bulgaria, the Czech Republic, Hungary, Lithuania, Poland, and Slovakia, among others, opportunities to shift away from state socialism and toward an integrated "European" social world that excludes Russia and other former Soviet republics.

As the authors of these essays document so convincingly, the reality is that political, economic, social, and cultural changes have unfolded in myriad ways across the postsocialist landscape. Taken together, these essays present striking differences as well as surprising similarities. Thus, the explicit and implicit comparisons invited by these articles challenge us to rethink the nature of "state socialism" and its successor systems, and to consider the many conflicting, overlapping, and distinctively unique trajectories of postsocialist processes as they take shape in different places at different times.

Building Socialism by Feeding the Nation

Tracing a coherent but sufficiently expansive narrative about "socialist" experiences with food is challenging, not least because the various countries belonging to the "state socialist" world joined at different times and for different reasons, an important detail often minimized in accounts of state socialism. Although the official "birth" of the state socialist world can perhaps be traced to the formal creation of the Union of Soviet Socialist Republics (USSR) in 1921, the socialist world on the European continent emerged only gradually over the twentieth century, primarily in the post–World War II period as East European countries were absorbed into the Soviet sphere of influence during postwar reconstruction, followed by the Soviet Union's empire-building efforts. Thus any accounting of the experience and impact of state socialism on daily life in this region is necessarily a partial one.

Putting aside this admission of partiality, one may still identify events and trends that have had significant consequences for the experience of state socialism more broadly. Both because of the importance of the Soviet Union as the dominant political and economic power at the center of the state socialist world, and because the institutional structures of state socialist food systems emerged with the very birth of the Soviet Union, it makes sense, perhaps, to start our narrative there.

Among the key changes affecting the creation of socialist food systems was the reorganization of Russia's food supply infrastructure immediately following the Russian Revolution in 1917. Accounts of the revolutionary activities of the early twentieth century point to the role of food in the political movements that subsequently led to the downfall of the aristocracy and the creation of the Soviet Union. Not only were citizens' political sentiments incited by severe food shortages, but political mobilization took place in the bread lines themselves (Davydoff 1971; Kitanina 1985; Lih 1990; McAuley 1991), foreshadowing the continuing role that food and food distribution sites would play in an emerging socialist form of political engagement.

Early Soviet efforts were directed at improving the efficiency and safety of the domestic food supply. In 1928 the Soviet Union's First Five-Year Plan, the first of many such blueprints for mapping out the complete reorganization of the country, expressly targeted food practices as an essential component in this process (Rothstein and Rothstein 1997:181). In keeping with the Soviet leaders' trust in the objectivity and rationality of science and technology, reformers in the food sector also appropriated philosophies and methods of scientific rationality. Soviet scientists, nutritionists, chefs, and food-services employees collaborated in the invention and implementation of a "scientific" food regime that revolutionized food production, distribution, and preparation; nutritional standards; culinary principles; and even the very arenas in which food was produced, prepared, and consumed (Borrero 1997; Rothstein and Rothstein 1997). Food "radicals" and other proponents of healthful food treated cuisine as a scientific discipline that drew from chemistry, physics, physiology, and other physical sciences (Rothstein and Rothstein 1997:184).

At the same time that Soviet leaders focused on reorganizing the physical infrastructure of this new social order, they also searched for practical ways to introduce and cultivate ideologies of communalism and egalitarianism among their citizens. One such method entailed radically reorienting the relationships of individual citizens to food and the relationships between people by moving food practices from the private sphere into the public sphere. Between the 1920s and 1940s private kitchens were replaced by workplace canteens and public dining facilities. In more extreme cases, reformers advocated eliminating kitchens and other facilities for food preparation from apartments, thereby forcing citizens out of their apartments and into public settings for eating (Borrero 1997, 2002; Buchli 1999; Rothstein and Rothstein 1997), where meal preparation and consumption were managed—and monitored—by professional staff. These changes were intended to accomplish several goals. First, the transformation of meal production and distribution activities into a public-service activity was meant to free workers from the time and inconvenience of preparing their own meals, thus increasing their efficiency for the state's labor needs. Second, moving consumption activities into a central location encouraged communalism and fostered camaraderie among workers. Third, these changes were promoted as a way to enhance women's liberation and gender egalitarianism: removing kitchens from private homes would free women from the drudgery of cooking and feeding their families. Nevertheless, Soviet citizens' accounts reveal that these utopian ideologies of food communalism were rarely matched by the realities of the food and service they received in public cafeterias (Glants and Toomre 1997a:xxi).

Soviet officials also endorsed new moralities, especially concerning ethics of personal responsibility, through explicit attention to the foods that people ingested in their bodies. Proponents of the Soviet temperance movement, which emerged and receded at different times during the twentieth century, sought to impose and enforce moral standards of responsibility and commitment. The primary targets of these campaigns, not surprisingly, were workers who were seen as shirking their responsibility by turning their attention and energies away from the state because of alcohol addiction.[2] Secondary targets were consumers who were diverting and wasting valuable resources—sugar, grains, and other ingredients—to satisfy personal needs rather than directing them to the greater good of society.

Over the course of the twentieth century, as the sphere of state socialism expanded to include the countries of Eastern Europe, food systems and food practices of these countries became increasingly entangled with the projects and policies of the Soviet Union. As part of its project of building a cohesive empire, the Soviet Union pursued initiatives that incorporated and celebrated the multicultural diversity of its citizens and its satellite states. Individual foods and culinary styles were potent symbols in the politically savvy hands of socialist leaders who wanted to facilitate the ideals of international communism and regional interdependence. In many respects, the wealth of the Soviet bloc could be measured in the quantities of foods produced and the culinary diversity of these regions. Ukraine, blessed with rich soil and a climate well suited for growing grains, was heralded as the "Breadbasket of the USSR," and Central Asia emerged as a prime source of fresh fruits and vegetables for the entire Soviet Union as well as Eastern Europe, Asia, and beyond. Bulgaria, Moldova, and Georgia were key wine-producing regions, and the Baltic republics were major suppliers of dairy products.

In perhaps one of the most compelling examples of this celebration of culinary diversity, food was prominently displayed in the exhibits at the All-Union Exhibition Center in Moscow (VDNKh), a permanent socialist version of a World's Fair celebrating the cultural, technological, and industrial accomplishments of the socialist world, with the USSR at the center. The USSR's fifteen republics were each represented by individual pavilions with exhibits highlighting the republics' unique traditions and contributions, including examples of regional culinary traditions with presentations on food production, preparation, and consumption (Glants and Toomre 1997a:xxiii).

This emphasis on regional culinary diversity also had a significant secondary importance. At the same time that the division of labor in food production for the socialist world provided a means to celebrate regional food specializations, it was also an effective management strategy for bringing each of the Soviet republics, as well as their satellite allies, into mutually interdependent relationships. As part of the larger process of political consolidation, the constituent members of the Soviet bloc became dependent on one another for their basic survival needs. This mutual interdependence facilitated not only the inward-looking focus of the Soviet Union and its satellite states but also strategic alliances with other socialist countries outside Eurasia. Allegiances among the Soviet Union, Eastern Europe, China, Cuba, and socialist African countries were fostered through the circulation of consumer goods—food, in particular.

Food also emerged as a key symbol in the mythologies of socialist states and socialist citizens. Farming implements, livestock, fertile grain fields, peasant farming traditions, and other agricultural themes became key symbols in socialist mythology. The successes of the socialist project were nowhere as visible as in the imagery of agricultural workers captured in paintings, frescoes, statuary, and even stamps throughout the Soviet bloc.[3] Even the nature of socialist time was embedded in agrarian themes, as citizens tracked the passage of time according to growing seasons for both domestic and wild foodstuffs such as potatoes, berries, and mushrooms (Paxson 2005; Pesmen 2000; Verdery 1996).

More generally, food emerged as a commemorative medium for documenting and preserving the victories and accomplishments of socialist citizens. In the Soviet Union, citizens were recognized for their contributions to the creation of the Soviet state with medals and honorary orders. One of the highest and most prestigious honor designations was that of "Hero of the Soviet Union," which was awarded to citizens who had served their country in the most exemplary ways possible: military personnel, politicians, socialist activists, and artists. Chefs and restaurant managers who had rendered exemplary service were also honored and awarded medals. The contributions of Soviet "Hero Chefs" were further recognized in a detailed exhibit in the Museum of Public Catering (*Muzei Obshchestvennogo Pitaniia*) in Moscow.

Even as food enjoyed public recognition as positive, celebratory, and patriotic symbols of state socialism, it also acquired salience as the ultimate emblem of the failures of that same system. More precisely, food practices often became the medium by which these failures were enacted across the Soviet bloc.[4] During the first decades of its existence the Soviet state's project of geographic, political, and economic consolidation included the forced collectivization of farms and other industries, an agenda that played out later across the socialist landscape. The intention behind these measures was to maximize the efficiency of the agricultural sector and harness its resources in ways that would distribute food resources more equitably among the population. However, the forcible seizure of private farm property and the removal of peasant farmers from their lands, followed by their replacement by state employees, resulted in the massive destruction of crops and livestock and the sabotage of farm equipment. These losses were compounded by a series of poor harvests. In the 1930s these events contributed to widespread food shortages across the Soviet Union but were particularly acute in Ukraine, the prime agricultural region of the USSR, where thousands of people died of starvation and by violence perpetrated by agents of agricultural reform. These incidents are frequently interpreted in Ukrainian national memory as the deliberate genocide against Ukraine by the Soviet Union (Dolot 1985).

After World War II perhaps the most common images of socialist failure across the socialist world (including Asia and Cuba) that were most recognizable to outside observers were empty store shelves and food-provision strategies such as queues, hoarding, and small garden plots. Because the state socialist economic system was skewed toward production and not consumption (Verdery 1996), for maximum efficiency factories were encouraged to produce large quantities of certain types of goods rather than a wide variety of products, resulting in little diversity. At the same time shortages of raw materials affected the quantity of goods produced, and inefficiencies in the distribution network prevented the goods that were produced from ever reaching their destination. Socialist production plans, based on political whim instead of ecological realities, further disrupted natural harvest cycles. Consequently the twentieth century was marked by periodic famines and food shortages throughout the socialist world.

These persistent shortages generated food practices relatively unique to state socialist societies. Queuing emerged as a necessary cultural practice among consumers who were forced to wait in line to acquire limited provisions.[5] While these queuing practices contributed to congenial social relationships and a cooperative attitude toward shopping among consumers with the common interest of filling their pantries, they also facilitated competitiveness among consumers literally battling to purchase scarce resources.[6] Through hoarding, socialist citizens accumulated stockpiles of staples such as flour, oil, sugar, and even bread, enabling them to "invest" their savings in these staples. During extreme shortages, socialist states introduced ration coupons to regulate the distribution of scarce foods and other goods.

The nature of shopping itself was also shaped by this need to manage the equitable distribution of scarce goods. Stores in some parts of the socialist world were organized around a three-queue system: customers first stood in line to inspect the available goods and decide what to buy, then moved to a second line to pay and receive receipts, and finally, stood in a third line to exchange their receipts for their purchases. Not only were foods and other items located behind glass counters, out of customers' reach, but classes of food items such as dairy, meat, canned goods, beverages, and so on, were also segregated in different sections. Thus customers could not interact directly with the products and had to rely on salesclerks for their purchases. Salesclerks, moreover, wielded considerable power, deciding not only whether to serve a particular customer but also which items to sell and of what quality. A further form of food segregation involved the creation of specialty stores, each selling only one type of food product. Consequently customers had to develop shopping strategies around visits to various stores and even stores in different parts of town.

Because socialist shoppers could never guarantee that the foods available in one store one week would still be there the following week, consumers learned to stockpile and improvise. Socialist consumers also developed extensive systems of informal exchange networks to circulate foods and other goods (Ledeneva 1998). Finally, the privations of the socialist period cultivated a strong reliance on personal gardens to provide for basic needs. Especially when food was scarce in the shops, socialist citizens intensively worked their tiny garden plots to produce tomatoes, cucumbers, squash, herbs, and fruits that could be turned into preserves to supplement their food supplies for the entire winter or longer (see Acheson 2007; Bellows 2004; Caldwell 2007; Hervouet 2007; Zavisca 2003).

Family dynamics and other social relations among socialist citizens were also structured by food and eating, most notably the different forms of kitchen culture. Kitchens were especially contentious places, as socialist-era housing shortages often forced multiple families into co-housing arrangements in which kitchen and bath were shared by all the residents. In these communal kitchens, which were particularly common in the Soviet Union, families negotiated for time and space to store food, prepare meals, and eat. Savvy apartment dwellers marked out and protected their respective spaces for storing food and cookware in these kitchens. As Katerina Gerasinova reports, losing control over one's physical space in the kitchen could mean a loss of status in the entire apartment (Gerasimova 2002).

At the same time that kitchens in communal apartments were places of conflict, kitchens in private apartments emerged as highly social and safe areas where close intimates could gather and talk more freely than in public spaces. In a society where free speech—and especially dissenting speech—was dangerous, this "kitchen talk" facilitated a sense of privacy and encouraged free expression (Ries 1997). In some cases the political discussions that were generated in kitchens over meals with friends became the very sustenance that nourished these socialist citizens. In a revealing vignette drawn from her personal experiences living in socialist Eastern Europe, Slavenka Drakulić describes a dinner party with several colleagues in Bulgaria. Drakulić writes that, even after the food had long been eaten, "nobody seems to mind that there is no more food on the table—at least not as long as a passionate political discussion is going on. '*This* is our food,' says Evelina. 'We are used to swallowing politics with our meals'" (Drakulić 1991:16).

Finally, despite the social egalitarianism expressed in the ideologies that socialist states promote, these societies were marked by striking social hierarchies articulated and maintained through differentiated access to food goods. In some parts of the socialist world, hard-to-get food items, including out-of-season produce, were available only in special stores with access determined by one's employment, party affiliation, or even political status. For instance, in the Soviet Union access to these special shops was a marker of social distinction, not always welcomed by ordinary citizens. A professor in Russia recalled a time during the 1970s when she was allowed into a closed cafeteria for a private dinner and, during that meal, ate her first banana. Later, when the professor described her encounter, an acquaintance scolded her for eating the banana; it was "unpatriotic," the acquaintance said, because bananas were beyond the reach of ordinary citizens. In other parts of the socialist world, access to special shops was restricted only by one's ability to pay. In Bulgaria "Show-Off Stores" (*pokazani magazini*) offered special, high-end luxury items to anyone who could afford them.[7]

Above all, socialist-era food consumption was characterized by ambiguity, unpredictability, and uncertainty in terms of availability and access (see also Patico and Caldwell 2002). Yet, if these features were important for the people who lived through these experiences, so, too, did they matter for the scholars who have studied these societies. In many respects we can track the development of the fields of socialist and postsocialist studies through the preoccupations of anthropologists, sociologists, political scientists, and other scholars with food scarcity and the resulting coping mechanisms employed by socialist citizens (e.g., Caldwell 2004b; Clarke 2002; Haukanes 2007; Osokina 2001; Patico 2002).

Nevertheless, the compelling nature of scarcity as an analytical subject may obscure the impact of another subject that has consistently informed most of the anthropological studies of socialist Eurasia: farming. Much as they have done for other areas of anthropological research, studies of rural farming communities have formed the backbone of ethnographic research in socialist Eurasia by indigenous and foreign anthropologists alike. In fact, the earliest ethnographic research projects in socialist countries done by Western anthropologists were typically conducted in collective farms and other agricultural communities. For instance, the first ethnographic monograph of daily life inside the Soviet Union produced by a fieldworking Western scholar was Caroline Humphrey's *Karl Marx Collective* (Humphrey 1983). Thus the Western scholars who created and shaped the field of socialist ethnography—Gerald Creed, Chris Hann, David Kideckel, and Katherine Verdery, among others—did so primarily by focusing on agricultural communities (Creed 1998; Hann 1980, 1985; Kideckel 1993; Verdery 1983, 2003).[8]

This interest in farming communities coincided to a great extent with broader anthropological concerns with locating "tradition" and "culture" in rural spaces, and with preserving peasant culture in the face of modernizing forces. For socialist states that were grounding their ideals of progress and modernity in urban settings, the impetus to document and preserve rural cultures before they disappeared was strong. Food played a critical role in these efforts. Ethnographic museums across socialist Eurasia are noteworthy for their detailed attention to farming implements and cookware in exhibits devoted to traditional peasant life. At the same time farming communities have often provided some of the most accessible field sites for foreign ethnographers forced to navigate the logistical and political difficulties of conducting research "behind the Iron Curtain." Regardless, even if these scholars were not focusing explicitly on food practices, the fact remains that food-production communities were, in profound ways, the birthplace of socialist, and later postsocialist, ethnography.

Food and the Postsocialist World

Given the centrality of food in socialist life, and in socialist ethnographic research, it would be understandable to speculate that the significance of food may have diminished in the postsocialist, capitalist period. If anything, however, food has become even more essential as a political medium and marker of the events unfolding in the postsocialist world following the fall of the Berlin Wall in 1989 and the collapse of the Soviet Union in 1991. The very negotiations between socialism and capitalism, communism and democracy, and the past and the present have been deeply and strikingly embedded in the food practices of postsocialist consumers.

Leading the way in this transformation was the arrival of fast food in the Soviet bloc. Through a joint-venture project established during the Soviet period, Pepsi-Co., Inc. and its subsidiary, Pizza Hut, had established a presence in the socialist world by the 1980s. They were followed in the late 1980s and early 1990s by McDonald's. As the bearers of capitalist ideologies and practices, fast-food restaurants represented the quintessential Other in the socialist world. Ironically, these fast-food establishments also played a part in the collapse of the socialist world. McDonald's arrival in the Soviet Union in 1990 preceded the demise of the Soviet Union by eighteen months. The company's active intervention in the Soviet economy—including rebuilding the physical infrastructure of Moscow public streets and utilities, stimulating and updating the domestic food-services sector, and funding local charitable initiatives—provided one of the prime vectors for economic transformation in the post-Soviet sphere. This influence has prompted speculation that these changes contributed to the downfall of the Soviet Union.[9]

Although the case of McDonald's is striking for its obvious material successes, the larger impact of this company and its peers is far more profound. Both symbolically and materially, McDonald's and other transnational food corporations helped usher in radically new models of consumption and political-economic activity across the postsocialist world. In some cases postsocialist citizens responded to the novelty and exoticness of foreign foods, and at other times they reacted to the symbolic value of a Western cultural experience (Barker 1999; Patico and Caldwell 2002; Patico 2002). Among the narratives recorded by Daphne Berdahl in her study of postsocialist East Germany is a letter from a young East German man who excitedly describes his first trip to McDonald's in West Germany (1999b). In still other cases postsocialist citizens responded to the new models of labor offered by McDonald's and other Western fast-food restaurants. In one striking scene of the German movie *Goodbye, Lenin*, set in East Berlin during the transitional period following the fall of the Berlin Wall, one of the main characters leaves college to take a job at Burger King.

At the same time that foreign food corporations provide striking examples of the political and economic transformations under way in postsocialist Eurasia, the impact of new food cultures has been far more profound and wide-reaching. Just as in the socialist period, food-related issues inform critical debates about the nature of postsocialist markets by influencing the everyday lives of citizens in these regions and revealing the similarities, and increasingly the differences, taking shape across this region.

Underlying discussions about the consequences of globalization and marketization on postsocialist food practices are important debates about the relationship between tradition and modernity. As Gediminas Lankauskas detailed in his analysis of a wedding in post-Soviet Lithuania,

negotiations over the beverages to be served at the post-wedding reception revealed generational conflicts about the nature of post-Soviet
Lithuanian identity. Members of the elder generation, including the parents of the newly married couple, insisted on serving alcohol and making
toasts, thereby linking their identity as Lithuanians to Soviet-era cultural
practices. By contrast, the younger generation—the bride, the groom, and
their friends—refrain from drinking alcohol and insisted on drinking juice
and soft drinks at the reception to emphasize their identities as post-
Soviet citizens who belonged to a global community of like-minded serious consumers (Lankauskas 2002). Krisztina Fehérváry tackles similar
issues about the nature of postsocialist identity in Hungary, where she
observes urban consumers actively remaking their kitchens according to
western European architectural and design standards as evidence of their
ability to converse and participate in European notions of modernity. As
her informants discover, however, the transformation of kitchens from
sites of social gatherings to aesthetic sites of food preparation brings
about an unintended loss of sociability, thereby illustrating that social
relations and social stability are at stake in shifts from "traditional" to
"modern" (Fehérváry 2002).

A related theme in these discussions of "tradition" and "modernity" is
that of "normalcy," as postsocialist citizens chafing under the perception
of having been "held back" by regressivist Soviet policies strive to identify
and achieve a "normal" life under capitalism. This "normalcy" takes many
forms but is typically rendered as being "Western," for instance, the ability
to enjoy the same foods and other goods, and the same quality standards,
as "Western" consumers (Jung 2005; Patico 2005; Rausing 2002). Another
aspect of "normalcy" is being able to participate in a global economy
more generally, such as Bulgarian consumers who enjoy the influx of
Chinese immigrants—and Chinese cuisine (Jung 2006).

Public awareness of these new food systems reveals another important
innovation in postsocialist life: branding. Although socialist states employed their own forms of marketing to promote their products and
educate consumers (see, especially, Jung's 2006 discussion of socialist
consumer cooperatives in Bulgaria), postsocialist companies have un-
veiled new measures taking these tactics to new heights. In order to
introduce unfamiliar, foreign products to postsocialist consumers, foreign
companies have employed such strategies as frequent shopper cards, in-

formational programs in stores and on television, advertisements in media outlets, and even "free samples." Branding has become an especially important aspect of these new marketing strategies, as Klumbytė describes for the growth of Lithuania's sausage market (Klumbytė, this volume) and Dunn for the case of Poland's juice industry (Dunn 2004).

The new styles of food packaging introduced by food transnationals have also contributed to the environmental movements that have emerged in postsocialist societies. Food companies are more than just the target of pro-environment and anti-globalization activists and have instead emerged as important partners in local green movements. As Krista Harper has documented for Hungary, McDonald's has actively participated in Hungarian efforts to introduce new environmental standards and reform consumers' recycling practices. In response to environmentalists' concerns about how its business strategies and production practices adversely affect both the natural environment and the cultural landscape, McDonald's actively sought out and encouraged new modes of production and consumption that have improved recycling efforts (Harper 1999). In eastern Germany, the Czech Republic, and elsewhere across postsocialist Europe, fast-food restaurants have been at the forefront in changing the ways in which customers dispose of trash. Unlike the American model where customers dispose of their refuse in a single trash can, European customers leave their trays on racks and restaurant employees then separate the wrappers, food bits, and other items into bins for paper and food trash. Other food and beverage companies have introduced packaging made from recycled materials.

Attention to industrial foods also sheds light on important concerns about safety and hygiene, both particularly prevalent issues among officials and consumers in European Union countries (Friedberg 2004). Despite the initial popularity of foreign foods in the postsocialist world, many consumers were skeptical about whether these products were healthy. Rumors circulated throughout postsocialist Eurasia, warning that imported foods, especially from the United States, contained harmful additives or had expired (Caldwell 2002; Patico 2001). Even domestic food industries came under scrutiny from consumers who were suspicious of the production process and voiced fears—sometimes based on personal observations—of how factory workers deliberately sabotaged the food supply (see Jung, this volume). Issues of food and healthfulness are also directly related to the responses of postsocialist states to environmental disasters. As Sarah Philllips has shown for post-Chernobyl Ukraine, consumers look to food as a means to manage and prevent radiation poisoning, thereby generating a market niche of protective food (Phillips 2002; cf. Pesmen 2000:27 for the case of Russia). Even the perceived consequences of economic disasters have been interpreted and alleviated through food. In a study of garden food in Russia, Cynthia Gabriel reports that one of her informants expressed his suspicions of commercially produced and distributed foods by calling them "capitalist food" (Gabriel 2005:186). In contrast to these "capitalist foods," garden produce that is grown, picked, and circulated informally by friends or relatives is seen as a safer and healthier, and hence preferable, alternative (Gabriel 2005; see also Caldwell 2007).

Beyond issues of food safety, industrial foods are also intimately connected to larger debates about labor and the relationship of postsocialist food-production systems to the global marketplace. In her work on factories in Poland, Elizabeth Dunn has documented the paradoxical consequences of national and international efforts to impose food regulation standards on postsocialist food industries. Even as implementation of these food standards on food industries promises to facilitate companies' participation in the global marketplace and their ability to engage in fair and free trade, these same efforts favor the interests of global capitalism and thereby threaten the viability of small-scale, local producers (Dunn 2003). At the same time, the introduction of Fordist labor techniques and capitalist models of autonomous workers into Polish food-manufacturing plants has dramatically transformed the ways in which factory workers relate to one another and to the products they are producing (Dunn 2004). Similar issues about the connections between industrial food systems, labor, and tradition have been taken up by Hans Buechler and Judith-Maria Buechler in their research on the economic implications of German unification on East German bakery traditions. As Buechler and Buechler document, the capitalist models introduced through unification processes entailed a Westernization of East German baking traditions that forced bakers to adopt new business styles and forms of property ownership that ultimately challenged their identity as East Germans (Buechler and Buechler 2000).[10]

As more postsocialist countries join the European Union, EU regulations concerning food quality and standardization will have profound effects on regional food specialties and the ways in which postsocialist societies link cultural identities with culinary practices. As Zsuzsa Gille has described for Hungary, EU laws threaten the very types of pepper that can be used in Hungarian cuisine (2006). Similarly, in Lithuania, EU laws governing dairy production threaten not only the livelihoods of small-scale farmers but also consumers who prefer raw milk and see it as healthier and cleaner than processed milk (Mincyte 2006).[11]

Even nationalist sentiments have been directly affected by postsocialist food trends. In multiple settings across the postsocialist region, consumers, worried about the potential saturation of their markets and the loss of their distinctive cultures, have sparked vibrant nationalist food movements. In Russia this movement began with the opening of *Russkoe Bistro,* an inexpensive Russian fast-food chain that set up shop directly across the street from the first McDonald's in Moscow and served "authentic" Russian dishes like meat pies and dumplings instead of more "traditional" fast-food fare such as hamburgers and french fries. Several additional chains quickly followed, offering "traditional" food; one chain even emphasized Russia's peasant history with decorations evocative of a rustic house in the midst of a village, complete with farm implements and stuffed chickens beside every table. Responding to consumers' interests in nationalist food, Russian officials launched a widespread "Buy Russia" campaign encouraging Russians to buy only domestic goods. Although the wide appeal of this campaign was to stimulate Russia's industrial sector and impel consumers to contribute their income—via consumer practices—to Russia's economy, food themes took center stage. Food companies have capitalized on this emphasis by launching brand names explicitly evoking nationalist ideals, historical events, and historical figures ranging from Peter the Great and Catherine the Great to Soviet-era artists and athletes.[12]

Similar concerns with food nationalism and food patriotism appear across the postsocialist world and are often linked to nostalgic reminiscences of the socialist past. In one of the most enduring and powerful events in the German film *Goodbye, Lenin,* the son attempts to counteract the postsocialist Westernization of food products—and prevent his ailing mother from knowing that her beloved East Germany no longer exists—by repackaging Dutch pickles in jars bearing socialist-era East German labels (Becker 2004). Daphne Berdahl documented similar attitudes to food in her article on *"ostalgie,"* the uniquely East German manifestation of nostalgia for the socialist past (1999a). Perhaps Lithuania provides the most striking example of these nostalgic trends, where sausages bearing the brand name "Soviet" line supermarket shelves, attracting a faithful following among consumers who long for the stability and healthfulness of the Soviet period (see Klumbytė, this volume). Even more than pointing to the dynamic relationships between past and present, and between socialist and postsocialist, these foods and food practices reveal the extent to which nostalgia itself has become a lucrative industry in the postsocialist world (see, especially, Boym 2001).

A notable example of the centrality of food to this nostalgia industry is the Museum of Public Catering in Moscow, which is devoted solely to preserving the culinary heritage of the Soviet Union. Part of the museum exhibits individual dishes and ingredients representative of the cuisines found across the Soviet Union, but most of the displays feature the role of food in national politics. The tour guides are retired chefs and restaurant managers who walk solemnly through exhibits packed with cooking appliances and implements, menus, and cookbooks from both famous Soviet-era restaurants and modest public eating places, before stopping in front of portraits of individuals who have been recognized as "Hero Chefs" for their exemplary service to the Soviet Union, particularly during the Great Patriotic War (World War II). These "Hero Chefs" are further acknowledged with exhibits devoted to menus, place cards, and other souvenirs from the restaurants where they worked, as well as artwork, postcards, and other personal effects of these individuals. Their portraits hang in a special Hall of Honor, and special recognition is given to members of the food-services profession who died in combat. The veneration paid to members of the food-services profession clearly underscores the importance of these individuals to the project of building the socialist state.

Nationalist foodways similarly occupy a central place in the Haus der Geschichte (House of History), a museum dedicated to East Germany's socialist past located in the town of Wittenberg in the former East Germany. Museum exhibits are explicitly structured around the evolution of socialism in East Germany, so that each suite of rooms in a former apartment presents daily life in a different decade. In each of the decades represented, exhibits devote considerable space and attention to cooking implements, appliances, kitchen furniture and furnishings, and even food packages that were representative of each period.

Finally, food is at the center of the latest identity trends at work in this region, namely, Europeanization. Despite the commonalities linking socialist states, the dissolution and fracturing of the socialist world has been solidified with European integration. Formerly socialist countries like Bulgaria, the Czech Republic, Hungary, Lithuania, Poland, and Slovakia have formally joined the European Union, a move that officially distinguishes these countries from their Soviet peers but also charts new trajectories of future development and further distancing from socialism, and even postsocialism. At the same time, as several contributors to this volume have documented both here and in other publications, the process of Europeanization is problematic as the diversity of Europeanness becomes ever more evident and contested. Despite ideologies of European "equality," typically rendered through ideologies about "standards," some postsocialist European countries have discovered the existence of rigid social hierarchies in which a socialist past is a liability, such as in Hungary (Gille, this volume). These hierarchies have been especially noticeable in the recent efforts by West European wine producers to preserve their share of the wine market by limiting, or even eliminating, wine production in "inferior" regions—all of which are, notably, East European countries such as Bulgaria, Romania, Hungary, and the former East Germany, all with historic and celebrated wine-making traditions of their own. In other cases, postsocialist consumers find the taste and quality standards implemented by the EU to be inferior to those of socialist states, as in the case of Lithuania (Klumbytė and Mincyte, this volume). Ultimately, as these various examples suggest, food will continue to be a prime battleground for the next stage of empire building in Europe.

These illustrations offer but a glimpse into the ways in which food continues to inform, reveal, and respond to the realities of everyday life across the postsocialist world. This discussion is not meant to be an exhaustive discourse on food politics or even food scholarship from this region, but, instead, the aim is to highlight several key themes and issues that have shaped this field. As noted above, food is an essential, perhaps the most consistent, element within postsocialist life. Moreover, food is the one element, perhaps even more than any other consumer trend, linking postsocialist communities together, materially, symbolically, and analytically, even as it delineates subtle and sharp differences between them.

Introducing the Volume

This volume has three primary goals. The first is a critical analysis of the significance of food issues for understanding the nature of postsocialist societies. Within the larger field of food studies, which has expanded significantly over the past fifteen years, research has noticeably concentrated on postsocialist studies, not just in the regions of the former Soviet Union and Eastern Europe but also in Asia and Cuba (e.g., see the essays in Watson and Caldwell 2005). One reason for this is because food offers a compelling—and concrete—lens with which to view these transformations and access how ordinary people experience them. The materiality of food practices, to a great extent, enables critical observation and analysis. A second reason for the critical mass of research on postsocialist food practices is that the specific institutional and cultural legacies of state socialism and postsocialism in these regions provide a critical and productive vantage point for understanding processes such as standardization, agricultural reform, food safety, consumer identity, and global capitalism more broadly than that offered by research in societies that have historically been organized around industrial capitalism. Consequently the essays in this volume are an important contribution to the field of food studies.

The second aim of the volume is to provide a comparative analysis of postsocialist societies through the lens of food issues. The ethnographic settings explored in the chapters broadly examine social formations across the former Soviet Union and Eastern Europe, and the subjects addressed represent a wide array of critical issues including everyday survival strategies, the evolution of taste preferences, gender relations, alcoholism, nostalgia, identity, and Europeanization, to name only a few. Despite their diverse topics and settings, the essays intersect in important ways. Not only do these cross-regional comparisons create opportunities for acknowledging and unpacking social and cultural differences, but they also present a necessary and timely intervention into the scholarly work on "socialism" and "postsocialism."

Third, while charting new directions in postsocialist societies, the book also engages and builds on older conversations about food practices in these regions. In particular, the essays draw on and update the pioneering studies of food in presocialist and socialist Russia and the Soviet Union collected in Musya Glants and Joyce Toomre's volume, *Food in Russian History and Culture* (1997). Not only does that volume offer critical historical and literary details about food practices in the prerevolutionary and Soviet periods, providing context for understanding the changes taking place today, but it also highlights the long history of popular and official preoccupations with food in these regions dating back to the mid-ninth century (Lunts 1997). Thus, in many ways, this book, and the research it presents, owes its inspiration and existence to this earlier volume.

All the authors in this volume are field-working anthropologists or sociologists who have conducted long-term ethnographic field research in their respective field sites. They are also scholars with enduring interests in the study of food, although each comes to the field from a different vantage point. This methodological and theoretical diversity is apparent in the chapters, as are the varied stakes of each author, and ultimately contributes to broader theoretical conversations about the value of approaching food topics through multiple perspectives and ethical standpoints. Further, the authors are knowledgeable of one another's work and have all engaged in frequent conversations through their involvement in this volume and in conferences and workshops.

Because of the authors' ongoing dialogue, their essays share numerous themes and issues of topical and theoretical significance, provoking intriguing questions about commonalities across diverse regions and historical contexts. The chapters also diverge on significant points, generating equally stimulating discussions about cultural particularities and the value of cross-cultural comparison.

Evident in each chapter is a serious commitment to understanding the nature and consequences of globalization on postsocialist societies. From the essays on the consequences of EU standards by Jung, Gille, and Mincyte to those on global and local negotiations by Caldwell, Klumbytė, Metzo, and Shectman, each chapter addresses the myriad ways in which global forces and local preferences are mutually intersecting and complex.

Another theme shared by many chapters, particularly those devoted to postsocialist countries that have recently joined the European Union, is that of standards. Taking up the case of canning practices in Bulgaria,

Yuson Jung critically examines the processes by which Bulgarian consumers decide when to engage in "traditional" Bulgarian practices of home canning and when to purchase manufactured canned goods from the shops. Jung suggests that the processes of standardization and normalcy in which canning debates are embedded, particularly in light of EU standardizing templates, have profound consequences on local identity, personal health, and national heritage.

Similar concerns with the effects of standardizing regimes on identity, health, and heritage are addressed in Diana Mincyte's chapter on informal dairy markets and the politics of raw milk in Lithuania. Through a careful study of the issues facing milk producers and consumers, Mincyte argues that negotiations over raw milk reveal larger conflicts between socialist and postsocialist "European" traditions of taste, labor, and gender. Specifically Mincyte presents a compelling picture of the adverse effects of these rigid milk policies on the women who depend on raw milk production and selling to support their families in a harsh, postsocialist economic environment.

In her chapter on Hungarian paprika, Zsuzsa Gille extends this discussion of the unintended and often adverse consequences of EU standardization. Gille documents how the elaborate standards of quality and hygiene adopted by EU regulators as a way to safeguard food safety, both for individual consumers and the European Union as a whole, have, in fact, undermined the very objectives they were enacted to meet. She also shows how these rigid standards regimes are paradoxical within the globalizing project of the European Union itself.

Stas Shectman similarly focuses on questions about the values attached to competing systems of standards in his chapter on the emergence of a new culinary arts culture in Russia. Beginning with a case study of cooking competitions, which represent the latest trend in Russia's professional food-production sector, and continuing with an exploration of the changing field of professional chefs, Shectman traces the evolution of new standards governing postsocialist cooking styles and taste preferences from their origins in a distinguished Russian culinary tradition to their current manifestation in some of the world's most avant-garde styles of *haute cuisine*. Shectman suggests that it is the ethics, techniques, and expertise of Russia's long-standing cultural heritage that make this culinary internationalism possible.

The intersections between past and present, Soviet and European, that emerge in Shectman's essay acquire a different form in Neringa Klumbytė's chapter on Soviet sausage in Lithuania. Here Klumbytė explores the issues of post-Soviet branding through a fascinating study of the popularity of "Soviet" brand sausages vis-à-vis their "Euro" brand competitors. In a context where Lithuania was the first republic to secede from the Soviet Union, the popularity of "Soviet" brand sausages reveals the consequences when post-Soviet pasts and European futures collide. My own chapter on the new publics formed in the changing consumer landscape also tackles questions about how postsocialist consumers navigate the changing spaces of food consumption in today's Russia, particularly as the emergence of coffeehouse culture, among other new food cultures, challenges Russians to reorient themselves and their comfort levels according to new distinctions between public and private consumption. Katherine Metzo pushes these themes of public and private in a different direction by investigating the problematic nature of women's drinking practices in today's Russia, with sensitive attention to the overwhelming silence accompanying women's alcohol consumption. In a moving essay detailing the struggles of a female acquaintance with alcohol addiction, Metzo calls attention to the consequences of the gendered norms shaping Russian experiences with drinking and alcoholism, norms that ensure that while men's drinking practices are normalized and made public, women's are silenced. Thus Metzo's chapter is powerful not only because it critically interrogates the factors contributing to these differences, but also because, in the very act of telling the story of her acquaintance, Metzo shatters the prevailing silence about women's experiences with alcohol.

Additional themes linking these chapters include the types of communities that emerge and disintegrate as new food practices arise or become radically transformed, as well as the types of identity (national, transnational, European, modern, traditional, female, and so on) that are constituted through and complicated by food practices. The processes by which taste preferences are cultivated, asserted, and legitimated are also recurring subjects, as are questions about the degree to which postsocialist consumers are fully and freely able to engage these new food systems. Finally, despite the celebratory nature so often associated with postsocialist food practices, these new cultural forms are associated with, and provoke, numerous hazards. Thus every chapter, either explicitly or implicitly, also provides insight into the risks accompanying these dramatic transformations.

NOTES

1. McDonald's operates more than 100 restaurants in Russia alone, and another 250 are scattered across Central and Eastern Europe. See http://www.mcdonalds.com/countries/russia.html; other country specific sites at www.mcdonalds.com, accessed on March 17, 2006.

2. In her study of homelessness in Soviet and post-Soviet Russia, Svetlana Stephenson (2006) discusses the stigmas attached to Soviet citizens who were seen as socially unproductive. Homelessness, criminality, and alcoholism were all factors that could cause Soviet citizens to be labeled as unproductive and parasitic, and lead to their expulsion from formal society.

3. For a longer and fascinating account of the themes of agriculture and industrialization in Soviet stamps, see Dobrenko 2003.

4. This holds true for China and Cuba, among other state socialist countries.

5. For other accounts of socialist queuing, see Pine 2002 and Hessler 1996.

6. See, for instance, the stories of competitive food shopping detailed in Cathy Young's memoirs (1989). See also Fitzpatrick 1999 and Osokina 2001.

7. Yuson Jung, personal communication.

8. Other scholars of socialism/postsocialism whose work also touches on rural and often farming communities include Martha Lampland, Deema Kaneff, and Frances Pine, among numerous others. This does not even begin to take into account the ethnography of Soviet and post-Soviet societies that has focused on hunting, fishing, and herding communities.

9. For a more detailed discussion of the arrival of McDonald's in the Soviet Union and its subsequent impact on postsocialist societies, see Caldwell 2004a and Cohon 1999.

10. See also Czeglédy's discussion of the implications of Hungary's new fast-food industry for division of labor (Czeglédy 2002).

11. Most recently Dunn has begun exploring issues of food safety and canned foods in Georgia with her work on botulism (Dunn 2008).

12. See Caldwell 2002 for a longer discussion of Russian food nationalism.

REFERENCES CITED

Acheson, Julianna. 2007. "Household Exchange Networks in Post-Socialist Slovakia." *Human Organization* 66(4): 405–413.

Barker, Adele Marie. 1999. *Consuming Russia: Popular Culture, Sex, and Society since Gorbachev.* Durham, N.C.: Duke University Press.

Becker, Wolfgang. 2004. *Goodbye, Lenin!* Columbia TriStar Home Entertainment.

Bellows, Anne C. 2004. "One Hundred Years of Allotment Gardens in Poland." *Food & Foodways* 12:247–276.

Berdahl, Daphne. 1999a. "'(N)Ostalgie' for the Present: Memory, Longing, and East German Things." *Ethnos* 64(2): 192–211.

———. 1999b. *Where the World Ended: Re-Unification and Identity in the German Borderland.* Berkeley: University of California Press.

Borrero, Mauricio. 1997. "Communal Dining and State Cafeterias in Moscow and Petrograd, 1917–1921." In *Food in Russian History and Culture,* ed. Musya Glants and Joyce Toomre, pp. 162–176. Bloomington: Indiana University Press.

———. 2002. "Food and the Politics of Scarcity in Urban Soviet Russia, 1917–1941." In *Food Nations: Selling Taste in Consumer Societies,* ed. Warren Belasco and Phillip Scranton, pp. 258–276. New York: Routledge.

Boym, Svetlana. 2001. *The Future of Nostalgia.* New York: Basic Books.

Buchli, Victor. 2000. *An Archaeology of Socialism.* Oxford: Berg.

Buechler, Hans, and Judith-Maria Buechler. 2000. "The Bakers of Bernburg and the Logics of Communism and Capitalism" *American Ethnologist* 26(4): 799–821.

Caldwell, Melissa L. 2002. "The Taste of Nationalism: Food Politics in Postsocialist Moscow." *Ethnos* 67(3): 295–319.

———. 2004a. "Domesticating the French Fry: McDonald's and Consumerism in Moscow." *Journal of Consumer Culture* 4(1): 5–26.

———. 2004b. *Not by Bread Alone: Social Support in the New Russia.* Berkeley: University of California Press.

———. 2007. "Feeding the Body and Nourishing the Soul: Natural Foods in Postsocialist Russia." *Food, Culture & Society* 10(1): 43–71.

Clarke, Simon. 2002. *Making Ends Meet in Contemporary Russia: Secondary Employment, Subsidiary Agriculture and Social Networks.* Cheltenham, UK: Edward Elgar.

Cohon, George. 1999. *To Russia with Fries: My Journey from Chicago's South Side to Moscow's Red Square—Having Fun along the Way.* Toronto, Ontario: McClelland and Stewart.

Creed, Gerald. 1998. *Domesticating Revolution: From Socialist Reform to Ambivalent Transition in a Bulgarian Village.* University Park: Pennsylvania State University.

Czeglédy, André P. 2002. "Manufacturing the New Consumerism: Fast-Food Restaurants in Postsocialist Hungary." In *Markets & Moralities: Ethnographies of Postsocialism,* ed. Ruth Mandel and Caroline Humphrey, pp. 143–166. Oxford: Berg.

Davydoff, M. I. 1971. *Bor'ba za Khleb.* Moscow: Mysl'.

Dobrenko, Evgeny. 2003. "The Art of Social Navigation: The Cultural Topography of the Stalin Era." In *The Landscape of Stalinism: The Art and Ideology of Soviet Space,* ed. Evgeny Dobrenko and Eric Naiman, pp. 163–200. Seattle: University of Washington Press.

Dolot, Miron, 1985. *Execution by Hunger: The Hidden Holocaust.* New York: W. W. Norton.

Drakulić, Slavenka. 1991. *How We Survived Communism and Even Laughed.* New York: Harper-Perennial.

Dunn, Elizabeth. 2003. "Trojan Pig: Paradoxes of Food Safety Regulation." *Environment and Planning—Part A* 35:1493–1511.

———. 2004. *Privatizing Poland: Baby Food, Big Business, and the Remaking of Labor.* Ithaca, N.Y.: Cornell University Press.

———. 2008. "Postsocialist Spores: Disease, Bodies, and the State in the Republic of Georgia." *American Ethnologist* 35(2): 243–258.

Fehérváry, Krisztina E. 2002. "American Kitchens, Luxury Bathrooms, and the Search for a 'Normal' Life in Post-socialist Hungary." *Ethnos* 67(3): 369–400.

Fitzpatrick, Sheila. 1999. *Everyday Stalinism: Ordinary Life in Extraordinary Times: Soviet Russia in the 1930s.* New York: Oxford University Press.

Freidberg, Susanne. 2004. *French Beans and Food Scares: Culture and Commerce in an Anxious Age.* New York: Oxford University Press.

Gabriel, Cynthia. 2005. "Healthy Russian Food Is Not-for-Profit." *Subsistence and Sustenance,* Special Issue of *Michigan Discussions in Anthropology* 15:183–222.

Gerasimova, Katerina. 2002. "Public Privacy in the Soviet Communal Apartment." In *Socialist Spaces: Sites of Everyday Life in the Eastern Bloc,* ed. David Crowley and Susan E. Reid, pp. 207–230. Oxford: Berg.

Gille, Zsuzsa. 2006. "The Tale of the Toxic Paprika: The Hungarian Taste of Euro-Globalization." Paper presented at Soyuz Symposium, March 2006, Bryant University.

Glants, Musya, and Joyce Toomre, eds. 1997. *Food in Russian History and Culture.* Bloomington: Indiana University Press.

——. 1997a. "Introduction." In *Food in Russian History and Culture,* ed. Musya Glants and Joyce Toomre, pp. xi–xxvii. Bloomington: Indiana University Press.

Hann, Chris. 1980. *Tázlár, a Village in Hungary.* Cambridge: Cambridge University Press.

——. 1985. *A Village without Solidarity: Polish Peasants in Years of Crisis.* New Haven, Conn.: Yale University Press.

Harper, Krista. 1999. "Citizens or Consumers? Environmentalism and the Public Sphere in Postsocialist Hungary." *Radical History Review* 74:96–111.

Haukanes, Haldis. 2007. "Katja's Canteen: Complex Intersections of the Public and the Private in the South Bohemian Countryside." *Focaal* 50:19–34.

Hervouet, Ronan. 2007. "Datchas et mémoires familiales en Biélorussie." *Ethnologie francaise* 37(3): 533–540.

Hessler, Julie. 1996. "Culture of Shortages: A Social History of Soviet Trade." Ph.D. diss., University of Chicago.

Humphrey, Caroline. 1983. *Karl Marx Collective: Economy, Society, and Religion in a Siberian Collective Farm.* Cambridge: Cambridge University Press.

Jung, Yuson. 2005. "Shifting Perceptions of Standardized Food in Postsocialist Urban Bulgaria." Paper presented at the American Association for the Advancement of Slavic Studies meetings, November 2005, Salt Lake City, Utah.

——. 2006. "Consumer Lament: An Ethnographic Study on Consumption, Needs, and Everyday Complaints in Postsocialist Bulgaria." Ph.D. diss., Harvard University, Cambridge, Mass.

Kideckel, David A. 1993. *The Solitude of Collectivism: Romanian Villagers to the Revolution and Beyond.* Ithaca, N.Y.: Cornell University Press.

Kitanina, T. M. 1985. *Voina, khleb i revoliutsiia.* Leningrad: Nauka.

Klumbytė, Neringa. 2006. "Deterritorializing Post-Socialist Nostalgia: Tradition, Memory, and Global Market of 'Soviet' Food Products." Paper presented at Soyuz Symposium, March 2006, Bryant University.

Lankauskas, Gediminas. 2002. "On 'Modern' Christians, Consumption, and the Value of National Identity in Post-Soviet Lithuania." *Ethnos* 67(3): 320–344.

Ledeneva, Alena V. 1998. *Russia's Economy of Favours: Blat, Networking and Informal Exchange.* Cambridge: Cambridge University Press.

Lih, Lars T. 1990. *Bread and Authority in Russia, 1914–1921.* Berkeley: University of California Press.

Lunt, Horace G. 1997. "Food in the Rus' Primary Chronicle." In *Food in Russian History and Culture,* ed. Musya Glants and Joyce Toomre, pp. 15–30. Bloomington: Indiana University Press.

McAuley, Mary. 1991. *Bread and Justice: State and Society in Petrograd, 1917–1922.* Oxford: Clarendon.

Mincyte, Diana. 2006. "Pasteurization of Lithuania: Of Raw Milk, Microbes, and Globalization." Paper presented at Soyuz Symposium, March 2006, Bryant University.

Osokina, Elena. 2001. *Our Daily Bread: Socialist Distribution and the Art of Survival in Stalin's Russia, 1927–1941.* Armonk, N.Y.: M.E. Sharpe.

Patico, Jennifer. 2001. "Globalization in the Postsocialist Marketplace: Consumer Readings of Difference and Development in Urban Russia." *Kroeber Anthropological Society Papers* 86:1127–1142.

———. 2002. "Chocolate and Cognac: Gifts and the Recognition of Social Worlds in Post-Soviet Russia." *Ethnos* 67(3): 345–368.

———. 2005. "To Be Happy in a Mercedes: Tropes of Value and Ambivalent Visions of Marketization." *American Ethnologist* 32(3): 479–496.

Patico, Jennifer, and Melissa L. Caldwell. 2002. "Consumers Exiting Socialism: Ethnographic Perspectives on Daily Life in Post-Communist Europe." *Ethnos* 67(3): 285–294.

Paxson, Margaret. 2005. *Solovyovo: The Story of Memory in a Russian Village.* Bloomington: Indiana University Press; Washington, D.C.: Woodrow Wilson Center Press.

Pesmen, Dale. 2000. *Russia and Soul: An Exploration.* Ithaca, N.Y.: Cornell University Press.

Pine, Frances. 2002. "Dealing with Money: Złotys, Dollars, and Other Currencies in the Polish Highlands." In *Markets & Moralities: Ethnographies of Postsocialism,* ed. Ruth Mandel and Caroline Humphrey, pp. 75–97. Oxford: Berg.

Rausing, Sigrid. 2002. "Re-constructing the 'Normal': Identity and the Consumption of Western Goods in Estonia." In *Markets & Moralities: Ethnographies of Postsocialism,* ed. Ruth Mandel and Caroline Humphrey, pp. 127–142. Oxford: Berg.

Ries, Nancy. 1997. *Russian Talk: Culture & Conversation during Perestroika.* Ithaca, N.Y.: Cornell University Press.

Rothstein, Halina, and Robert A. Rothstein. 1997. "The Beginnings of Soviet Culinary Arts." In *Food in Russian History and Culture,* ed. Musya Glants and Joyce Toomre, pp. 177–194. Bloomington: Indiana University Press.

Shevchenko, Olga. 2002. "'In Case of Emergency': Consumption, Security, and the Meaning of Durables in a Transforming Society." *Journal of Consumer Culture* 2(2): 147–170.

Stephenson, Svetlana. 2006. *Crossing the Line: Vagrancy, Homelessness and Social Displacement in Russia.* Aldershot, England: Ashgate.

Verdery, Katherine. 1983. *Transylvanian Villagers: Three Centuries of Political, Economic, and Ethnic Change.* Berkeley: University of California Press.

———. 1996. *What Was Socialism, and What Comes Next?* Princeton, N.J.: Princeton University Press.

———. 2003. *The Vanishing Hectare: Property and Value in Postsocialist Transylvania.* Ithaca, N.Y.: Cornell University Press.

Watson, James L., and Melissa L. Caldwell, eds. 2005. *The Cultural Politics of Food and Eating: A Reader.* Malden, Mass.: Blackwell.

Young, Cathy. 1989. *Growing Up in Moscow: Memories of a Soviet Girlhood.* New York: Ticknor & Fields.

Zavisca, Jane. 2003. "Contesting Capitalism at the Post-Soviet Dacha: The Meaning of Food Cultivation for Urban Russians." *Slavic Review* 62(4): 786–810.

ONE

From Canned Food to Canny Consumers

Cultural Competence in the Age of Mechanical Production

YUSON JUNG

"Burkanite" (The Jars)

One clear fall afternoon, the appetizing smell of roasting bell peppers permeated the entire building in downtown Sofia. While riding in the elevator up to the sixth-floor apartment I shared with my seventy-eight-year-old landlady Katya, I speculated about which neighbor was roasting peppers on a weekday afternoon.[1] My first thought was that it must be Nadiya, our downstairs neighbor and one of the few people in the building who would be home and cooking during this time of day. On entering my landlady's apartment, however, clearly the wonderful smell was coming from our flat. I peeked into the kitchen on the left side of the apartment halfway along the hallway but did not see anyone or any sign that the stove was in use. Proceeding along the hallway and into the living room, I finally saw Katya sitting on a chair on the balcony off the living room. She was bending over an old and clearly much-used *chushkopek* (literally, "pepper grill"), a cylindrical electrical device about the size of a large stock pot. Lying next to the *chushkopek* was a small pile of roasted red bell peppers.

At first Katya barely noticed me but, when she finally did, she proudly smiled and said she was having her "*burkan*" day.[2] After greeting Katya, I told her that she should have waited for me to help her; but she said that she had left the tomato canning business for me. I watched as she placed a red pepper into the hole in the middle of the electric grill, where it was roasted until the skin of the pepper was burnt. Katya then removed the pepper and wrapped it in newspaper so that the steam would loosen the peel and facilitate its removal. As I commented with fascination about the machine, Katya responded plainly that it was just a "typical" old thing that every Bulgarian household had. I watched as she finished up with the last several peppers and then I carried them to the kitchen.

In the kitchen Katya had already set aside a large tray full of small empty glass jars (the size of the smallest Smucker's jam). Beside the tray was a large bowl of tomatoes and a metal food mill resembling a pasta maker. The food mill was fastened to the kitchen table with a screw. Katya first boiled the tomatoes and peeled the skins before putting them into the food mill, which she held with one hand while slowly turning the handle with the other. I offered to help but she refused, claiming that only she knew how to do it without getting hurt. Smiling, she softened her response by saying it was an old machine. She then directed me to sit and peel the skins of the roasted peppers, which I happily did. When I completed my task, I was allowed to pour the pureed tomatoes into the jars. I then started boiling water in a large pot that would sterilize the jars after they were sealed to ensure preservation. After several more hours Katya froze the roasted peppers and canned the tomato puree in the jars, ending her simplified session of making *burkani,* or "jar foods." The pickled vegetables known as "*turshia*," which are part of typical canning sessions among Bulgarians, were not among the day's yield. Katya, with a sigh, told me that she did not have the energy and money to make *turshia*. She would buy them from the store, since store-bought *turshia* was actually "pretty good" these days.

In urban Sofia, jarring foods at home to preserve vegetables and fruits

Figure 1.1. A *chushkopek* and grilled red pepper. Photograph by Yuson Jung.

Figure 1.2. Below. Making jars (*burkani*). Photograph by Yuson Jung.

for the winter is occurring less frequently. Among families strongly connected to the villages that still have resources, such as older parents
or other relatives with social relations to villagers, *burkani* like *turshia*,
purees, and *kompot* (fruit in syrup) are still produced in the villages in
large quantities and then brought to the city for consumption. Increasingly, however, Sofians have begun resorting to standardized jars now sold
in various grocery stores. This seems at odds with past attitudes toward standardized food in Bulgaria. For most Bulgarians, buying factory-
produced jars was unimaginable during socialist times despite the affordability and understanding of "standards and control" often positively
associated with the socialist state's food safety.[3] How can we explain these
changing attitudes toward standardized food among Bulgarian urban consumers? Is this simply a consequence of the homogenizing effect of globalization associated with capitalist development in the aftermath of socialism, an explanation most commonly applied to emerging consumerism in
transitional economies (cf. Watson and Caldwell 2005)?

In thinking about the making and consuming of *burkani,* I am concerned with shifting perceptions of standardized food in postsocialist
Bulgaria. By standardized food, I refer to industrially produced food that
follows specific protocols of production standards that have been applied
under both socialist and capitalist systems. My focus is on standardized
jar food (more commonly understood as canned food) and frozen food
because they link the past to the present in terms of the industrialized
food sector during and after state socialism.

Food lets us access the intimate experiential levels where social and
economic changes are being felt. It is a compelling marker for understanding the intensive transformation from a socialist system to a capitalist
market system. And food, especially the smells of roasting pepper and
fresh ripe vegetables and fruits in the fall, invokes a sense of nostalgia in
postsocialist Sofia. As Seremetakis (1994) points out, senses are tangled
with history and memory. Memories, like those of my Bulgarian friends
preparing jars for the winter, are nostalgic. Nostalgia, however, is not just a
romantic sentimentality confined to a bygone past (Seremetakis 1994).
More important, it speaks of changing ideas on everyday activities and
their current relationships to these activities. It is the memories and
increasingly nostalgic, rather than necessary, practices of such activities as
preparing jars of vegetables and fruits for the winter and freezing fresh

fruits and roasted, fresh vegetables that reveal the changing and seemingly contradictory understanding of notions such as standardization among Bulgarians.

These shifting notions indicate that Bulgarians grapple with what was once perceived as typical or distinctive socialist ideas and seek to transform and embrace these ideas in their daily practices in a new social and economic environment. The increasing acceptance and normalization of buying and consuming standardized jars and, to a lesser extent, processed frozen food in urban Bulgaria suggests a more nuanced process that cannot simply be labeled as a form of globalization where transnational flows of goods and ideas lead to homogeneous practices (Walters 1985; Tomlinson 1991; and Appadurai 1996; cf. Ritzer 2004), thus overlooking the experiences of the people undergoing these changes. Nor can these changes be viewed merely as a result of an interaction of local and global forces (e.g., Hannerz 1996; Watson 1997), as Bulgarians do not associate these changes with cultural innovation in the face of globalization. One should also be cautious of labeling this process "Europeanization," which implies a one-way process devoid of local agency.

Instead, by focusing on the notion of standardization and discussing it in relation to theories of globalization, I argue that a growing consumer competence enabling people to execute their own control over the food they consume is a significant aspect of changing attitudes toward standardized food. This approach differs from other postsocialist studies of food and consumption that have emphasized globalizing forces and trends, on the one hand, and resistance and adaptation to them on the other (e.g., Caldwell 2005; Gille, this volume; Patico 2001). It also departs from dichotomized readings of food practice in terms of socialist/ Soviet/indigenous versus postsocialist/European/foreign (e.g., Patico 2003; Klumbytė, this volume). I suggest, instead, that increasing consumer competence among urban Bulgarians reflects consumers' rationalizing tendencies originating in their experiences of modernization during the socialist period, and then developing further under neoliberal capitalist processes. This analysis also shows a local understanding of globalization itself that is not confined to the visibility of homogeneous global brands and logos such as McDonalds and Nike, which are often the focus in consumption studies. Furthermore, with this analysis I propose to go beyond the oppositional rhetoric of capitalism versus socialism commonly employed in accounts of postsocialist consumption practices (see also Humphrey 2002; Verdery 1996). By contrast, urban Bulgarians carefully reconsider, reorient, embrace, and reevaluate preexisting ideas associated with "standards and control" through their own consumer experiences, and they create new meanings for their changing consumption practices regarding standardized food.[4]

Standardization and Globalization

The notion of standardization has been discussed mostly in the context of industrial production, focusing on the implementation of standards in the production process (Dunn 2004) in relation to governmentality within the global political economy (Dunn 2005, Gille this volume). These studies discuss the context of global market regimes where standards are authored and written down (usually in the developed "West") and then imposed on the production process in various parts of the world. These studies focus on the effects of standardization for local producers in the newly evolving economies in postsocialist Eastern Europe. Such an examination poses significant questions and challenges to transitional economies attempting to restructure their industries in order to gain access to the global economy. Two aspects of the notion of standardization, however, have been given little attention: the idea that "standardization" was discussed and implemented not only in the capitalist economy but also in the formerly socialist world; and the perception and implication of the idea of standardization for consumption practices and consumers. These aspects offer significant insights into changing consumption attitudes in the postsocialist world. I suggest that the shifting perceptions of standardized food in urban Bulgaria provide a window into these aspects that have not been examined previously.

Standardization can be best understood as the implementation of technical standards to create compatibility within the context of modernization and industrialization. The literal definition of the word *standardize* in English is "to make objects or activities of the same type have the same features or qualities" (*Oxford Dictionary*). It is particularly the aspect of creating similar qualities in objects and activities that was exemplified in Fordist management techniques. These techniques entered the industrialized production process not only in the capitalist system but also in its socialist counterpart (see, especially, Dunn 2004:8–23, and Buechler and Buechler 1999).[5] Given this historical backdrop, standardization is hardly a unique idea applied only to socialist economies. Notably, however, many Bulgarian consumers perceived the homogenizing effects of standardization as a "typical" socialist idea, as I discuss below. For instance, many Bulgarian consumers used the terms "sameness" (*etnakvost*) and "dullness" (*ednoobrazie*) to describe socialist products and attributed these characteristics to standardization. The notion of standardization is intimately related to industrialized mass production with its rationalizing tendencies for the production system and process. One could therefore think of standardization as a form of rationalization. This institutional rationalizing system and its principles raise critical issues of control, quality, and choice, which in turn offer ways to think about standardization in relation to globalization and homogenization.

A common and popular understanding of globalization describes it as a natural, inevitable, and economics-driven process on a global scale (Ritzer 2004). In the core of this process lies the hegemonic rule of American-led capitalist developments throughout the world, which is related to the Weberian notion of the "rationalization" of modern society. Ritzer (2004) argues that this principle of rationalization is central to the ways in which modern society is organized and suggests that we should understand globalization in terms of forms versus content. Thus, although globalization appears to be linked with the idea of homogenization, only the homogenized "form," which he calls "nothing" (2004:3), is really affected. In other words, the consumer world we now experience as a place where identical commodities sweep local markets with the transnational flow of goods and services based on capitalist principles provided by global corporations is only one aspect of globalization based on "form." The "content" aspect of globalization is far more complicated and cannot be explained in simple terms.

This insight suggests a meaningful approach to understanding the comment of my Bulgarian friend, Darya, a woman in her early thirties: "Wherever you go, you can find McDonalds, Coca-Cola, Colgate toothpaste, Danon yogurt, and so on." She also added that Bulgaria now had them as well and that Bulgarians were globalized consumers ("*Nie sme globalizirani*"). Darya, like many other Sofians, was sometimes critical of these globally branded products, but she also consumed them and had started to buy *burkanite* from the stores.[6] Yet, despite her assertion, Darya refused to explain her changing attitude toward consuming store-bought *burkanite* and other standardized food as an *inevitable* consequence of globalization or global capitalism. She agreed that these changes have brought about more choices, but she did not consider her changing attitude toward the consumption of global brands and standardized food to be the result of globalization. Rather, as I will discuss below, the idea of "control" explains the changing consumer attitudes of many Bulgarian consumers.

Although the term "globalization" has become a mega-trope (Tsing 2005) popularly used in public and academic discourses worldwide, it has little meaningful content to which people commonly subscribe. Scholars, however, seem to accept the following general definition of globalization: "the worldwide diffusion of practices, expansion of relations across continents, organization of social life on a global scale, and growth of a shared global consciousness" (Ritzer 2004:160; for similar definitions, see also Walters 1995 and Appadurai 1999). Another common buzzword for this global process is "McDonaldization," which has been defined as "the process by which the *principles* of the fast-food restaurant are coming to dominate more and more sectors of American society as well as the rest of the world" (Ritzer 2004:1; my emphasis). Ritzer lists these principles as efficiency, calculability, predictability, and control through nonhuman technology, and he argues that this rationalization process has proven to be globally irresistible in the neoliberal milieu (Ritzer 2004). This approach to globalization, however, hardly takes into account that socialism, just like capitalism, sought the same principles under the discourse of modernization and experimented with "scientific management," most commonly understood as Taylorism and Fordism, to reach modernity (cf. Dunn 2004; on socialist food sciences in the Soviet Union, also see Rothstein and Rothstein 1997). Although the neoliberal practices of globalization may be historically new phenomena for postsocialist citizens, the underlying principles of globalization, such as the notion of standardization, are very familiar. In this regard, standardization and globalization are hardly identical processes, but they evolve under the same principle of rationalization. This aspect of rationalization, I suggest, deserves more attention in order to understand consumers' attitudes toward consumer choices, which cannot be labeled simply as a homogenizing practice influenced by the global flow of goods in a capitalist market economy.

The Law on Standardization

The standardization behind mass-produced commodities employed by Fordist managers to support the principles of efficiency, calculability, predictability, and control was, in fact, also actively adopted by state socialist planners (Dunn 2004:17), albeit with quite different consequences. The principles of standardization were often compromised by the shortage and irregular supply of ingredients for industrial production under the socialist state (Dunn 2004). This meant that the outcome and quality of goods could not be predictable or controlled and were not always homogeneous. And yet socialist consumers' perceptions of standardized products were affected not so much by the inconsistent outcome but more by the ideas of "control" and "quality."

In Bulgaria the idea of standardization is generally meaningful in reference to the Law on Standardization (*Zakon na Standartizatsiya*) enacted by the Bulgarian Communist State in 1964 to control virtually every consumer item produced. Until an amendment to the law was announced in 1998, and a subsequent change in the form and content of the legislation was enacted in 1999, the same year that a Consumer Protection Law was created and passed in the Bulgarian Parliament, the Law on Standardization had a profound impact on the everyday consumption practices of Bulgarians because it regulated the standards of every single consumer product and service available for consumption.[7] For ordinary consumers, therefore, standardization is associated with state control. As my good friend and key informant Yassen once told me,

> *Can you imagine, they [i.e., the socialist regime] had laws . . ., recipes were written as laws . . ., for* lyutenitza *[a Bulgarian pepper-tomato puree that is consumed as spread or garnish and commonly produced as jar food]. One spoon of salt, two spoons of water, and so on. So, any factory [zavod] that would produce* lyutenitza *would have the same result and taste. . . . Basically, they [i.e., the socialist regime] could control everything.*

Recipes would not typically be codified as national laws in capitalist systems but would remain within the production protocols for the producers. But under socialist systems like that in Bulgaria, where the state was also the producer, industrial food recipes were technically codified as law.

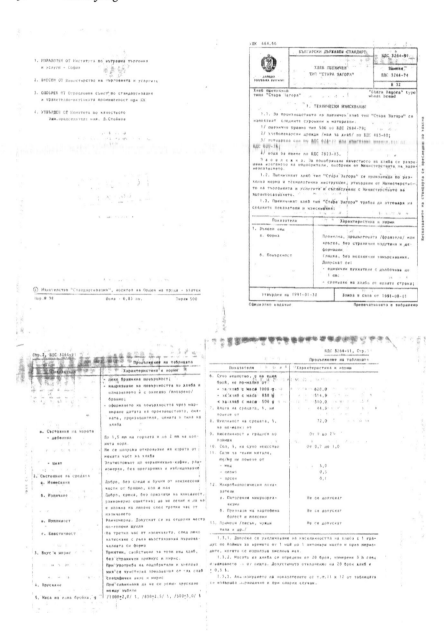

Figure 1.3. Bulgarian State Standards for the bread type *"Stara Zagora."*
Photograph by Yuson Jung.

These laws of standardization worked as follows: the communist state codified fixed standards for every item in the market. Take for example, the most common staple food, bread: according to the Bulgarian State Standard (BSS), all breads that are called "type *Stara Zagora*" should be made of wheat flour "type 500" according to BSS 2684-79, yeast for bread according to BSS 483-80, cooking salt according to BSS 628-77 or crystal salt according to BSS 629-76, drinking water according to BSS 2823-83, and so on. The list under this type of bread even states the thickness of the dough (the bottom dough should be no thicker than 2 mm and the top no more than 1.5 mm), how to work the dough (one should give a light push with the hands after three hours to get the proper texture), and how it should taste and smell (a nice, unique taste and smell for this type of bread), to mention just a few instructions from a long list (BSS 3264-91, revised from 3264-74, Republic of Bulgaria, pp. 1–3; my translation).[8] All producers were obliged to follow this standard approved by the Committee for Standardization and Quality. Consequently the state technically had control over everything that went to the market.

To Bulgarian consumers this system meant, theoretically, that both the basic quality of and trust in consumer products were assured. At least consumers knew that these products were safe to consume. The fact that one could purchase a loaf of bread for 10 *stotinki* (a very low price), for example, did not mean one had bought "garbage" and was risking one's health. This sort of guarantee allowed ordinary people to have a normal life—like in the "normal Western countries," as Bulgarians often said. A "normal life," Bulgarians simply explained, is a life without anxiety (*spokoistvie*). This is not to suggest, however, that consumers did not complain about the quality of standardized products during the socialist period, as I discuss below. On the contrary, consumer frustration over the quality of available products was widespread throughout the socialist period (e.g., Creed 2001; Jung 2007). Yet when Bulgarian consumers describe the quality of products from the postsocialist time as "garbage," they evoke the principles of standards and control that were prevalent during the socialist period and then contrast their present material circumstances to those of the past. They continue to assess socialist products as having superior quality compared to the postsocialist products that ordinary consumers can *afford*.[9] Consumer complaints, therefore, must be understood relative to the circumstances and values of each political-historical context.[10] In any case, standardized food, for Bulgarian consumers, was associated with the state through the Law on Standardization of the socialist period, and with control and quality.

The Evolution of Standardized Food in Bulgaria

Traditionally Bulgaria has been an agricultural society that takes great pride in the agricultural products grown in its high-quality soil (Creed 1998). The development of Bulgaria's modern food industry can be traced back to the second half of the nineteenth century, when the first mechanized mills were established in the cities of Karnovat and Varna (*Enziklopediya Bulgaria* 1982). The food industry, however, became fully industrialized only after the Communist Party nationalized the industry in 1947, with particular emphasis on the production of export-oriented food products. Production protocols were gradually developed and codified throughout the 1950s to the 1970s as part of the socialist industrialization process. It is within this context that Bulgaria's canning industry developed.[11]

Unlike in the former Soviet Union, where the state was concerned with domestic food services and consumption (Rothstein and Rothstein 1997), the emphasis in Bulgaria was on exports within the food sector, which made industrial food and food science less of a domestic issue. During socialism, as Creed (1998) discusses, the large-scale agricultural production of strawberries and the canning of fruits and vegetables was centered on the international market. The Bulgarian state promoted the socialist project of modernization in regard to liberating women from multiple duties of child rearing, housekeeping, and employment. In doing so, it offered standardized food products in the domestic markets. Certain standardized foods such as jar food and frozen food, however, were never popularized. On the one hand, this was because of consumers' increasing distrust of the state owing to the irregular distribution of goods; on the other hand, consumers came to distrust the quality of products, despite the state's "standards and control." Regardless of the state's promotion and the affordability of standardized food products, people continued to make their own jar foods and freeze their own vegetables and fruits.

With the influence of modern technology, especially freezing technologies, and the Communist government's need to demonstrate the progress of its society, frozen food was introduced to Bulgarian consumers in the late 1960s and early 1970s. These food products included fresh fruits and vegetables frozen with added sugar or salt, for example, frozen strawberries or frozen green beans, as well as ready-made food such as yogurt cucumber soup (*tarator*), stews (*yastie*), and near-ready food (*polifabrikana hrana*) such as meatballs (*kyufte*) and sausages (*kebabche*) which only needed grilling. Although the quality of frozen food had declined gradually by the 1980s, a brief period ensued when urbanites were fascinated with the technology and grew quite fond of it. Tanya, a woman in her late eighties, still reminisces about the frozen *gyuvech*, a traditional stew dish, from the late 1960s and early 1970s, in which the vegetable ingredients came washed, cut, frozen, and ready for cooking in a baking pan. This dish saved her much labor after a long workday. Yet Tanya also remembered that frozen foods of a decent quality slowly disappeared, for later she could not find this particular dish. Some younger Sofians now in their late fifties and early sixties asserted that the frozen vegetables and wrapping in the frozen *gyuvech* that they bought in the 1980s were of pathetic quality. According to other Sofians in their seventies and eighties, frozen foods in Bulgaria during the late 1960s and early 1970s were considered modern and were envied by people from other *soz lager* (the Bulgarian expression for the other formerly socialist countries of Eastern Europe and the Soviet Union) such as Yugoslavia, where they did not have this technology yet. Tanya suspected that the frozen-food industry did not prove profitable enough for the socialist state especially regarding the export sector, and so the state gradually focused more on producing jar foods.

Consumer Perceptions of Standardized Food

It is questionable how well the state's system of standards and control actually worked (for a discussion of how standardization planning operated from the production side in socialist Poland, see, especially, Dunn 2004:16–17). Bulgarian consumers reacted skeptically to the idea of standardization under socialism, although later the same people often spoke nostalgically about the "safe and reliable" socialist past. But more important is the perception that state control is implied in the notion of standardization and is associated with reliability. It is interesting to note what and when people choose to remember certain things but not others. Even though urban Bulgarians were skeptical of the quality of jar foods produced in state plants (*durjavni zavodi*), they nevertheless associated socialist production with qualities such as "safe and reliable," in sharp contrast to the present period of capitalist transition (*prehod*). As their attitudes and actions reveal, Bulgarian consumers electively evoke the past based on their current experiences.

As noted previously, my friend Yassen and other Bulgarians were convinced that standardization was a uniquely and distinctive socialist practice associated with state control. As I learned later, however, standardization was "a Western management technique as Fordist managers deployed and as state socialist planners wanted to do" (Dunn 2004:17). Unlike the popular perception of many Bulgarians, socialist and capitalist production practices had much in common.[12] The consequences of these identical production processes, however, proved to be quite different for consumers.

Despite the implied meaning of control and its positive association with reliability and safety, standardization during socialism reflected the lesser value that people placed on "standardized socialist products" such as jars or frozen food produced in state plants. Bulgarian consumers realized that despite the Law on Standardization and socialist planners' best intentions, the food products from these plants did not always result in identical taste, nor were consumers convinced that the products were reliable. As many of my Bulgarian informants, representing a pool of both genders and all ages, repeatedly told me, "God knows what people actually put in those jars or whether they actually washed the veggies." Snezhanka, a woman in her late forties, recalled her work-brigade days during summer breaks in the late 1960s (the so-called heyday of socialism) when she was assigned to work in a canning factory.[13] Snezhanka said that she had never bought jars during socialist days after witnessing how workers labored in the plants with unwashed hands and cigarettes dangling from their mouths, without care where ashes might fall. Some of her friends even put insects into the jars just for fun, and nobody noticed. When I naively asked whether there were any control systems to maintain quality, she laughed at my comment and said: "Oh, socialism had all sorts of systems—but so what? It is not the system that is unreliable, but the people!"

This distinction between the system and the people who work in and for the system echoes Herzfeld's (1992) idea of "secular theodicy," where he examines Greeks' attitudes toward bureaucracy and bureaucrats.[14] As Herzfeld observes, bureaucracy as a system is perfect; it is the bureaucrats who make it imperfect. Bulgarians exhibit similar attitudes toward the state or the system when compared to the people who work in them.[15] Hence standardized food was associated with lower value and quality, despite the implied meaning of control in the notion of standardization. In other words, socialist consumers were skeptical of the actual practices of control in the production lines. As a result, Bulgarians relied on homemade jars for their own consumption, whereas factory-produced jars were primarily export items.[16]

Such attitudes toward standardized food also held for frozen foods, especially during the 1980s. Sofians in their fifties and sixties said that the appearance of frozen foods available in the 1980s was "awful." Regardless of the Law on Standardization, these Bulgarians claimed that they did not trust the quality of these food items.[17] Although making *burkani* was a labor-intensive and time-consuming task far removed from the "efficiency" promoted by Bulgaria's modernization advocates, authorities could not convince Bulgarians to buy factory-produced jars during socialism. Bulgarian consumers displayed similar attitudes toward frozen food as its quality became questionable throughout the 1980s.

Skepticism about standardized food was also reflected in the lesser prestige attached to salespeople in stores selling ready-made food. Unlike salespeople working in more ordinary stores offering a range of products, including fresh foods, staples, and other household goods, who exercised power over consumers because of the constant shortages in the socialist economy, salespeople working in ready-made food stores held little power. Daniela, a woman in her late twenties whose ex-boyfriend's mother had worked as a seller in a ready-made food store, explained it to me as follows:

> Ivan's mom worked in those ready-made food stores that were regarded as the lowest level of store because nobody actually bought from there. Poor woman, she was not powerful like the other sellers in other stores. Nobody trusted the quality of such food sold there, and it was believed to taste awful. They really did not look good either. You know communist-style [i.e., presented in minimal and basic wrapping]. . . . What can taste better than homemade food, anyway, right?

In the first decade or so after the end of state socialism, Bulgarian consumers lamented the lack of quality control by the government. Although there were no longer shortages and stores had become filled with products, many of the goods affordable to average Bulgarians were suspected of poor quality and even at times of being "false/fraudulent" (*mente*) and therefore harmful to consume.[18] Under these circumstances, Bulgarian consumers were nostalgically referring to the socialist past and the Law on Standardization, when the government would at least protect consumers from hazardous products. Ironically Bulgarian consumers seemed to have forgotten their skepticism about factory-made jars that were supposed to be controlled by standardization law during socialism.

Changing Attitudes toward Standardization

It is no secret that Bulgarians are proud of their vegetables and fruits, which are believed to taste better than food grown anywhere else. According to a local Bulgarian saying, if God gave one thing to Bulgaria, it was the great Bulgarian soil. Given Bulgarians' pride in their vegetables and fruits, I was somewhat surprised by the actions of Lili, a woman in her early fifties, when we shopped at the wholesale outdoor vegetable market not far from her neighborhood in the fall of 2001. Lili and I were there to buy vegetables to make *turshia* (pickled vegetables). Lili purchased two kilograms of onions from a seller whose prices were significantly lower than those of other vendors. Her decision to purchase such inexpensive onions seemed odd, particularly as Bulgarian informants had repeatedly warned me that if products are sold too cheaply one should suspect their origins (for a similar observation in Russia, see Patico 2003). In fact, Lili told me afterward that she thought they were not Bulgarian, but she admitted that she had to buy the cheapest products because of her financial constraints. This was a reality many Bulgarians shared. After the changes from socialism to capitalism, when cheap imported products from Turkey or Greece flooded into the domestic market, financial constraints outweighed national pride and forced many average Bulgarians to buy cheaper products that were inferior in quality and taste (cf. the "Buy Russia" campaign in postsocialist Russia described in the introduction to this volume and in Caldwell 2002).

Owing to the popularity of *burkani* among my Bulgarian acquaintances, I expected that Lili and I would return home with large bags of vegetables for making jar foods. Yet after we made our first round in the surprisingly deserted market, Lili announced that she would only produce a small amount of *turshia* this year, as good-quality Bulgarian vegetables were becoming increasingly expensive to buy in Sofia and she could not afford to spend a lot of money right then. Smiling, she said that making jars was more for nostalgic reasons now, because it had been a ritual for so many years.

On our way home I asked Lili whether the vegetables we had bought would be enough for her winter supply, and she responded that she would get some from her mother and buy some from the store. Surprised, I asked whether she would actually consume store-bought jars. She laughed and replied that some brands actually produced "nice" (*hubavi*) things that were affordable and reliable to consume these days. As soon as we arrived at her home, she took a jar of *lyutenitza* out of her refrigerator. "Taste this," she offered, "it's actually pretty good!"

Later I learned from other friends that Lili was not the only one buying jars from the store, and that this had become a much more acceptable practice. When I brought up comments I had heard about standardized food during socialist times, acquaintances nodded in affirmation but explained that certain brands are reliable. Generally Western brands from Germany and France, for example, were unquestionable but less affordable, whereas Greek brands were acceptable and definitely more affordable. Bulgarian brands (including some supported by foreign investment) were very affordable, reliable, and had decent taste. When it came to factory-made jars, my friends preferred and trusted jars made by "Deroni,"[19] which was believed to be a Bulgarian company supported by foreign investment and therefore did a proper job with quality control.[20] When I asked how consumers could be so sure, one person answered: "Of course, you can never be sure, but you know, it will not be like under communism. You will not get away with jars that have cigarette ashes or bugs!"

This comment reflected a growing consumer competence that has evolved from consumers' socialist experiences.[21] Now that standardization was not imposed from the top, that is, from the state, and companies had *voluntarily* adopted certain standards, Bulgarian consumers started to reconsider their understanding of standardized food.[22] Their growing consumer competence is related to companies controlling food production and their own consumption choices controlling quality.

One might wonder about food security in these changing attitudes toward standardized food, especially because the socialist system was notorious for irregular production and distribution, despite its planned nature. In other words, one could argue that socialist citizens typically resorted to homemade jars because they could never be guaranteed a consistent supply of daily necessities such as food. Sofians did not deny the aspect of irregular supply but emphasized that they did not feel threatened by starvation during socialism.[23] In fact, not until the *collapse* of socialism did they feel compelled to secure food in fear of starvation because of rising market prices, growing unemployment, low wages, and plummeting living standards. Although stores brimmed with products, many ordinary consumers knew they could not afford them.

With the end of the Cold War and the triumph of neoliberalism, which itself is a consequence of the Cold War, one might easily attribute the shifting attitudes of Bulgarian consumers to the appeal of globalization as promoted in the triumph of capitalism over socialism. Yet I suggest that doing so obscures consumers' individual agency as well as local understandings of globalization. This knowledge is significant because one should not assume that, as is popularly believed, globalization imposes a monolithic one-way, top-down process on everyday consumption practices. Thus the shifting perceptions of standardized food should be understood in a more nuanced way than as an inevitable consequence of global capitalism.

The experience and perception of standardization in Bulgaria must be understood historically. The basic ideas of standardization are hardly new to postsocialist citizens. Although the principles of globalization and standardization are related to the idea of rationalization, they are not identical processes. As discussed previously, globalization is a historical phenomenon tied to neoliberal capitalist practices based on rationalizing tendencies. Standardization, however, is not exclusively linked to one mode of production. Experiences with standardization during the socialist period familiarized Bulgarian consumers with rationalizing practices that guided their perceptions of "control" and "quality."

It is not surprising, therefore, that Sofians do not explain their changing perceptions in relation to a newly shared global consciousness—in other words, they do it because the rest of the world does it. As Lili and other friends pointed out, they experimented with the standardized jars and frozen food out of curiosity and necessity, and then realized that the food could be acceptable for consumption in terms of quality and taste given the daily constraints of time and money. If they did not like a particular brand, there was another they could try. They were not simply purchasing standardized food to emulate what other people did around the world or because it was merely a new lifestyle. Nor did they do it because they believed in quality control exercised by private companies under the capitalist system, for many still believed that market competition did not function these days to eliminate completely all unqualified or substandard products. What now compels them to consume standardized jars is the idea that because they have choices they participate in the control of acceptable standards and standardization. This reflects a growing consumer competence among Bulgarian urbanites,[24] which may be explained further through several common shopping strategies employed by Sofians.

Growing Consumer Competence

In the spring of 2007 Sofia's popular *Bila* supermarket was crowded with consumers returning home from work. Not only had the store expanded its shelves for jars of preserved vegetables and its sections for frozen food, but noticeably more consumers were purchasing these jars and frozen food. Especially striking were the consumer-choice criteria used by my friend Mila when we went shopping together. Mila stopped me as I was trying to select a jar of pickles from the shelf, instructing me first to scan the prices of the various brands before choosing one in the mid-range of prices. Unlike a few years ago, Mila confidently stated that these were the brands that one could consume "*spokoino*" (without anxiety).

When I asked informants about their *burkani* sessions that spring, even the strongest advocates for homemade jars announced that they consumed store-bought jars. Their choice was based on the cost of these items and their own enhanced consumer competence. Over the past several years high-quality fruits and vegetables have become more expensive and increasingly out of the reach of ordinary consumers, but at the same time more varieties of *affordable* standardized food are available from which consumers can choose according to the standards they personally deem important. My friend Snezhanka, who claimed that she had never bought standardized food under socialism because of her personal experiences in the student brigade, said that she began buying jars because she found nice ones she could afford and that fit her standards for taste and quality. Like Mila, when Snezhanka goes to the market she first scans the prices of the different brands of jars and eliminates the most expensive and the cheapest ones. Among the mid-range priced jars, she tries different brands until she finds one that pleases her taste. The previous hierarchy of products that put Western items (typically German and French) at a higher level than domestic goods has apparently become less meaningful.[25] In other words, there is not an immediate preference for Western over domestic products even if the former are within the range of affordable purchase criteria. Snezhanka sometimes consults newspapers and television and also listens to advice from friends, but ultimately she relies on her own experiments. When I asked how she could be sure of the reliability of the jars she chooses, particularly their quality, she replied, simply, "My experience [opit]."

Many other friends echoed this attitude, although some added comments such as the following one: "Among the mid-range priced jars, I further see whether the companies are certified to export to the European Union." More recently, especially with Bulgaria's membership in the EU, Internet-savvy consumers have begun asking consumer advocacy organizations (nongovernmental) or consumer affairs agency (governmental) whether they could publicize the brands and companies that make certain products and have certificates to export to the common market. Unlike previous periods, standards have now become a matter of voluntary adoption by private manufacturers, and the fact that manufacturers are seeking out EU standards provides consumers the added assurance that the jars they choose are reliable both in taste and quality. In this regard, the paradox of standards for consumers in postsocialist Bulgaria lies in its voluntary aspect. Bulgarian consumers like my informants insist that, by recognizing certain manufacturers that have voluntarily adopted certain standards to appeal to consumers, they reevaluate the meaning of standardization and embrace the normalization of standardized food.

Critics are correct when they describe globalization as consisting of multiple factors such as corporate hype, media excitement, and social commentary (Tsing 2005), or when they question whether this phenomenon is as novel as it claims to be (on historical precedents, for example

Figure 1.4. A variety of standardized *Lyutenitza* jars available in a
Sofia grocery store, May 2007. Photograph by Yuson Jung.

see Graeber 2002). According to my informants, globalization in the local
context certainly carries the connotation of Westernization, which is
viewed with suspicion. But their changing attitudes for standardized food
are hardly perceived as Westernized practices. My argument here is not
about resistance to an inevitable global phenomenon; on the contrary,
Bulgarian urbanites are increasingly accepting the normalization of standardized food which they once deemed impossible. The local explanation
of these changing attitudes, however, should not be ignored in favor of a
popular notion of globalization that precludes Sofians' historical experiences. Sofians insist that they are not merely yielding to a globalizing
force. The idea of standardization based on its cultural and historical
understanding accounts for the shifting perceptions and practices around
the consumption of standardized food.

Concluding Remarks: Changes and Continuities

One might suggest that the cooperative aspect of making and consuming jars is changing. Commensality, or the sharing of food, in Bulgaria, however, was rarely centered on making the jars together, as each household prepared them separately. The jars certainly became treats if one had guests visiting, but the jars themselves were not circulated or exchanged for the experience of commensality among friends, families, and neighbors in urban Bulgaria.

Store-bought jars have not completely replaced homemade jars in Sofia, but urban Bulgarian consumers clearly are reconsidering their preexisting ideas on standardized food. This is not to suggest an exoticized or romanticized image of socialism when people used to produce homemade jars to secure their food. Although the irregular distribution systems of the socialist period cannot be ignored, these changing attitudes are closely linked with historical understandings of standards and standardization. The notion of standardization still carries the implication of control, but not necessarily by the state. Certain factory-produced jars are perceived as reliable not because of the Bulgarian state's control but because the brand gained consumers' trust in the control of the quality of the factory's products. The increasing acceptance of buying and consuming factory-produced jars cannot simply be understood in terms of urban Bulgarian consumers trusting the capitalist system more than the socialist system. Rather, it is a reflection of consumers' rationalizing tendencies based on their own growing competence. Bulgarian consumers do not buy factory-made jars because their perceptions are altered by the force of globalization. Instead, they learned that standardized jars could be reliable and suitable for their taste.

Standardization itself is acquiring different meanings based on changing ideas of the effects of control and reliability on quality. It is not simply the state or even the system that acts as the agent of control and the object of reliability. The agent of control is more ambiguous, as Sofians are buying standardized jars not because they were assured that the quality of jars was controlled by the government or by a uniquely Bulgarian version of capitalism. Like many Sofians, my informants still believe that the capitalist system in Bulgaria does not work and that the government is too corrupt and weak to exercise control. Instead, Sofians recognize their own

Figure 1.5. Frozen food available in a Sofia grocery store, May 2007.
Photograph by Yuson Jung.

ability to choose certain brands that produce reliable and affordable products that taste good without necessarily associating these brands with
certain interests. As consumers, they execute their own control over food
consumption. It is sufficient for them to realize that standardized food has
re-obtained its original meaning as controlled reliable food. An extra
incentive is that these foods may also have a pleasant taste. In this regard
urban Bulgarians are reconsidering the low value associated with standardized food and are developing a positive relationship with it. Although
standardized jars occupy a lower status in the hierarchy of value than
homemade jars, the consumption of the former is no longer deemed
unimaginable.

Bulgaria's membership in the EU, in January 2007, further assured consumers who consider EU standards as another validation for the choices
they make. This form of standardization by an abstract entity like the
European Union may invoke the standards and control by the state during
socialist times, prompting consumers to be skeptical about whether the
system of control actually works. As I have argued, however, that con-

sumers believe they exercise ultimate control through their own competence significantly colors their shifting attitudes toward the practical consequences of standardized food. In this regard, the cultural logic of consuming or disdaining standardized food is not so different during and after socialism. Sofian consumers have always actively examined their options, given their circumstances, and have chosen the most efficient and reliable means for themselves.

ACKNOWLEDGMENTS

The research for this chapter was supported by a Krupp Dissertation Fellowship at the Minda de Gunzburg Center for European Studies at Harvard University; a Harvard University Graduate Society Research Fellowship; Andrew Mellon Pre-Dissertation Grants administered by the Department of Anthropology at Harvard University; and summer research grants from the Davis Center for Russian Studies and the Minda de Gunzburg Center for European Studies at Harvard University. Additional support for write-up was provided by a Dissertation Writing Fellowship at the Minda de Gunzburg Center for European Studies. I also acknowledge the technical assistance of the Center for East European, Russian/Eurasian Studies at the University of Chicago and the Woodrow Wilson International Center for Scholars in Washington, D.C., during the revision of earlier drafts. None of the above organizations is responsible for the views expressed here. This essay has greatly benefited from the careful and critical readings of friends and colleagues. I thank especially Melissa Caldwell and Neringa Klumbytė for their detailed comments. Portions of the research have been presented at the Annual Meetings of the American Association of Advancement of Slavic Studies (2004) and the American Anthropological Association (2006). I am grateful to those who participated in the panels, especially Elizabeth Dunn and Gabriela Vargas-Cetina, for their constructive feedback, which helped develop ideas for this chapter.

NOTES

1. All names have been changed to protect and respect the identities of my informants.

2. In referring to preserved vegetables and fruits I prefer the local Bulgarian term "jar" (*burkan*) over "can," the more commonly used expression in the English-speaking world, because Bulgarians store vegetables and fruits in jars rather than cans. I also use the term "jar

food" rather than "canned food" for the same reason. For descriptions about jars in Bulgaria, see Smollett 1989.

3. According to my Bulgarian friends, "food safety" was not an issue during socialism, but consumers often complained about the poor quality and shortage of food. Food safety, unlike poor quality, was associated with "danger" (*opasnost*).

4. This discussion is based on almost twenty months of ethnographic fieldwork in Sofia between 1998 and 2007, including thirteen months of extended fieldwork between September 2001 and October 2002. Supplemental data come from archival research at the City Library of Sofia, the Agency for Standardization and Metrology in Sofia, Bulgaria, and the U.S. Library of Congress.

5. Dunn (2004) notes how capitalism and socialism shared specific ways of organizing industrial work because of the influence of Henry Ford, whom both Lenin and Stalin admired. This fascination with Fordism profoundly shaped the organization of state socialist industry and characterized Soviets' ideal of modernity. Along with Taylorism, which popularized "scientific management" to improve efficiency on the shop floor, Fordism had a huge impact on the industrial systems in the socialist world (ibid., 9–18). See Buechler and Buechler's discussion (1999) of the emphasis on Taylorism in the GDR in bread production.

6. Danon yogurt was one of the global brands perceived particularly negatively by Bulgarian consumers. Bulgarians consume a lot of plain yogurt (*kiselo mlyako;* literally, sour milk) and believe that the Danon brand has an unnatural taste and is made artificially (from dried powder, not from natural bacteria that turns milk into yogurt).

7. According to my informant and friend, Dimitar, a lawyer who has participated in writing the new consumer law while working at the former Agency of Standardization and Metrology (Agentziya na standardizatsiya i metrologiya), the old Law on Standardization with compulsory standards was not effective between 1991 and 1999. During the turmoil of the early transition period, no one actually adhered to those regulations.

8. The Law on Standardization also regulates the kind of paper in which products are wrapped as well as how they are wrapped, stored, and transported. For instance, with regard to frozen food, every government standard (*durjaven standart*) under this law identified the temperature for manufacturing, transporting, and storing the frozen products.

9. The consumer products presently available for purchase should be distinguished from those that ordinary consumers can actually afford.

10. One should be careful not to make simplistic statements about the quality of products during the socialist period. Even though postsocialist consumers often acknowledge the inferior quality of their socialist products compared to "Western" products sporadically available to socialist consumers (for example, if one had access to foreign currency, one could purchase Western products through a Foreign Currency Store [in Bulgaria's case, *KOREKOM;* akin to "Dollar Stores" in the Soviet Union]), they also point out the superior quality of socialist products compared to what they can afford in the postsocialist context because of financial constraints limiting them to cheap products often of inferior quality (see more about consumer complaints in Jung 2007:55–57, 86–89).

11. The first canning industry is documented as having been the small canning industry in Varna in 1899; about 250 small enterprises exported their canned products to Germany during World War II. This emphasis on exports continued throughout the socialist period, comprising 75–80 percent of production (*Enziklopediya Bulgaria* 1982:551).

12. For further discussions on standards and standardization as modern production practices and their impact on control and circumvention of governing principles in the EU and the global political economy, see Dunn 2005.

13. In the 1980s socialist Bulgaria produced and exported a lot of foodstuffs and processed food to the former Soviet Union and East Germany, as well as to some Western European markets. Most of the industrial food production was for export, and an urban myth claims that the processed food for the domestic market was of poor quality (i.e., second quality), which affected Bulgarians' negative attitude toward standardized food.

14. Herzfeld is drawing on Weber's ideas about theodicy, which Weber uses to explain why religion continues to be important to people even though it may not explicate everything perfectly.

15. I In further discussion of the common dichotomy of the state/system versus the people during and after socialism in Bulgaria, see Jung 2007:72–79. For discussions on this dichotomy in the literature of postsocialism, see Verdery 1996 and Yurchak 2005.

16. Under the socialist regime, Bulgaria took part in the SIV (Suvet za Ikonomicheska Vzaimopomosht, or the Council for Economic Mutual Aid) led by the Soviet Union. This meant, for example, that Bulgaria exported food and foodstuffs in exchange for oil and natural gas from the Soviet Union or for machines from East Germany. Jars and cans were chief export items under this economic practice during socialism.

17. According to Sofians, declining consumption of standardized frozen food in the 1980s could also be attributed to the increased manufacture of refrigerators that included a separate freezing section. By the late 1980s stand-alone freezers had become more available in individual homes. In the final years of socialism and the early days of the postsocialist period (i.e., the late 1980s and the first half of the 1990s), electricity supplies became unreliable and eventually so expensive that many people stopped using separate freezers.

18. In the summer of 1999 I observed a widespread obsession with "false/fraudulent products [mente]." On grocery shopping excursions my friends made sure that the items we bought (especially those with global brand recognition such as Coca-Cola, chocolates, and yogurt, or alcohol such as Bulgarian wine and brandy [rakiya]) were not mente. My acquaintances were profoundly knowledgeable in distinguishing mente products, knowledge that was also publicly disseminated through daily newspapers and a specialized magazine titled Mente. Already by the following year, however, the obsession was slowly fading, though people still mentioned it, and I could no longer find the magazine Mente in the kiosks. For further discussion on the "mente" phenomenon, see Jung 2007:122–126.

19. The food industry has revitalized enormously since 2002, and, according to my observations in 2007, many more domestic brands are gaining popularity among Bulgarian urbanites.

20. Although Bulgarians generally express skepticism that the country will undergo any positive change, there is also a common belief that Westerners would implement reliable quality control.

21. I view consumer competence differently from purchasing power, as the latter assumes consumer power through money. In the postsocialist context, it is still difficult to say that ordinary consumers have purchasing power in the way it is used in wealthier societies.

22. The voluntary aspects for adopting standards have different implications for the producers. See Gille, this volume; and Dunn 2005.

23. For descriptions of common socialist shopping practices such as hoarding, see, for example, Caldwell 2004 and Humphrey 2002.

24. Similarly Berdahl (1999) explains these changing consumption practices in terms of a growing cultural fluency that postsocialist consumers develop.

25. Some acquaintances explained that "Western/global" brands have become less meaningful in the hierarchy of products because consumers believe that some of the global products

are produced differently for different markets. For example, even the same ketchup brand such as "Heinz" would not taste the same in different countries because the ketchup would have been produced at different sites.

REFERENCES CITED

Berdahl, Daphne. 1999. *Where the World Ended: Re-Unification and Identity in the German Borderland.* Berkeley: University of California Press.

Buechler, Hans, and Judith-Maria Buechler. 1999. "The Bakers of Bemburg and the Logics of Communism and Capitalism." *American Ethnologist* 26 (4): 799–821.

Caldwell, Melissa L. 2002. "The Taste of Nationalism: Food Politics in Postsocialist Moscow." *Ethnos* 67(3): 295–319.

———. 2004. *Not by Bread Alone: Social Support in the New Russia.* Berkeley: University of California Press.

———. 2005. "Domesticating the French Fry: McDonald's and Consumerism in Moscow." In *The Cultural Politics of Food and Eating: A Reader,* ed. James L. Watson and Melissa L. Caldwell, pp. 180–196. Malden, Mass.: Blackwell.

Creed, Gerald. 1997. *Domesticating Revolution: From Socialist Reform to Ambivalent Transition in a Bulgarian Village.* University Park: Pennsylvania State University.

———. 2002. "(Consumer) Paradise Lost: Capitalist Dynamics and Disenchantment in Rural Bulgaria." *Anthropology of East Europe Review* 20(2): 119–125.

Dunn, Elizabeth. 2004. *Privatizing Poland: Baby Food, Big Business, and the Remaking of Labor.* Ithaca, N.Y.: Cornell University Press.

———. 2005. "Standards and Person-Making in East Central Europe." In *Global Assemblages: Technology, Politics, and Ethics as Anthropological Problems,* ed. Aihwa Ong and Stephen J. Collier, pp. 173–193. Malden, Mass.: Blackwell.

Enziklopediya Bulgaria. 1982. Sofia: Sofiyal Press.

Gille, Zsuzsa. n.d. "The Tale of the Toxic Paprika: The Hungarian Taste of Euro-Globalization." Unpublished manuscript.

Glants, Musya, and Joyce Toomre, eds. 1997. *Food in Russian History and Culture.* Bloomington: Indiana University Press.

Graeber, David. 2001. *Toward an Anthropological Theory of Value: The False Coins of Our Own Dreams.* New York: Palgrave.

Herzfeld, Michael. 1992. *The Social Production of Indifference: Exploring the Symbolic Roots of Western Bureaucracy.* Oxford: Berg.

Humphrey, Caroline. 2002. *The Unmaking of Soviet Life: Everyday Economics after Socialism.* Ithaca, N.Y.: Cornell University Press.

Jung, Yuson. 2007. "Consumer Lament: An Ethnographic Study on Consumption, Needs, and Everyday Complaints in Postsocialist Bulgaria." Ph.D. diss., Harvard University, Cambridge, Mass.

Klumbytè, Neringa. n.d. "The Cold War in the EU Market: 'Euro' and 'Soviet' Brands in Lithuania." Unpublished manuscript.

Patico, Jennifer. 2001. "Globalization in the Postsocialist Marketplace: Consumer Readings of Difference and Development in Urban Russia." *Kroeber Anthropological Society Papers* 86:127–142.

———. 2002. "Consuming the West but Becoming Third World: Food Imports and the Experience of Russianness." *Anthropology of East Europe Review* 17(1): 31–36.

Ritzer, George. 1996. *The McDonaldization of Society.* Thousand Oaks, Calif.: Pine Forge.

———. 2004. *The Globalization of Nothing.* Thousand Oaks, Calif.: Pine Forge.

Rothstein, Halina, and Robert A. Rothstein. 1997. "The Beginnings of Soviet Culinary Art." In *Food in Russian History and Culture,* ed. Musya Glants and Joyce Toomre, pp. 177–194. Bloomington: Indiana University Press.

Seremetakis, Nadia. 1994. *The Senses Still: Perception and Memory as Material Culture in Modernity.* Chicago: University of Chicago Press.

Smollett, Eleanor. 1989. "The Economy of Jars: Kindred Relationships in Bulgaria—An Exploration." *Ethnologia Europaea (Journal of European Ethnology)* 19(2): 125–140.

Tomlinson, John. 1997. *Cultural Imperialism.* Baltimore, Md.: Johns Hopkins University Press.

Verdery, Katherine. 1996. *What Was Socialism and What Comes Next?* Princeton, N.J.: Princeton University Press.

Waters, Malcolm. 1995. *Globalization.* London: Routledge.

Watson, James L. 2006. "Transnationalism, Localization, and Fast Foods in East Asia." In *Golden Arches East: McDonald's in East Asia,* ed. James L. Watson, pp. 1–38. Stanford, Calif.: Stanford University Press.

Watson, James L., and Melissa L. Caldwell, eds. 2005. *The Cultural Politics of Food and Eating: A Reader.* Malden, Mass.: Blackwell.

Yurchak, Alexei. 2005. *Everything Was Forever Until It Was No More: The Last Soviet Generation.* Berkeley: University of California Press.

TWO

The Tale of the Toxic Paprika

The Hungarian Taste of Euro-Globalization

ZSUZSA GILLE

In 2004 eight former communist countries, followed by two more in 2007, entered the European Union, a supranational organization whose members formerly constituted these countries' ideological nemesis. The process of meeting the requirements for accession to the EU, although arduous and fraught with conflicts, was seen as one in which the East would adopt the laws, policies, political institutions, and even political culture of the West; the actual accession, although repeatedly delayed, was a foregone conclusion. Policy analysts and social scientists succumbed to the inevitability of this radical redrawing of Europe's political map and, as a result, found the accession process unremarkable and lacking merit for serious, theoretically informed, and critically attuned analysis. Most of what social science scholarship has produced about this development belongs to the realms of comparative political science approaches or international relations studies relating the Eastern enlargement to previous instances of accessions, largely framing it as part and parcel of a worldwide trend of democratization.

As a native Hungarian who has conducted research in Eastern Europe for fifteen years but has also lived in the United States, I experienced the era from 1989 to the present as a profound transformation in everyday practices, in mentality, and even in cognitive maps applied to political arguments. Given my informants' experiences, I never understood the capitulation of the social sciences in treating the accession process as a black box. Granted, many aspects of molding Eastern Europe to a Western shape were complex and hard to keep pace with even for the most committed experts; that, however, does not justify relinquishing the effort to understand, evaluate, and critique the process. In fact, I argue that the enlargement process, if viewed through the correct analytical lens, can provide new insights into the workings of this mighty global supranational institution, into the nature of its power and its relationship to globalization.[1] In my view, one problem has been the fallacy Anna Tsing (2000) calls "globalism," namely, that to understand global and large-scale processes we must analyze them on a global level. My analysis in this essay takes the opposite tack, making use of an unexpected little spice to examine the practices and processes of Europeanization, demonstrating that a more restrictive perspective can provide a better understanding of the EU accession. I examine the 2004 paprika scandal and what it tells us about the nature of globalization embodied in the European Union.

On October 27, 2004, the Hungarian government shocked the public by banning the sale of paprika powder, its use in restaurants, and, until further notice, its household use as well. The chief Hungarian public health authority (ÁNTSZ) had found that of the seventy-two commodities regularly sold in Hungary, thirteen contained aflatoxin B1, a carcinogenic microtoxin produced by mold. The concentration of the substance was sometimes sixteen times larger than the threshold permitted by the European Union (5mg/kg). To extend the testing to all products, their sale was banned. The testing, and thus the ban, lasted three days, during which ÁNTSZ gradually released the list of products found to be safe. Ultimately forty-eight products tested positive for the chemical, although how many of these were legally toxic—that is, above the EU limits and whose sale would thus constitute an act of crime—is unclear. Aflatoxin, which in public discourse had primarily been linked to repeated EU bans on African or Brazilian nuts, can only grow in peppers produced in Mediterranean or tropical climates. Hungarian consumers were astounded to learn, however, that the famous Szeged and Kalocsa paprika, sold worldwide as a *Hungaricum*, a unique product marketed and protected as originating in Hungary and embodying national traditions, actually contained peppers imported from Brazil and Spain. Experts, too, were dumbfounded that contaminated products could find their way to the grocery shelves undetected despite the elaborate food safety measures adopted to meet EU standards. The processes associated with EU accession that led to this scandal are explored in the following sections.

Making Paprika European

Hungary produces, on average, eight thousand to ten thousand tons of paprika every year (from six times this amount of fresh peppers).[2] In 2003 fifty-three hundred tons were exported, indicating that the industry is strongly export-oriented. Germany imports an average of 30 percent, and other important buyers are Austria, Holland, Slovakia, and Romania. Thus Hungary accounts for 10 percent of the world's paprika exports. Although paprika does not constitute as great a share of Hungary's exports, even of food exports, as one would expect based on its fame, it is an economically important product. First, paprika is a unique product that enjoys worldwide brand-name recognition, thus contributing positively to the image of Hungarian products. Second, it is used in many other products that Hungary exports such as Pick salami and Gyulai sausage. In fact, Szegedi Paprika owns Pick. Third, as a national symbol, paprika is an asset in promoting tourism. Therefore, not only is the production of paprika a pull sector in Hungarian exports, but its great visibility (even greater than its quantitative economic significance) also renders its successes and failures consequential for several economic sectors. And, in terms of its failures, there have been several recently.

Two scandals erupted in the 1990s. In the first, lead was found in paprika sold mostly at farmers' markets.[3] The source of the contamination was a lead-containing paint that sellers had mixed in with paprika. In the second incident, powdered brick was found in paprika. In both cases the obvious rationale for the adulteration was to enhance the color of the spice, and, according to news media, the culprits were known to be Ukrainians and Romanians.[4]

Many such scandals were seen as the manifestation of the "Wild East" phenomenon, which, depending on one's political attitude, was chalked up either to liberalization and the collapse of the state or to Eastern Europeans' newly liberated and thus excessive and gullible consumerism. But all this was supposed to end with Hungary's accession to EU membership. After all, the European Union constantly emphasized that it was not letting Eastern European food products, known to lack hygiene and quality, into Europe. News like this abounded in the Western media as the accession grew closer:

> A food agency chief has warned that welcoming new members could bring down food standards across the European Union. The chairman of the Food Standards Agency, Sir John Krebs, said consumers could face risks from fraudulent traders and contaminated food unless standards were upheld. (BBC, January 15, 2003)

In response to these fears, EU officials proclaimed, if not threatened, that

> Food safety is an element of the enlargement process where the EU made clear from the beginning that it will not accept a situation that might lead to lower food safety standards or to any risks for consumers. The new Member states recognize that compliance with the Union's acquis on food safety is essential. (EU Enlargement: Questions and Answers on food safety issues Memo/ 03/88, Brussels, December 5, 2003, p.1)

Well before the fifteen-member EU and the candidate countries' publics formally voted on their membership, Hungary already not only had adopted eighty thousand pages of legislation and case law into its legal framework but had also replaced Hungarian food-safety laws with those of the EU. In addition, many corporations had gone beyond minimum requirements by adopting so-called voluntary safety and quality standards. Most notable among these standards was the HACCP (Hazard Analysis Critical Point System).[5] HACCP is a risk management tool based on the identification and monitoring of critical points where biological, chemical, or physical risks arise. To achieve HACCP accreditation, producers and service providers first identify the source of health risks in their production process with the help of expert consultants. They then adopt new procedures and even new appliances to prevent these risks or reduce them to an acceptable level. Regulation entails the implementation of alternatives to such "critical points" and their systematic monitoring, which is self-administered and must be kept on written record. Authorities in charge of surveillance do not control or test the actual production process or products; they simply "audit the books" to get an immediate glimpse of the state of hygiene and safety in a particular place (Unnevehr and Hirschhorn 2000; Unnevehr 2000).[6]

As the deadline passed for food-related facilities to acquire HACCP accreditation (January 2003) and deadlines for various extensions grew near, my interviews made clear that emotions ran high among farmers selling their own produce, butchers, salespeople, and managers of small grocery shops. The mere mention of the words "standards" and "the EU" brought forth a veritable flood of complaints. People found the imposed standards ridiculously impractical, for example, having to change color-coded uniforms between cutting a chunk of meat for a customer and handling the cash involved in the transaction. They were all insulted by the costs of the consultation, training, and accreditation, as well as by the expenses involved in actually implementing the required changes in the physical layout of their facilities, new materials such as cleaning supplies, new equipment such as refrigerators meeting the new guidelines, and the administration of the self-monitoring itself.[7]

Other anxieties concerned the implications of newly adopted EU standards for Hungarian cuisine and national traditions of feeding and slaughtering animals. Questions abounded in the media as to whether Hungarians would be able to produce and eat *foie gras,* poppy seeds, or home-made sausages (i.e., feed hogs swill and slaughter them without prior sedation). The official pro-EU campaign not only made such qualities the central themes in its various infomercials, but it also used food-related imagery even in its messages unrelated to food.[8] The message was that we can be Hungarian *and* European at the same time—Hungarian by holding onto our gastronomic traditions and European by observing high standards of quality and hygiene as well as adhering to strict animal rights. The answer was to vote yes to the accession.

Beaten into Hungarian heads was that a brave new world was coming where food will be better and safer without insulting local taste buds. It came as a shock, therefore, that just as practices officially came to be sanctioned as European-Hungarian, paprika, the pride of the nation, was found to be toxic. Or was it really *Hungarian* paprika that was toxic? Apparently Europeanizing Hungarian paprika did not make it safer and better but just the opposite. To understand how Europeanization produced results contrary to its intended purpose, we must view the process as Janus faced, a development I term "Euro-globalization."

Globalizing Paprika

Hungary had been subject to what Harvey (1991) calls "post-Fordist capitalism" or what McMichael (1996) terms the "globalization project from the late 1980s."[9] In what sense, then, can we argue that paprika become more globalized than it was prior to EU accession? To answer this question, I elaborate on the following aspects of the case: the pressure to privatize; increased free trade, especially the radical reduction of import duties; the insistence to maintain flexible production; the replacement of national with international or foreign authorities to monitor the safety of imported food; and the ensuing relaxation of national food safety standards.

PRIVATIZATION   Whereas Western European market economies are often credited with the term "capitalism with a human face," the European Union, in many of its practices vis-à-vis extra-EU states, embodies a more laissez-faire, more liberal, more, if I may, American model of the market economy than what it prefers for itself. I need only mention Cancún for even a cursory observer of world news to recall the bitter debates about the double standards involved in the EU's agricultural and trade policies.[10] Let us remember that one criterion of EU membership for former socialist countries (as laid down in the Copenhagen criteria in 1993) was a functioning market economy. The EU saw the structural adjustment programs of supranational agencies, such as the International Monetary Fund (IMF) and the World Bank, as the right path to meeting the accession criteria, especially those requiring a thoroughly liberalized economy. Although the existing, Western members of the EU retained much of their welfare system and production subsidies, if you were to read the texts of various aid and loans packets provided by them to former socialist countries, you would be hard-pressed to say which came from the explicitly neo-liberal financial institutions (the IMF and the World Bank) and which from the bastion of tamed capitalism (the EU). To the extent that it advocated economic growth through reduced state spending, privatization, price liberalization, and free trade, the European Union acted as an agent of neoliberal globalization in Eastern Europe.

In the case of Hungary, paprika-producing land was progressively privatized after 1989, although substantial fields remained in agricultural cooperatives. As for the two key paprika-processing firms, Kalocsai Fűszerpaprika, and Szegedi Paprika, they were transformed into shareholding corporations. The Hungarian state retained significant shares in the former, and members of paprika-producing cooperatives also bought shares in these processing companies.

FREE TRADE   A key element of neoliberalism is free trade. Although trade between Hungary and EU member countries had been gradually liberalized by the time of the formal accession, some pockets of "protectionism" remained until May 1, 2004. One was the high import duty levied on paprika. Overnight this was reduced from 44.2 percent to 5 percent, radically increasing the appeal of cheap Latin-American imports. Two major sources of imports were apparent immediately prior to the scandal. Hungary "imported" twenty-two tons from Spain in September 2004. Whereas the same trade event would have been considered imports just a few months earlier, after May 1, 2004, that is, after Hungary's formal accession to the EU, it no longer counted as imports because Spain and Hungary, as EU members, now shared the same customs borders. This has great significance for food safety, as I will illustrate below. The other, this time "real," exporter is Brazil from where Hungary had imported eighty-eight tons since December 2003. Eight tons of this tested positive for Aflatoxin B 1.[11]

That importing paprika was the decision of paprika processors seems well established,[12] but their rationale for doing so is less clear. Some argued that a poor harvest the previous year (2003) as a result of a drought cut the harvest by 60 percent, making importing necessary. Others pointed out that imports were needed because the peppers were insufficient in color, a problem also attributed to bad weather, since the more sunshine peppers receive before harvest, the greater their pigment. In order to retain paprika's appealing color, processors mixed the Hungarian peppers with peppers from Spain and Brazil, as the pigment content in the latter is almost twice that of Hungarian peppers.

A third argument came not from the processors but from the producers. In my interviews with two directors of farms that produce paprika on a large scale (100 hectares),[13] one of them, the chief of the Paprika Produce Council[14] and a member of the Committee on Identifying Paprika Species at the time, told me that the processors imported paprika from Brazil because it was much cheaper than Hungarian peppers. The second director added, approvingly, "This processor invited us, producers, for a meeting. He [the representative of the processing firm] put paprika powder made from Brazilian peppers on the table and pointed out how colorful it was." The threat was clear: either they cut their prices or their contracts would be lost to the Brazilians. Producers were also aware—and paprika processors emphasized this point—that foreign distributors were already engaged in mixing Hungarian paprika with Latin American peppers to lower their costs without necessarily lowering the price. Consequently Hungarian processors simply wanted to do what seemed to make good economic sense: keep the profits that arise from mixing to themselves rather than yielding them to their foreign wholesale customers.[15]

Although these tactics were a powerful incentive and despite food producers everywhere finding themselves in ever fiercer competition with one another in the so-called race to the bottom, Hungarian producers did not give in. They knew that taste was on their side and that Brazilian and Spanish peppers could never win against the paprika from Szeged and Kalocsa. Banding together, rather than competing, they refused to lower their prices. After the paprika scandal, news came that small producers stopped selling peppers to the indicted processors and instead established their own processing facilities. Ironically processors were now desperate to keep producers on their side because, in the words of one informant, "We are being hurt together."

Certainly this is a temporary reconciliation. Small producers see no solace in the case of Spain, where spice pepper production fell by one-third after EU accession because of cheap imports. In fact, Hungary's spice paprika production is apparently decreasing. According to my data sources thus far, in 1996 the annual harvest was fifty-two thousand tons compared to no more than thirty-seven thousand tons harvested in 2004, a good-harvest year.

FLEXIBLE PRODUCTION VERSUS FLEXIBLE INFORMATION

Another criterion for accession included the candidate country's ability to withstand competitive pressures on the unified market. Given swift changes in consumer demands—and an increasing number of demands in niche markets—as well as shifts in raw material and stock prices, withstanding these competitive pressures requires great flexibility in production. Paradoxically, it is precisely the EU's emphasis on and Western European consumers' demand for standard quality and thus trustworthiness that required Hungarian paprika processors to implement more flexibility in their production. According to various news reports and interviews, some processors started importing peppers in 1997, and others did not begin until 2003 and then only in small quantities to compensate for natural misfortunes such as poor harvests or low pigment content, as noted above. Although this flexibility may be desirable from a neoliberal perspective, it is clearly at odds with EU regulations requiring that the packaging lists ingredients and source countries. No processor complied with this labeling law, because, as the president of one processing company argued in a TV interview, the composition of the paprika that is sold varies more frequently than they could accommodate through printing new packaging (*A Szólás Szabadsága,* October 29, 2004). Although many viewed this argument as a poor excuse, in the market climate of ever increasing competition any cost-cutting measure will seem rational, even the expense of reprinting labels. In the end, in March 2008, Szegedi Paprika lost its appeal against a court ruling fining the company 3 million Forints (U.S.$20,000) for falsely advertising its paprika as exclusively Hungarian (MTI Econews 2008).

DISEMPOWERING NATIONAL AUTHORITIES AND RELAXING NATIONAL FOOD SAFETY STANDARDS The common assumption is that, with EU membership, a candidate country's food-safety regulation will improve, but in many cases the opposite was true. Although member countries are generally free to enforce stricter standards than those imposed by the EU—whether regarding food safety or the environment—I know of no new member country that retained its standards when they were stricter than the EU's. This was the case in Hungary, for example, regarding the legal definition of fresh milk, certain emission standards, and nature protection laws. Obviously this has much to do with these countries' hunger for capital and with their poor bargaining positions in the world and in the EU. This explains why the replacement of national standards with EU standards effectively resulted in a relaxation of norms.

Let us consider some consequences of this relaxation of standards. First, because Spanish peppers are not "real" imports, they are no longer checked when entering Hungary. This became a problem in August 2004, when through random testing—the only kind of testing done since EU accession—one Hungarian processor discovered the presence of ochratoxin, a liver- and kidney-damaging microtoxin also produced by molds. To avoid a scandal, the affected products were silently removed from grocery stores. Note that this discovery came about only because Hungarians traditionally tested for ochratoxin in paprika, even though the EU had no limits for ochratoxin in peppers and spices.

Second, as trade experts argue, even when peppers are imported to Hungary from Spain, we cannot know for certain whether they were actually grown and dried in Spain or whether Spain imported them from elsewhere (*Index*, October 28, 2004). Unknown origins naturally make tracing a problem and resolving it much more difficult, further weakening the power of national food safety authorities.

Third, after accession, even peppers comprising real imports are removed from the jurisprudence of national authorities, because authorities at the entry port, in this case Rotterdam, carry out the prescribed controls. Spice peppers, however, are not on the list of imported goods that must be tested. Furthermore, the amount of information on pepper that is required has decreased. As my informant argued, "Before EU accession we tested the peppers for twenty to thirty things; now, however, we don't, because the EU does not prescribe such tests." As the director of the Hungarian Food Safety Bureau (MÉBH) pointed out, the certificates accompanying the peppers imported from Latin America "are useless, because they only indicate whether there are any additives in them. Since the EU does not test for mold toxins [in peppers], the certificates obviously don't address them" (*HVG*, November 6, 2004, p. 97).

Here it is useful to examine three reactions to the paprika scandal of 2004. First, the Hungarian government submitted a proposal to the EU Food Safety Committee to perform Aflatoxin tests on imported peppers at EU entry ports. The Committee turned down the request, disagreeing that the available information provided evidence that paprika originating from Brazil was the main source of contaminated paprika on the EU market. Therefore restrictive measures regarding paprika products originating from Brazil were unjustified (Standing Committee on the Food Chain and Animal Health, Section on Toxicological Safety and Section on General Food Law, Summary Record of the meeting of February 14, 2005, p. 3). The Committee effectively deferred this case, and all such cases, to national competence, stating that "Member States [are] recommended to reinforce the controls on the presence of aflatoxins in paprika and paprika products placed on the market" (ibid.).

As a second response to the scandal, the requirement that manufacturers indicate a product's place of origin on its label if it is marketed as being from a specific geographical location, though in place since accession, will now be more strictly enforced, as indicated by the above-mentioned court ruling. And, in a third reaction, the prime minister placed the Hungarian Food Safety Bureau (MÉBH) under the supervision of the Ministry of Health, arguing that its previous superordinate ministry, that of Agriculture and Regional Development, "is dominated more by the interests of the processors."[16]

That these steps did not go far enough quickly became obvious. Even before the police closed the paprika case, a new pepper-related scandal broke out in February 2005 in which white peppers from Morocco were found to contain residues of pesticides already banned in the EU. This time, Hungarian authorities went further than they had in the fall of 2004, explicitly criticizing the EU's standards that had been relaxed in the name of free trade and calling for the reinstitution of national surveillance. In a TV program the director of the Hungarian Food Safety Bureau (MÉBH) dared to draw a connection between free markets and failures in food safety: "Since May 1 [2004], all products can come in the country unimpeded, what is more, this is the basic principle of the common market, that is, we should not obstruct this; and this is why there is no obligatory examination [at the national borders]" (*Index*, February 26, 2005). Moreover, the director of ÁNTSZ pleaded, though timidly, that, "we *would like to* ensure that *some* control *would still be allowed* at the internal borders" (*Index*, February 26, 2005; my emphasis).

The Nature of Euro-Globalization

What does all this tell us about the nature of capitalism in the European Union? Is it enacting a largely neoliberal globalization project, the model of the race to the bottom, or a kind of protectionist capitalism in which standards are proliferating at a dizzying speed, effecting what World Bank analysts called the "race to the top"?[17] We can understand the question in one of two ways: Does it refer to the kinds of project that the EU intends to realize in Western and Eastern Europe, or is it referring to the "actually existing" Europeanization, regardless of the EU's intentions? As Martha Lampland (2004) reminds us, models of economic and social transformation never materialize in a pure form untainted by local conditions either in the project's place of origin or where it is transposed for implementation. I therefore choose to focus on the "actually existing" Europeanization.

Table 2.1 organizes and summarizes the above-detailed claims concerning the effects of globalization and EU accession on paprika production and trade, separating and contrasting the elements that belong to each model along five key dimensions.

To the extent that we can find elements of both models in Hungarian paprika production, we might conclude that in order to decide which model is prevalent we need to look at which explains the case better or which seems to have won out over the other. It would be compelling to argue, then, that neoliberal capitalism prevails, because Hungary could not protect consumers from toxins repeatedly found in imported peppers. Nor could it protect the paprika producers from cheap competition. In my view, however, we are better off seeing "race to the bottom" and "race to the top" as two sides of the same coin. I do not intend this to mean that they are centrifugal tendencies, especially not in the sense of the former being the dominant force to which the latter is simply a defensive reaction. I prefer, instead, to look at their dynamics as mutually enabling and restricting. Were we to concentrate on practices rather than ideologies of each "race," we would find not so much a struggle of two seemingly conflicting economic models but the emergence of a new model that provides a judicious and strategic mix of these two models. Here I elaborate on the ways in which the two projects, "race to the bottom" and "race to the top," work together in the paprika case, enabling, rather than merely constraining each other.

Table 2.1. "Race to the Bottom" versus "Race to the Top"

	Neoliberal Capitalism Race to the bottom	"Protectionist" Capitalism Race to the top
Flexible production	Demand for flexibility leads to imports and changing ingredients in paprika	Requirement to inform consumers of ingredients
Trade	Promotion of free trade leads to the import of the cheapest products even when there is sufficient domestic produce; and the radical reduction of import duties, further cheapening imports	Quality and safety standards in place to limit sub-standard imports; HACCP and ISOs were adopted by paprika producers and retailers
Regulation of production	Decreased regulation and monitoring of production and goods in circulation; fewer tests done on peppers	New practices are required to standardize testing and monitoring; HACCP and ISOs were adopted by paprika producers and retailers
Level of surveillance	Only supranational (EU-level or WTO) arbitration in the regulation of production and trade; disempowerment of national authorities in monitoring paprika safety	Those outside these supranational organizations still view this surveillance as an act of protectionism; call for the possibility of national surveillance
Source of profit	Increased circulation of goods and capital (both spatially and temporally) increases turnover and thus profits; mixing cheap imports into Hungarian paprika increased profits	Certifications, trademarks, audits, and other self-monitoring systems become a value-added and, by excluding competitors without those certificates, increase profits; paprika is a Hungaricum and thus has great value-added

First, quality and safety standards, rather than impediments to free trade, actually increase the circulation of goods. With the blessing of HACCP and the ISO,[18] the Szeged and Kalocsa paprika can now enter previously closed doors or doors that otherwise may have suddenly been shut. Furthermore, competitors elsewhere in the world will find that in order to enter new markets or retain old ones now protected in the name of these standards, they will have to adopt the same standards. At the same time, to the extent that safety and quality standards originate in the global North/West, they require the replacement of local, domestic standards still in place in the global South/East, which, whether stricter or looser, disadvantage domestic producers in the latter: as a result of added expenses or lost markets they might go out of business. More generally, one aspect of protectionist capitalism, safety and quality standards, works against another of its aspects, namely, the preference and subsidy for domestic production.

Lowering national standards hurt the image of Hungarian paprika, even though the source of the toxins was not Hungarian. This, in turn, reduced the commercial value of paprika-processing firms. The head of a paprika farm described this pattern as "neo-privatization," the intentional cheapening of Hungarian assets so they can then be bought at much reduced prices—presumably by foreigners. Even as it is, he complained, only 80 percent of the paprika industry is in Hungarian ownership. The interpretation of the ever more numerous food scandals according to which Hungarian agricultural products are intentionally contaminated either for a cheap sale or to eliminate competition for Westerners was repeated by several informants. Indeed, there have been a few major transfers of the shares in Szegedi Paprika since the time of the scandal, bearing out my informant's prediction that the scandal would facilitate cheap sales.[19] In the paprika case, the lowering of standards had actually halted paprika exports and damaged the image, which contradicts the idea that lower standards facilitate the circulation of goods.

Second, that paprika is a Hungaricum is a value-added and therefore a key source of its producer's profit, although primarily the processors and distributors profit. As with other expensive brands, this invites producers in other parts of the world to make cheap copies. This trend, in the sociology of consumption literature, is called "chase and flight," the phenomenon in which elites constantly struggle to keep up their distinction through specific consumer practices and commodities, which the lower classes struggle to imitate; here the phenomenon is repeated on a global level (Corrigan 1997). In fact, the very uniqueness of Hungarian paprika depends on the distinction that well-informed consumers are supposed to be able to make between cheap, mass-produced commodities and unique, traditional, handicraft-type goods largely produced for niche markets. As the head of the Hungaricum Club put it, "It's important to retain the value of the Hungaricum name. If someone visited Hungary, let's say, and on the way from the airport to the hotel came across 426 Hungaricums, then Hungaricum would mean nothing" (Laforest 2004). The identity of a Hungaricum depends on the concept of cheap mass products—"Chinese" products, as they are now referred to in Hungary—even though China may not be the actual source of these products. As Derrida would say, a trace of "Chinese" always exists in the concept of Hungaricum. In sum, high-quality, certified products facilitate the circulation of uncertified goods.

Third, we must also remember that although many of the quality, safety, and environmental standards are recommended by national governments, or are endorsed and required by supranational organizations such as the EU, they were designed in the corporate sector, are self-administered, and are voluntary. The spread of such standards in the area of environmental protection has been identified in sociology as a key element of ecological modernization, in which state and corporations are increasingly "partners" and in which social movements shed their skin of confrontational activism to become NGOs, "stakeholders," and expert consultants. In fact, this new symbiosis is now so prevalent that Gereffi talks of the rise of the industrial-NGO complex, Conroy (2007) speaks of a certification revolution, and Berstein (2001) refers to the "compromise of liberal environmentalism." All these developments seem to confirm Hajer's fear already voiced in 1995 that ecological modernization may turn technocratic. By this he means that legitimate safety and environmental concerns may turn into corporate quality and labor management tools, which will then leave corporations in charge of all regulation. Standards and certifications, therefore, are not the manifestation of greater state or social control that one might associate with protec-

tionism or a Polanyian self-protection of society; instead, these are a sign
of diminished public scrutiny over production consistent with the neoliberal model.

Finally, far from demanding the withdrawal of the state, corporations
interested in patenting or otherwise protecting their products constantly
demand legal protections. What defines a product's "Hungarianness" is
a set of legal practices, however incoherent. In the 1990s and early 2000s
a dozen various labels were in existence, certificates floating around in
tended to distinguish a commodity as Hungarian.[20] Some of these were
initiated by politically motivated civic initiatives, others by corporate
NGOs, but they were all aspiring to be state-recognized and thus legal.
Some practices are restricted to the "realm of culture and identity" and
have no corresponding legal existence, such as Hungaricums (Axel 2004),
whereas others "exist" both legally and culturally, such as brands or the
award "Excellent Hungarian Product."[21] My point is not that the state
is still "doing favors" for capital even in more liberal globalized contexts (Sassen 1995) but rather that the state is increasingly expected to
do so on corporate terms, that is, by adopting corporate management
rationalities, which, in my view, signals a new relationship between the
economy and the state (Clark 2004; Brown 2003). In the case of Hungaricums, the state's role goes beyond simply funding and operating the
infrastructure that gives legal muscle to some of these labels and awards.
First, in Hungary, even after the extensive privatization wave of the early
1990s, the state held onto so-called golden shares in companies producing iconographic Hungarian products, such as Kalocsai Fűszerpaprika,
or strategically crucial Hungarian energy firms and banks. The golden
shares allowed the state to veto strategic decisions such as changes to
registered capital, acquisitions, and liquidations, thereby effectively exer-
cising state control in an allegedly liberal economy. Only recently, in
2006, did the Hungarian Parliament, responding to the EU's critique that
the golden shares limited the free movement of capital, convert these
shares into regular ones downgrading the state to a normal economic
actor. The second extended role of the state is to provide funds promoting
a Hungarian image, following the practice of many Western states in
nation-branding that operates synergistically with corporate standards,
labels, and certificates.[22] Thus the state has a different, if not neces-

sarily greater, role to play not only in image enhancement but in generally fine-tuning the balance between the "race to the bottom" and the "race to the top" models.

Conclusion

As we have seen in the case of the Hungarian paprika scandal, Euro-globalization is neither a neoliberal model encapsulated as the "race to the bottom" model nor a welfare/Keynesian/protectionist capitalist model described by some as the "race to the top." Rather, from Hungarians' perspective, the European Union stands for a unique mixing and match-ing of both models in such a way that those powerless relative to Western European actors and EU institutions, in this case Hungarian producers and consumers, receive the worst of both worlds: they cannot freely participate in EU-level trade, as their product is now tainted and their laboratory tests no longer accepted when exporting paprika, nor can they persuade the EU to implement greater regulation, namely, the testing of imported peppers for Aflatoxin at the new EU customs borders. Finally, the Hungarian state and Hungarian producers cannot even carve out a legally binding protection from the EU for their products labeled as Hungaricum, such as the Kalocsa and Szeged paprika.

The European Union is not simply advocating trade liberalization at the same time that it demands the removal of non-tariff barriers to trade in the developing world and in postsocialist Eastern Europe. Instead, it is establishing, in a strategic manner, what Agamben (1998, 2005) calls "states of exception." Depending on the dictates of the most powerful interests, the EU creates a calculated mosaic of economic fields: in some, free-trade principles are ruthlessly enforced, whereas, in others, economic actors are granted exemptions from these very same principles. It is not neoliberalism, nor protectionism, that renders the EU an increasingly muscular economic power; rather, it is the strategic juxtaposition and the productive dynamic between these states and spaces of neoliberalism and those of exception. I call this "Euro-globalization." It is my hope that this argument contributes not only to a more nuanced understanding of East-West power relations but also to existing and nascent critical political praxis in Europe.

ACKNOWLEDGMENTS

Research for this chapter has been supported by the International Research and Exchanges Board, and by the Campus Research Board of the University of Illinois at Urbana-Champaign. I am also grateful to Martha Lampland for constructive feedback on earlier versions of this essay.

NOTES

1. The increasing pool of notable exceptions, including Böröcz (2003), Böröcz and M. Kovács (2001), Dunn (2004, 2006), Mincyte (2006), Verdery (1996), and Schwartz (2007), is gratifying.

2. "Average" here applies to the years between 2000 and 2004.

3. Although the tainted paprika was not found in supermarkets and grocery stores, these incidents have great significance for public health, since most people, though an ever decreasing proportion, still buy their groceries at farmers' markets, street vendors, or at small mom-and-pop shops.

4. I have not yet found written evidence for this claim; the media reported that people believed it to be true.

5. The HACCP originated in 1971; in 1993 the Codex Alimentarius Committee of the Food and Agriculture Organization (FAO) and the World Health Organization (WHO) made it public. In Hungary, adoption of the HAACP was required by all food industrial facilities after 1996 and, in 2002, by all food-related facilities including those in the food-service industry. Note that its adoption was obligatory only in the new candidate countries, not in the EU generally. When I asked why this was so, experts in the certifying agencies explained that conditions in Western Europe were sufficiently safe and hygienic to render the standards moot. However, small shop owners and salespeople told me on several occasions that, when traveling in Greece or Italy, they noticed that the food displays and services would never meet the required HACCP conditions. Clearly, in the eyes of Hungarians, a truly European practice is colored by traditional cognitive mapping—that is, only Western Europe is truly European—as well as cultural, ethnic, and even racial biases.

6. For a Foucauldian analysis of the auditing and quality management in a Polish factory, see Dunn 2004; and for a similar analysis of HACCP, see, especially, Busch 2004.

7. Although government financial aid was available for the adoption of the HACCP, applying for these funds incurred additional effort and costs and so no one I spoke with applied for them or knew anyone who received them.

8. I analyze this imagery in a forthcoming book tentatively titled *Pigs, Paprika, and Predestination in Hungary: The Cultural Politics of the Eastern Enlargement of the European Union.*

9. Both descriptions are consistent with a commonly accepted notion of neoliberalism, according to which the role of the state and labor unions, and generally all limits placed on production and trade, are significantly reduced with the stated goal of encouraging commerce. Mass production is replaced by small-batch, flexible, just-in-time manufacturing in order to adjust to ever faster changes in the world market. Especially outside the most developed countries, development aid such as subsidies for food, health care, housing, and education are radically diminished in order to observe new free-trade regulations and to ensure that develop-

ing countries repay their loans. Economic and social policies are subordinated to fiscal policy, which in turn are designed and monitored by supranational organizations such as the World, Bank, the IMF and the WTO. In former state socialist countries, perhaps even more accentuated than elsewhere, the globalization project and post-Fordist flexible accumulation regime have manifested themselves in privatization of state assets, liberalization of prices, elimination of state regulation of production, and a radical reduction in welfare spending. Although the European Union had traditionally only allowed a limited reign to neoliberalism, it, too, has succumbed to these trends, and its corporate constituents, who had demanded these policies, have benefited.

10. For example, developing countries are not allowed to subsidize their farmers whereas the EU continues to do just that, effectively increasing the cost of developing countries' exports and thus impoverishing their farmers who are increasingly forced by structural adjustment programs to make a living from commodity production of export goods rather than from subsistence crops.

11. Note that imported peppers enter the country in the form of dried peppers and not as already ground spice, so the portion of Brazilian paprika in the overall volume of ground Hungarian paprika was, at the most, 0.002 percent if one assumes its equal distribution in the annual production. Although this seems an insignificant proportion, in reality some batches contained a much higher ratio of imported peppers.

12. See Parliamentary Session minutes quoted in *Index*, October 28, 2004; and the interview with the former head of Paprika Produce Council in *HVG*, November 6, 2004, p. 95.

13. In contrast, other countries produce peppers on small farms and therefore use different techniques. In Spain, for example, the largest table of paprika is 2 hectares.

14. Produce Councils are corporate nongovernmental organizations (NGOs) that not only represent the interests of their members (both producers and processors) and the segment of the food industry in which they work, but they also execute governmental functions such as collecting data, administering EU grants, monitoring EU production quotas, and training members in new safety and hygiene standards.

15. Mixing is common practice in the European Union. A few years the revelation that *Bertolli's* "Italian" olive oil contained a large proportion of African-grown olives outraged consumers.

16. It is not clear from this source whether processors' interests are seen to dominate more strongly than the interests of producers or consumers. In my opinion, both would be a fair interpretation of the prime minister's words. The rationale for this switch in authority was that during the investigations it became clear that the National Food Safety Bureau had enough information to act much earlier: regional agencies of ÁNTSZ confiscated certain shipments, levied a fine on one of the processors, and launched a criminal investigation already in August, two months before the ban. Also true, however, is that the National Food Safety Bureau (MÉBH) was established experimentally a few years before not as an authority but rather as an agency to coordinate various authorities, to analyze risks, and to operate the Rapid Alert System for Feed and Food (RASFF) which, according to most media analysts, it failed to do with sufficient speed (*HVG*, November 6, 2004). In my interview with the director just a few months prior to the paprika scandal, he emphasized the same lack of authority to act.

17. The term was actually coined in direct reference to another Aflatoxin contamination case. The World Bank analysis bitterly criticized the EU's seemingly unfair and protectionist exclusion of African peanuts from European markets on the grounds that African producers could not meet the EU's Aflatoxin norms (Wilson and Otsuki 2001; Otsuki, Wilson, and Sewadeh n.d.).

18. ISO refers to the International Organization for Standardization which designs and sanctions wide-ranging technical and organizational standards of safety and quality.

19. As far as I can tell, however, the majority of shares are still in Hungarian ownership.

20. Kovács and Zsarnóczay (2007) provide a summary of some of these.

21. A few years ago this award was granted to a "Hungarian" pineapple juice brand. Given that pineapples do not grow in Hungary, this case is rather curious.

22. For an excellent analysis of nation-branding in Latvia, see Dzenovska 2005.

REFERENCES CITED

Agamben, Giorgio. 1998. *Homo Sacer: Sovereign Power and Bare Life*. Translated by Daniel Heller-Roazen. Stanford, Calif.: Stanford University Press, 1998.

——. 2005. *State of Exception*. Translated by Kevin Attell. Chicago: University of Chicago Press.

BBC, January 15, 2003.

Berstein, Steven. 2001. *The Compromise of Liberal Environmentalism*. New York: Columbia University Press.

Böröcz, József. 2001. "Introduction." In *Empire's New Clothes: Unveiling EU Enlargement*, ed. J. Böröcz and M. Kovács. Central Europe Review. http://www.rci.rutgers.edu/eu/ Empire.pdf (accessed February 26, 2009), pp. 4–50.

——. 2003. "Goodness Is Elsewhere: For a Sociology of Imperial Kitsch." Paper presented at the EUtopia conference Enlargement and the Politics of European Identity, April 10–12, University of Illinois, Urbana-Champaign.

Brown, Wendy. 2003. "Neo-liberalism and the End of Liberal Democracy." *Theory and Event* 7:1.

Busch, Lawrence. 2004. "Grades and Standards in the Social Construction of Safe Food." In *The Politics of Food*, ed. Marianne Elisabeth Lien and Brigitte Nerlich, pp. 163–178. New York: Berg.

Clarke, John. 2004. "Dissolving the Public Realm? The Logics and Limits of New-Liberalism." *Journal of Social Policy* 33(1): 27–48.

Corrigan, Peter. 1997. *Sociology of Consumption*. London: Sage.

DiMaggio, Paul. 1994. "Culture and Economy." In *Handbook of Economic Sociology*, ed. N. Smelser and R. Swedberg, pp. 27–57. Princeton, N.J.: Princeton University Press.

Dunn, Elizabeth C. 2004. *Privatizing Poland: Baby Food, Big Business, and the Remaking of Labor*. Ithaca, N.Y.: Cornell University Press.

——. 2006. "Standards and Person-making in East Central Europe." In *Global Assemblages: Technology, Politics, and Ethics as Anthropological Problems*, ed. Aihwa Ong and Stephen J. Collier, pp. 173–194. Malden, Mass.: Blackwell.

Dzenovska, Dace. 2005. "Remaking the Nation of Latvia: Anthropological Perspectives on Nation Branding." *Place Branding* 1(2): 173–186.

Gille, Zsuzsa. 2003. "The Pig That Died for Europe: Making Hungarians into Europeans." Paper presented at the EUtopias conference Enlargement and the Politics of European Identity, April 10–12, University of Illinois, Urbana-Champaign.

——. 2004. "Operationalizing Freedom in the EU: The Making of the Homo Europaeus." Paper presented at the Conference of Europeanists, Council for European Studies, Chicago, March 11–13, 2004.

Gille, Zsuzsa, and Sean O' Riain. 2002. "Global Ethnography." *Annual Review of Sociology* 28:271–295.

Hajer, Maarten. 1995. *The Politics of Environmental Discourse: Ecological Modernization and the Policy Process.* Oxford: Clarendon.

Halász, Zoltán. 1987. *Kis magyar paprikakönyv* (Little Hungarian Book of Paprika). Budapest: Corvina.

Halkier, Bente. 2004. "Handling Food-related Risks: Political Agency and Governmentality." In *The Politics of Food,* ed. Marianne Elisabeth Lien and Brigitte Nerlich, pp. 21–38. New York: Berg.

Harvey, David. 19991. *The Condition of Postmodernity: An Enquiry into the Origins of Cultural Change.* New York: Wiley-Blackwell.

Kovács, Ágnes, and Gabriella Zsarnóczay. 2007. "Protected Meat Products in Hungary—Local Foods and Hungaricums." *Anthropology of Food.* Available at http://aof.revues.org/docu ment500.html (accessed February 26, 2009).

Laforest, Nancy. 2004. "Hungary's Dowry." *Business Hungary,* May 2004, 18:5. Available at http://www.amcham.hu/BusinessHungary/18-05/articles/18-05—38.asp (accessed February 26, 2009).

Lampland, Martha. N.d. "Working Models, Hybrid Practices: The Science of Work and the Transition to Socialism in Hungary (1920–1956)." Unpublished manuscript.

Mato, Daniel. 1997. "On Global and Local Agents and the Social Making of Transnational Identities and Related Agendas in 'Latin' America." *Identities* 4(2): 167–212.

McMichael, Philip. 1996. "Globalization: Myths and Realities." *Rural Sociology* 61(1): 25–55.

Mincyte, Diana. 2006. "Small-scale Farms, Large-scale Politics: The Changing Landscape of Rural Lithuania." Ph.D. thesis, University of Illinois at Urbana-Champaign.

MTI Econews. 2008. "Court Rejects Appeal by Szegedi Paprika against Competition Office Decision." March 12.

Otsuki, Tsunehiro, John S. Wilson, and Mirvat Sewadeh. N.d. "A Race to the Top? A Case Study of Food Safety Standards and African Exports." Washington, D.C.: The World Bank.

Popovics, Anett, and Imola Kisérdi Pallóné. 2004. "Hagyományos és tájjellegű élelmiszerek ismertségének vizsgálata" (Survey of the knowledge of traditional and characteristic regional foods). *Élelmiszeri Közlemények* (Journal of Food Investigations) 50(1): 28–36.

Sassen, Saskia. 1995. "The State and the Global City: Notes Towards a Conception of Place-centered Governance." *Competition and Change* 1:31–50.

Schwartz, Katrina. 2006. *Nature and National Identity after Communism: Globalizing the Ethnoscape.* Pittsburgh: University of Pittsburgh Press.

Tsing, Anna. 2000. "The Global Situation." *Cultural Anthropology* 15(3): 327–360.

Unnevehr, Laurian J. 2000. *The Economics of HACCP: Costs and Benefits.* St. Paul, Minn.: Eagan.

Unnevehr, Laurian, and Nancy Hirschhorn. 2000. *Food Safety Issues in the Developing World.* Washington, D.C.: The World Bank.

Verdery, Katherine. 1996. "What Was Socialism, and Why Did It Fall?" In *What Was Socialism and What Comes Next?* Princeton, N.J.: Princeton University Press.

Wilson, John S., and Tsunehiro Otsuki 2001. "Global Trade and Food Safety: Winners and Losers in a Fragmented System." Washington, D.C.: The World Bank.

THREE

Self-Made Women

Informal Dairy Markets in Europeanizing Lithuania

DIANA MINCYTE

My first day of fieldwork in Lithuania started early: I woke up in my apartment complex to an unusual commotion coming through open windows. Looking outside, I saw ten to twelve elderly neighbors mingling and talking around the entrance to the apartment building. Suddenly a noisy, blue German car pulled in and all the talk ended. A woman in her mid-fifties with a sunburned face jumped from the car, opened the trunk, and, with the help of the neighbors, pulled out a large metal milk container. Everybody silently bent down, one after another, to place empty jars in front of the woman who then filled them with raw milk. At times the woman stopped and shook the containers to mix in the cream floating at the top. There was something graceful about the healthy farmer surrounded by fragile bodies of pensioners and the sharing of the fresh milk.

I soon learned that the woman—a farmer from a village some twelve miles away—drove to my building three times a week and sold unpasteurized milk along with other dairy products such as farmers' cheese, milk curd, and sour cream for almost half the price of those same products in the supermarkets. She also often brought seasonal vegetables. I also discovered that her case was not unique, that most of the living quarters in Lithuanian cities had their own local dairy suppliers. In every interview and conversation about dairy, urbanites living in the apartment complexes claimed to know exactly when, where, the price, and the quality of raw milk flowing to their neighborhoods. Some consumers did not consider buying the milk, but, for many, unofficial raw milk became the staple diet. Exceptions were the capital of Vilnius and the city of Klaipėda— Lithuania's largest, busiest, and most "globalized" cities (Sassen 1995) where many drove or took buses to shop at the supermarkets. In every other city, farmers distributing milk on the street curbs have become an inseparable part of the local urban fabric.

In the context of Lithuania's recent accession to the European Union (EU), the ubiquity of informal food markets is counterintuitive. As large milk processing companies fiercely compete in European and global markets, it is surprising that official dairy enterprises such as the Lithuanian companies Žemaitijos Pienas, Pieno Žvaigždės, and Rokiškio Sūris, as well as the French company Danone, have not yet captured a relatively large proportion of local dairy consumers. With the implementation of EU agricultural reforms, especially the new accounting-administrative requirements, the number of unreported incomes, unaccounted cows, and unregistered farmers is expected to drop quickly. Finally, with a zero-tolerance policy toward uncertified food in the EU, the Lithuanian Public Health Agency is fiercely fighting the distribution of milk from uncertified and less than meticulously clean containers on the streets. Yet, despite these obstacles, the raw milk market in Lithuania is stronger than ever. Why have dairy markets failed to incorporate raw milk delivery systems into its official structures? How does culture enable informal dairy markets, and what do these markets tell us about the processes of Europeanization in post-Soviet Lithuania?

Motivated by these questions, I consider how local actors experience and participate in the Europeanization of Lithuania through raw milk production, distribution, and consumption. Inspired by studies of the social life of things (Appadurai 1991; Barndt 2002; Lind and Barham 2004), I follow the circulation of milk in the lives of small-scale producers, distributors, and consumers.

In the course of my research, I found that most consumers, producers, and distributors in this economy were women. Hence, gender seems to be deeply implicated in the emergence of informal food economies in Lithuania. My main finding is that local dairy economies operate as sites for self-making by enabling women to control their nutrition and bodies. In so doing, the marginalized members of postsocialist economies—mostly women with low incomes who are often isolated from public life or more profitable economic endeavors—have carved a niche not only in local economies but also in social hierarchies.

On the surface this argument resonates with two common ideas. First, it has been widely argued that women's participation in the economy is emancipatory; by earning incomes, women gain economic independence and thus contribute to transforming structures of domination over women's bodies, labor, and social status (Epstein 1993; Friedan 2001; de Beauvoir 2002; Gal and Kligman 2000). Second, sociologists have shown that small-scale, semi-formal markets are valuable assets for local communities, as they incorporate actors, enliven neighborhoods, and build social capital among its participants (Cross 2000; Staudt 1998). Referred to as a "peddler economy" (Geertz 1963), such markets play an important role in integrating marginalized, and often racialized, communities into the lives of American cities (Morales 2000). From this perspective, raw milk markets in Lithuania enable women to strengthen their social ties, gain financial independence, and significantly improve their social standing. Similarly dairy delivery points emerge as community building sites and one of the safe public spaces where women convene to claim a place in the fast-deteriorating urban districts.

At the hub of the informal milk markets in Lithuania, however, lies a different kind of self-making project defined not so much by financial success or emancipation as by the ability to sustain oneself, especially through nourishment. Central to such projects is the experience of autonomy that rests on self-sufficiency. By producing and consuming milk that flows outside the formal economy and by convening in unsupervised, illegal places to socialize, women are claiming their bodies and public spaces. For the marginalized groups involved in Lithuania's raw milk economy, these embodied experiences of autonomy allow them to deal with challenges posed by the new regulatory regime, increasing globalization of the markets, and deepening social inequalities.

To pursue this argument, I begin with a discussion of my methodology and follow this with a brief overview of the scholarly work on food politics and self-making. I then move to three portraits of women who are involved in the unofficial dairy network in Panevėžys to examine how the raw milk helps them to build their autonomy, dignity, and postsocialist bodies. The concluding section returns to the question of how, through the raw milk economy, we can conceptualize the Europeanization of everyday life in Lithuania.

Methodology and Data

The focus of this ethnography is on the informal milk flows around Panevėžys, the fifth-largest city in Lithuania, located in the North Central part of the country known both for its spectacular industrial growth under socialism and for its decline in the early postsocialist period to economic depression, high unemployment rates, and soaring crime rates.[1] I used classical ethnographic techniques for studying how this informal economy fits in the daily lives of the milk producers, deliverers, and consumers; how these individuals define healthy and wholesome foods; how they understand success in the context of an increasingly globalized and liberalized economy; and how they see themselves fitting in the landscape of Europeanizing Lithuania. I began by observing the farmer whose milk is delivered to Panevėžys. While living on the farm, I observed and learned about caring for the cows and their well-being, about how to prepare milk for deliveries by filtering and separating the cream in the milk, and why the raw milk economy was so important in the life of the postsocialist village. I also traveled with the deliveries from the village to Panevėžys to understand the organizational logic of this raw milk network and its social, economic, and political realities. Finally, I observed consumers waiting for the milk, which included following their discussions, participating in heated debates, and convening for informal conversations. I conducted semi-structured interviews outside the milk collection points, and, of course, observed and learned about the tastes and smells of raw milk and the making of yogurt, milk curd, and farmer cheese.

More formally, in addition to participating in and observing the urban consumers' community, I conducted interviews with five milk-delivering farmers; visited and stayed on their farms; interviewed three managers from the milk-processing companies and five representatives from the Ministry of Agriculture; and collected and analyzed formal reports about dairy production, processing, and distribution from governmental Web sites, newspapers, radio, and television.

As with other ethnographies, findings from this research are not easily generalized to other parts of the diverse postsocialist region that is being integrated into the political, social, and economic structures of the EU or the world. Rather, the purpose of this research was to understand the specificities of how European/global food politics intersect with local foodways to produce new markets, diets, bodies, and human subjectivities in Lithuania.

Global Markets, Local Identities

To talk about unofficial, unprocessed, and untested foods in today's world means to engage in a debate about food safety (Lien and Nerlich 2004; Haukanes 2004; Gille 2006). The stakes here are high. Global politics heads straight for our stomachs, as demonstrated by the recent outbreak of bovine spongiform encephalopathy, the use of highly toxic agents such as Aldicarb, Altar, and dioxins in foods, and controversies surrounding genetically modified foods. At the heart of this problem is the industrialization of food (and agriculture) (Kimbrell 2002; Busch, Lacy, and Burkhardt 1991; Nestle 2003). As Lawrence Busch (2004) has powerfully shown, globalization has caused a paradigmatic shift in the production, consumption, and distribution of foodstuffs. Most of the food consumed in North America and Western Europe is no longer grown locally, but in mega-sized farms scattered around the globe. Traditional processing methods have been replaced by assembly lines and biochemical treatments. By the time packaged food reaches shelves at local supermarkets, it has passed through long chains of supply and retailing. Precisely because today's food supply is exposed to so many different environments and comes from so many different places the risk of its susceptibility to microbes, viruses, and microorganisms has enormously increased.

In the case of raw milk markets, this classical approach does not apply to food safety and quality. Since livestock is grown on small-scale farms, the dangers of industrialized farming are not present. All the fodder is grown locally; hormones and antibiotics for cows as well as pesticides and fertilizers for feed are rarely used because they are too expensive (Dunn 2005). From the perspective of the consumer, the safety and quality of the products are ensured through intricate mechanisms of trust and face-to-face interactions (Mauss 1954).

The issue of safety, however, enters the lives of Lithuanian farmers through the back door. As Dunn's study (2005) shows, local producers are forced to comply with standards issued by the EU and the International Standards Organization to ensure the safety (and quality) of the products as defined by these institutions. Local small-scale farmers are unable to afford the technologies needed to comply with these requirements, and so large mechanized farms and global corporations—for instance, Iowa's Animex, in the case of the Polish meatpacking industry—are pushing local producers outside the boundaries of the official economy. Similarly Busch (2004; Gille 2006) has shown that standards "tilt" food markets in favor of large producers by preferentially treating companies that can afford the expensive tests and technologies needed for producing records of food-control procedures.

The social implications of such processes are far-reaching and devastating. In her article Dunn (2005) draws a fundamental connection between standardization and identity politics. She argues that the implementation of standards in the meat-processing industry requires realigning work practices with multilayered auditing techniques (Miller 1994; Strathern 2005; Hacking 1990; Rose 1996). In order for products to comply with international food-safety requirements, for example, all meat batches are continuously tested for consistency, safety, and quality. Along with testing, workers leave paper trails where they record observations and, by so doing, transform themselves from knowledgeable workers into subjects of administrative supervision, management, and control. Through their participation in the panoptic-like work environment, the workers experience profound disempowerment. At its core, EU standards are acting as agents of social engineering that are transforming Polish men and women into self-disciplined citizens (see also Dunn 2003, 2004).

While Dunn highlights the deskilling of food production and, more broadly, the expansion and consolidation of West Europe's cultural and economic domination over new member countries as key factors driving informal food markets, I argue that informal foods are also manifestations of alternative economies and identities. In a way that differs from Dunn's article, I suggest that informal food markets are significant not because they are by-products of the EU food policies or manifestations of subalternity but because they are sites where local actors claim control over their bodies. My interviews and ethnographic research demonstrate that in many cases the impinging new regulations and supervision mechanisms in Lithuania have produced not inferior, self-disciplined subjects (Foucault 1995 [1978]) but also autonomous, self-made, and well-nourished individuals who function outside these panopticon systems.

On Autonomy and Self-Making

It is commonly argued that the archetypal story of the "self-made man" belongs to North American cultural and political mythology,[2] but that story has also become a powerful identity-producing vehicle in postsocialist and Europeanizing Lithuania. Newspaper headlines, television shows, radio programs, and stories circulating in public transportation, workplaces, and at dinner tables are often about the achievements of those who are succeeding in the new economy through economic success and gaining political capital. In a different way than in Western myths of the "self-made man" that emphasize the rise from "rags to riches," Lithuanian stories often obscure the social origins of their heroes and focus on their spectacular deals. The Lithuanian version is a story of an autonomous actor who cunningly outmaneuvers competitors, fearlessly takes risks, and defeats all obstacles to gain power. The end of these stories is often laced with detours through newly built palaces (Humphrey 2002) and insights into lavish nouveau riche lifestyles.[3]

In addition to the success stories of the privileged, marginalized actors also construct themselves as "self-made people." As with all stories of splendor and power, the stories of farmers, raw milk deliverers, and consumers are centered on the autonomy of one's life in the context of larger political and economic systems. Unlike magazine covers praising one's ability to gain economic capital and political power, however, farmers construe their autonomy in terms of physical sustenance by growing their own food and earning income through their labor. In these stories, self-making means providing food for one's family, earning money by selling the produce, or working on somebody else's farm, not striking deals, buying property, playing political games, or applying for EU funding.

By autonomy here I mean not only farmers' ability to procure food and control their bodies through diet but, more important, their very subsistence and physical survival. An emphasis on self-sustenance and physical autonomy is not unique to Lithuania. For example, Tiina Silvasti (2003) argues that Finnish farmers are also critical of the EU's agricultural politics of subsidies and direct payments, because these political measures make them feel that they are not "really farming" but are only "pretend farming":

> Under the Common Agricultural Policy (CAP), sale prices of agricultural products in Finland are so low they hardly cover production costs—and the majority of farm income is achieved, "behind the desk," by filling in forms for subsidies. This [practice of earning a living by applying for EU support] has devalued the social value of farming, and is a threat to the cultural script of hard work and the notion of real farm work. (Silvasti 2003:145)

Silvasti suggests that Finnish farmers resent CAP because its reforms require them to earn a living not from farming but from "behind the desk," which goes against their values of hard physical labor and industriousness. Similarly, in the context of East and Central Europe, Martha Lampland (1991) points out that under socialism Party secretaries (and other collective farm members) who did not keep pigs on their household farms or work on subsidiary plots were considered "do-nothings," thereby implying moral corruption and social rejection. The value of physical labor on subsidiary farms far exceeded the incomes it brought, as it was also a way of earning social capital in the villages.

In Lithuania, too, hard physical work on the land has earned respect in the community. Today, however, the value of this work lies not simply in industriousness, productivity, or devotion to farming or homemaking but in people's ability to sustain their sources of what they consider wholesome food. The following section introduces portrayals of three women engaged in the informal economy who work to nourish their bodies.

Raw Milk Economy: Portraits of Three Women

Aldona, Ona, and Marytė are connected through the raw milk economy. Aldona, is a farmer who keeps four cows and delivers the surplus of milk to her neighbor, Ona, to sell it in Panevėžys. Ona is the entrepreneur farmer who not only delivers and sells the milk but also keeps her own farm. She is the most important conduit in the informal dairy economy linking Aldona's farm to consumers' diets. Marytė, a retiree residing in an apartment building in Panevėžys is one of Ona's oldest and most regular customers. Through portraits of these three women I seek to demonstrate that the raw milk economy enables these women to control their nourishment and also become independent, self-sustaining subjects. More broadly, the women's portrayals reveal connections between the informal economy, gendered politics, and experiences of embodied autonomy in postsocialist Lithuania.

PORTRAIT OF A FARMER: ALDONA   The story of the milk starts with the cows on Aldona's farm. Living fifteen miles from Panevėžys, Aldona is one of Lithuania's many small-scale farmers struggling to find a place in the changing structure of agricultural production. Her strategy has been to diversify her farm, which enables her to provide her family with food from the farm and also to earn cash by selling the surplus.

Three generations live in Aldona's home: Aldona and her husband, her seventy-four-year-old mother, and her teenage son and daughter. Aldona's mother, Veronika, is of considerable help to her daughter, spending most of her time working around the house, cooking, cleaning, sowing, feeding the hens, and gardening in the kitchen garden in the summer. In the winter she is the first to rise and start the fire. She often says, "While I can, I work." Her work combines difficult household chores with caring for the family. Her life consists of much warmth but also hardship.

The son and daughter, Justas and Paulė, go to school. Justas is one of the brightest students in his class, and the family is pinning its hopes on him. Should he study dentistry? Or is statistics a better career? These questions are often entertained at the dinner table. Last summer Aldona bought a computer, "So that the kids are like everybody else." To be a "normal teenager" in a Lithuanian village, as in many places worldwide, means having access to the Internet. Justas willingly shares his e-mail address, but he rarely goes online. Phone calls are expensive, and he is well aware of what it takes to earn money to cover these costs. He, too, works on the large farm during summers.

The women's voices hush as they speak of Martynas, Aldona's husband. Yes, he commutes to a shop in the nearby town where he works as a mechanic, but he is of little help on the farm. Martynas spends a considerable amount of time and money on drinking. Last year he had a car accident driving while intoxicated and had to relinquish his license. He was fined 2,500 Litas [LT] (about U.S.$1,000), which he is still paying off, an amount exceeding the cost of a non-purebred, Lithuanian cow. In Martynas's absence, Aldona alone must fend for herself and her family.

Aldona is in her late thirties but looks ten years older. She is the heart of her family, and she runs the farm comprising 7 ha of land on which there are four cows, two calves, three sows, a couple of goats, and a hen house. The farm also includes a 100-ares garden just outside the village and a tiny kitchen garden by the house.[4] Although Aldona is not officially employed, she earns about 65–80 percent of her family's income, of which milk constitutes the largest and, significantly, the most stable part of her earnings.

Aldona's day starts at 5:30 AM when she gets up to feed the animals and milk the cows. In the summer she rides her bicycle to the pasture, but in the winter the cows are in the barn close to home. Sitting on a small bench by the cow, she washes the teats and manually milks the cow letting the milk flow into a bucket. She then pours the milk into a container she had carried with her on the bike and moves on to the next cow. After milking, she takes the cows one by one to the new pasture, fastens the cows, and brings them water for the day. Including the trip, all this usually occupies about three hours. Back home she separates the milk for her own consumption and for sale. She carries her milk inside to the refrigerator, leaving the remaining milk in the shed for her neighbor, Ona, to pick up.

Ona picks up the milk three times a week to be delivered in Panevėžys. Aldona receives 1 LT for a liter of her milk, of which she keeps 0.80 Lt/liter; 0.20 LT/liter goes to her partner, Ona, to cover travel expenses and the time it takes Ona to sell the milk. On other days Aldona takes her milk to the Žemaitijos Pienas collection point in the central part of the village, near the old pharmacy, where she earns 0.52 LT/liter. Žemaitijos Pienas, one of the four largest dairy producers in Lithuania, pays a relatively high price for the milk. In other villages, especially in smaller and more remote areas, collection prices are considerably lower, only 0.39 LT/liter.[5]

Working around the cows is only part of Aldona's busy day. Besides her housekeeping duties, working on the land, gardening, and taking care of animals and children, she also nurses an old neighbor whom she visits twice a day to feed and look after. The neighbor's children have moved to the city and pay Aldona to care for their mother. Most important, in the summer she takes temporary jobs on one of the large village farms where she weeds, waters, thins, harvests, sorts, and cleans—everything that needs to be done in the warm summer months. In the summer of 2005 she was paid 25 LT per day, or about 4 LT per hour (approximately U.S.$1.50). The minimum hourly wage in 2005 was 3.28 LT (around U.S.$1.22), which is considered a *good* wage for those living cheaply in rural communities.

Despite the various sources of income, Aldona worries about her future. She does not pay social security taxes, so when she reaches retirement age—sixty years old for women in Lithuania—she may only receive the minimum support from the state, which is not sufficient to live on. This is one reason why Martynas still works. Even though he does not make much money, he is "in the system," as she explains it, meaning that he pays social security.

Most surprising about Aldona is that she does not even aspire to expand her farm or buy new technologies to facilitate her work on the land and with animals. "Why?" she asks, throwing her hands up in the air. When asked why she is not applying for EU support that would enable her to buy more land, she explains: "We have enough. We are busy as it is with getting everything done in time." Aldona, like many of her neighbors, wants to live off her farm and, at least for now, she is getting by.

At the center of Aldona's life is food self-sufficiency. She proudly states that they do not buy food in stores:

> *Pork is so cheap that it is hard to say whether it is worth raising pigs anymore. But we would never buy a pig from the store, even if it was more profitable. . . . It's tastier and healthier. . . . How can you live in the countryside and not grow your own food? . . . [For the farmer], to buy food is a crime [Lith., nusikaltimas].*

In Aldona's world, farmers have to be able to feed themselves and their families. Buying what can be grown on one's land implies being a "bad" farmer. The same logic applies to producing milk:

ow can you buy milk while you live on the farm? . . . [Milk] is so good for your health . . . You always want to get fresh milk—your own milk—not something from the store that comes from God knows where . . . True, it is a lot of work to keep cows, but you can feed your own family and sell it for a little bit of cash.

Here, as in many other interviews with small-scale farmers in Lithuania, the recurrent themes are of sustenance and nourishment. The good farmer can procure food for the family for the entire year; good food comes not from the stores and "God knows where" but directly from the farm and through difficult labor.

The informal dairy economy is deeply embedded in these cultural and economic rationalities. Selling milk brings the much-needed cash incomes into the homes of small-scale farmers and makes their diversified farms economically sustainable. Further, selling milk, a product of one's grueling labor, is seen as a dignified way of surviving in the new economy. Living off one's labor ensures one's economic autonomy, sustenance, and self-respect. Most important, milk production and consumption on the farm make Aldona and her family independent from EU subsidies, market fluctuations, and the national and international political climate. Producing, consuming, and selling milk is an embodied experience of independence and self-sustenance. For Aldona to survive in the new economy is not to buy the cheapest food available, but to provide her family with what she produces on the land. Aldona's responsibility for feeding her family is a manifestation of gendered practices in Lithuania's villages that heavily weigh on women to nourish and sustain the bodies of their kin.

PORTRAIT OF A DISTRIBUTOR: ONA Petite, with short red hair, Ona radiates optimism and confidence. She is forty-nine and runs her unpasteurized dairy business as a professional. Although she was born and grew up in the countryside, she went to school in Panevežys. Trained in nursing in the early 1980s, up until the mid-1990s she worked as a school nurse before she lost her job. Ona then moved back to the village where her parents lived, started a farm, and now has three cows, two sows, a dozen hens, 3 ha of land away from her house where she grows potatoes and grain, 3 ha of pastures, and a large 1-ha garden by the house where she has a beautiful orchard with apple, pear, and cherry trees as well as currant bushes.

Ona has a fifteen-year-old son, although he is of little help to her. He likes to join her on her trips to Panevėžys, but he does not help with sales and just wanders off to the shopping centers, clothing stores, and second-hand technology and furniture markets on the outskirts of the city. Ona half-jokingly comments that Lithuanian men are interested in shopping and luxury more than women. Coincidentally Ona's husband, like Aldona's, "rarely sobers up." As in Aldona's household, Ona is the engine of her family life.

Ona's day starts at 5 AM, feeding the animals, milking the cows, and preparing milk for deliveries. After carefully filtering and separating the cream, she pours the bulk of the milk into one large metal container and three smaller plastic containers. She likes to leave a considerable amount of cream in this milk because "her people" like it that way. Ona explains that the "neighbors"—as she calls the consumers—usually skim the cream off their milk and use it to make their own sour cream.

The second task in her milk routine is to work with the fatty part of the milk to prepare sour cream and cheeses. In fact, cheese is Ona's specialty. With little guidance, and through trial and error, she developed a recipe for a sweet milk cheese that is comparable to the best-tasting and most expensive cheeses sold in international delis. She sells about 15 kg of the cheese every week.

After sorting the milk, Ona makes her last preparations for the trip. She pours the sour cream into jars and weighs the cheeses so that she knows the price of every cheese before she sells it. To do so, she affixes a price tag on every cheese packed in a plastic bag. She then loads everything into the car and drives up to Aldona's to pick up her milk.

Unlike Aldona, Ona's primary income comes from dairy sales. Not surprisingly she feels particularly threatened by the new food safety and quality regulations and trade laws. But Ona is bold and does not plan to give in: "My neighbors [meaning consumers] want my milk, and I will continue delivering milk at night, if need be," says Ona. For her, the unofficial market provides desired income, stability, independence, and, most important, respect.

Similar to Aldona, Ona does not plan to expand her operation. When asked why she did not apply for EU funding to expand her farm (she is eligible because she owns more than 5 ha) or start a business of milk deliveries, she argues that EU money is not for "ordinary people":

*Y*ou have to have a good consultant to prepare a business plan and an
accountant to work with the National Payment Agency. You have to have
matching funds. Who can afford this?! . . . And then you need to know how to
run the [large-scale] farm, to hire good people, and to buy the machines. You
need to buy good seedlings from the new companies that insure that they will
grow, you need good fertilizers, you need Roundup [the herbicide] . . . Otherwise,
how can you compete with a farm like Vytas's [the large-scale producer who runs
a nearby industrial farm]? . . . You have to be rich in the first place . . . to get the
EU money.

Ona's statement demonstrates the difficulty of small-scale farmers to succeed in the new system. To obtain EU funding, one needs start-up capital,
and to get start-up capital, one has to own valuable real estate to secure a
loan. EU funding is outside the reach of small-scale farmers, who generally are unable to obtain loans.

Although Ona recognizes that she is in an inferior economic position
compared to her neighbor who runs a large-scale industrialized farm, she
claims to be morally superior to him because she sustains herself through
her own work. In fact, Ona says she is proud she is not applying for EU
money but is making it on her own by delivering the milk. She wants to be
what she calls *"pati sau valdžia,"* which translates into the powerful statement "I am my own government." But Ona is not an anarchist. What she
means here is her ability to get by without the support and supervision of
bureaucrats. Like Aldona, Ona values self-sufficiency through her work on
the farm.

Tellingly, the phrase "I am my own government" has been used frequently in Lithuania's media. For example, a newspaper article told
the story of a twenty-five-year-old woman who keeps ten cows with
the help of her seventy-eight-year-old grandmother and has not applied
for EU funding. The young farmer claimed that she does not want to
depend on payments from the EU: "It is best to be your own government," she stated ("Žaidimas su Gyvūnais Virto Ūkiu" ["Games with
Animals Turned into Farming"] 2004). The notion of self-government is
illuminating because it suggests that the alternative agro-food systems
are not simply black markets supported by marginalized groups but that
they emerge as sites through which women reconstitute self-governing
subjects driven by the experiences of moral superiority, health, and
autonomy.

PORTRAIT OF A CONSUMER: MARYTĖ   Like most of her neighbors in the Panevėžys apartment building, Marytė was born in a village before World War II. Similar to many others of her generation, she fled a countryside decimated by collectivization from 1948 to 1951 in order to attend college. She received a degree in accounting and was assigned to work in the Panevėžys hospital in the late 1950s. Soon after getting married, she and her husband moved into a three-room apartment where she lives now, years after her son left to go to college and start his own family and after the death of her husband. Today Marytė is retired, and her life is centered on her home.

Marytė's daily routine consists of cleaning, cooking, taking care of the various tasks involved in maintaining a home, communing with her neighbors and relatives, and watching television. Significantly Marytė has also maintained a dacha garden outside Panevėžys, where she has a small, three-room brick house built in the middle of a 6-ares plot. Although she has to take two buses to get to the garden, she willingly travels there every other day during the summer, even if she only stays for two or three hours. Marytė's gardening is not only a hobby but also provides healthy foods for herself and her grandchildren. She is a master of preserving, making strawberry, cherry, currant, gooseberry, or plum jams, preparing apple, pear, and even zucchini compotes, and pickling cucumbers and cabbage.

Raw milk from the farm fits comfortably into the matrix of Marytė's food values and practices. Just like berries, vegetables, and fruits from her garden, milk comes "raw" directly from the farm, allowing her to use her knowledge, craftsmanship, and labor to transform it into food. Unlike the ultra-pasteurized milk of homogeneous consistency that comes from the store, Marytė values the milk from the farm because it comes with fat and microorganisms, enzymes, and bacteria. This milk is organic and therefore much more conducive to fermentation. Using these material qualities of the raw milk, Marytė skims it, leaves the "fatty" portion of the milk for her coffee and soups, and uses the rest to make yogurt, milk curd, and sometimes, cheese.

This does not mean that Marytė and her neighbors are unaware of the dangers posed by un-pasteurized milk. On the contrary, pasteurization is a highly debatable subject among those consuming it at the beginning of deliveries. When I conducted my research, most of the neighbors had already taken sides and resisted changing them. Marytė does not drink milk without pasteurizing it. She uses a method of what is known as "slow pasteurization." Immediately after picking up the milk from the farmer, she pours it into a pot and slowly heats it to about 75°C. She uses the thermometer for precision to prevent overheating, thus preserving the milk's natural elements. But even Marytė, an avid supporter of pasteurization, often sips the milk before pasteurizing "to taste the real thing."

In addition to understanding that the milk from the farm is better to cook with, Marytė and other consumers value raw milk from the farmer because it is a clean, healthy, and safe food that comes from nature. Just as in Caldwell's (2004a) analysis of Russian consumption practices, where food products collected directly from the ground are considered healthier than those bought in stores, Marytė says that milk coming straight from the farm is "better":

> *I don't have to tell you that milk [from the farm] is healthier [than milk from the store]. We get it the same day after milking the cows, it has all the bacteria that gets killed when they pasteurize the milk in the big companies . . . And we need food that comes from the farm! How many people are complaining about their digestion—you know why?—because they are eating the foods that come from who knows where.*

Marytė makes it clear that she buys milk from Ona because she trusts her. She has been buying milk from Ona for more than four years, and although she tried other suppliers she likes Ona best because she knows her background (Marytė claims to know someone who knows Ona's mother). Every time we spoke, Marytė emphasized that she likes the socializing with her farmer and neighbors that occurs in milk delivery spots. In other words, the milk from the farmer is embedded in face-to-face interactions and social relationships, not anonymous institutions and the industry. The milk flows into the homes of consumers through trusted networks, and it comes to their tables as a fresh food filled with microorganisms and social history.

Similar to Aldona and Ona, Marytė is preoccupied with self-sufficiency through nourishment. Even though she shops in the store for meats, fish, and breads, she reestablishes control over her diet by growing and preserving her vegetables and buying milk from the farmer. At the center of her everyday food practices is labor, not consumption. Through her hard work in the garden and through transforming "raw" foods into a "healthy" meal, Marytė is making herself into a self-sufficient, independent agent.

Keeping in mind that Marytė lives in the city, her ability to act self-sufficiently is surprising. Indeed, although living in the countryside obviously enables one to be self-sustaining by growing food and selling the surplus, living in the city makes urbanites dependent on food deliveries. Yet Marytė's case illustrates that alternative agro-food systems open up opportunities for gaining more control over one's food intake and thus one's body.

Conclusion: The Politics of Milk

Throughout this essay I have demonstrated that the unofficial raw milk economy is deeply embedded in how local actors define health, labor, and success. As an economic practice through which producers, distributors, and consumers establish their autonomy and control over their diets, the unofficial raw milk economy is a site for self-making and renegotiating body politics. Women involved in informal dairy markets gain control over their world in a context of increasing inequalities, social isolation, and growing regulatory regimes.

This argument has political and economic implications. In her analysis of the emergence of industrialized organic dairy in U.S. markets, Melanie DuPuis (2000, 2002) contends that by choosing to drink organic milk consumers refuse the intake of hormones and antibiotics found in milk produced on "conventional" industrialized farms. When one consumes organic dairy, even if it comes from industrialized organic farms where animals are treated just as inhumanely as at conventional organic farms, one seeks to protect one's body against possible toxic pollution. At the heart of these consumption practices, DuPuis argues, lies the politics of "Not-in-my-Body," a concept echoing the widely quoted notion "Not-in-my-Backyard" pertaining to the refusal to have toxic facilities built next to one's residency. Such consumption is deeply political and forces consumers to figure out what is risky and what is safe.

Women involved in informal dairy markets in Lithuania seem to practice the politics of "Not-in-my-Body." By engaging in the raw milk economy, women are protecting the autonomy of their bodies and the bodies of their kin. By choosing to consume milk from trusted sources, they closely guard the boundaries between their world and the outside. To push this point further, I argue that by consuming dairy from unrecorded, unregulated, and untested farms, women are building bodies that are also outside the EU's supervision.

The notion that "I am my own government," which surfaced in many interviews, newspapers, and conversations, is also relevant here in that women draw powerful connections between the raw milk economy and governmental practice. Just as with "Not-in-my-Body," the unofficial raw milk economy is about nutrition as much as it is about unplugging the body from the political-economic-industrial complex. In this sense, women's bodies in Lithuania are materially self-made and politically ungovernable.

Unlike the industrialized organic farming sector in the United States (and other parts of the global North) that operates as a highly profitable niche market, Lithuania's raw milk economies are criminalized economic activities that are increasingly marginalized and disciplined. Just as with many other small commodity chains (Goodman and Redclift 1985; Friedmann 1978a, 1978b) that previously dominated the region's economy, this "moonshine" milk is being pushed to the outside of the formal economic sector by political sanctions, financial instruments, and well-funded institutional supervision. Women who have been engaged in these local (food) production-consumption-distribution chains are increasingly losing these economic niches and finding themselves at the bottom of the social ladder. For them, raw milk consumption is not a reflexive, risk-management practice but an embodied experience of sovereignty. This is because risks lie not in the food but in the new economy.

To conceptualize the political and economic processes taking place in the region more broadly, use of the term "pasteurization" may be helpful.[6] Pasteurization allows us to target certain elements in the milk—microbes, viruses, and bacteria—as "risky" ingredients that must be contained at negligible levels. Similarly, in Lithuania informal food markets and ungovernable bodies are construed as dangerous and potentially harmful and therefore must be removed from the legal arena. The result is a new kind of Lithuania, a country with nicely packaged food, bigger supermarkets, and sharper boundaries between social classes.

ACKNOWLEDGMENTS

This chapter is based on my dissertation research, and I gratefully acknowledge funding support from the University of Illinois, Urbana-Champaign Graduate College, for Dissertation Research and Dissertation Writing Grants. Earlier versions of this chapter were presented at the Soyuz conference at Bryant University, Smithfield, Rhode Island, in March 2006 and the Sustainable Consumption and Society Workshop in Madison, Wisconsin, in June 2006. I also thank Zsuzsa Gille, Andrew Pickering, Heather Paxson, Jenny Leigh Smith, Neringa Klumbytė, Gediminas Lankauskas, and especially Melissa Caldwell for insightful comments and helpful suggestions on this essay. I am also thankful to all my informants for sharing their time and lives and for teaching me about milk, informal economies, and self-making.

NOTES

1. To better understand the specificities of raw milk communities in Panevėžys, I also studied raw milk consumption in Kaunas, Lithuania's second largest city located in the central part of the country (population 362,000), and in Marijampolė (population 71,000), the capital city of the Suvalkija ethnographic region that historically has been the richest and the most technologically advanced region. The community in which I stayed in Panevėžys is rather homogeneous in terms of gender, age, and ethnic composition. Of the nineteen most frequent consumers, fifteen are women. Only one Russian family was buying the milk. Most participants were retired. Despite the perceived demographic homogeneity of this group, it offers a relatively good representation of raw milk consumers in Lithuania. Women—comprising 54.3 percent of Lithuanian urbanites—consider raw milk more suitable for cooking, and so they are prone to buy milk directly from the farmer. Most of the raw milk consumers are retired and do not work outside the home (only 2.4 percent of women and 6.2 percent of men over sixty-five are still working in Lithuanian cities).

2. Historians of American culture often assume that the mythology of the "self-made man" goes as far back as the writings of Benjamin Franklin who, in his *Autobiography* (2003), described his rise from humble origins as the son of a candle maker to later become a wealthy and highly respectable citizen. This kind of myth is deeply tied to two other major archetypal stories—"Rags to Riches" and "the American Dream"—both emphasizing the importance of hard work and self-improvement to succeed in the world. In his recent and widely discussed *European Dream*, Jeremy Rifkin (2005) argues that the American dream has been eclipsed by the European dream that bears community values and emphasizes consensus rather than individual prosperity and autonomy. This topic, of course, is beyond the scope of this essay, but it is indeed puzzling why Lithuanian success stories are drawing on the American version of the dream rather than its European counterpart.

3. Examples of such stories are abundant across a wide range of media. Television shows, radio programs, and magazines celebrate the winners of the postsocialist transition. For

example, one of Lithuania's most popular magazine that comes as an insert in the country's largest daily, *Lietuvos rytas*, is devoted to what Bonnell (1995) calls the winners of the post-socialist transition. Titled *Stilius* (Style), the magazine focuses solely on the achievements of the new businessmen, politicians, managers, and celebrities. Another similar magazine that became popular more recently is *Žmonės* (People). As one interlocutor pointedly suggested, the very title *Žmonės* seems to imply that those who do not make it to its pages are somehow subhuman.

4. 7 ha = 17.3 acres; 100 ares = .25 acres.

5. Ramanauskas (2006) compared milk collection prices: in Finland farmers were paid an average of 1,070 LT/ton; in Ireland, 1063 LT/ton; in Denmark, 854 LT/ton; in New Zealand, 527 LT/ton; in Estonia, 827 LT/ton; in Poland, 813 LT/ton; in Russia, 701 LT/ton; in Latvia, 632 LT/ton; and in Lithuania, 606 LT/ton.

6. The term "pasteurization" for those in science studies evokes Bruno Latour's *The Pasteurization of France* (1988). In his brilliant study, Latour sheds light on processes through which Louis Pasteur's theory of microbes became accepted as a valid approach to understanding diseases. Latour's story is centered on political conflicts, public use of science, and the agency of the yeast, rather than on Pasteur's ingenious ideas.

REFERENCES CITED

Appadurai, Arjun. 1988. "Introduction: Commodities and the Politics of Value." In *The Social Life of Things: Commodities in Cultural Perspective,* ed. Arjun Appadurai, pp. 3–63. Cambridge: Cambridge University Press.

———. 1990. "Disjuncture and Difference in the Global Economy." In *Global Culture: Nationalism, Globalization and Modernity,* ed. Mike Featherstone, pp. 295–310. London: Sage.

Bagdanavičiūtė, Violeta. 2005. " 'Rokiškio Sūris' Pelno Ieško Latvijoj." *Verslo Žinios,* December 29.

Barndt, Deborah. 2002. *Tangled Routes: Women, Work, and Globalization on the Tomato Trail.* Lanham, Md.: Rowman & Littlefield.

Bonnell, Victoria. 1996. "The Winners and Losers in Russia's Economic Transition." In *Identities in Transition: Eastern Europe and Russia after the Collapse of Communism,* ed. Victoria Bonnell, pp. 13–29. Berkeley: University of California Press.

Borneman, John, and Nick Fowler. 1997. "Europeanization." *Annual Review of Anthropology* 26:487–514.

Bourdieu, Pierre. 1985. "The Social Space and the Genesis of Groups." *Theory and Society* 14(6): 723–744.

Brenner, Neal. 1999. "Globalization as Reterritorialization: The Rescaling of Urban Governance in the European Union." *Urban Studies* 36(3): 431–451.

Bromley, Ray. 2000. "Street Vending and Public Policy: A Global Review." *International Journal of Sociology and Social Policy* 20(1/2): 1–28.

Busch, Lawrence. 2004. "Grades and Standards in the Social Construction of Safe Food." In *The Politics of Food,* ed. Marianne Elisabeth Lien and Brigitte Nerlich, pp. 163–178. New York: Berg.

Busch, Lawrence, William B. Lacy, and Jeffery Burkhardt. 1991. *Plants, Power, and Profit: Social, Economic and Ethical Consequences of the New Biotechnologies.* London: Blackwell.

Castells, Manuel. 1996. *The Rise of the Network Society.* Vol 1. Cambridge: Blackwell.

———. 2001. "Information Technology and Global Capitalism." In *On The Edge: Living with Global Capitalism,* ed. Will Hutton and Anthony Giddens, pp. 52–74. London: Vintage.

Caldwell, Melissa L. 2002. "The Taste of Nationalism: Food Politics in Postsocialist Moscow." *Ethnos* 67(3): 295–319.

——. 2004a. *Not by Bread Alone: Social Support in the New Russia.* Berkeley: University of California Press.

——. 2004b. "Domesticating the French Fry: McDonald's and Consumerism in Moscow." *Journal of Consumer Culture* 4(1): 5–26.

Clarke, John. 2004. "Dissolving the Public Realm? The Logics and Limits of New-liberalism." *Journal of Social Policy* 33(1): 27–48.

Creed, Gerald, 1998. *Domesticating Revolution: From Socialist Reform to Ambivalent Transition in a Bulgarian Village.* University Park: Pennsylvania State University.

Cross, John. 2000. "Street Vendors, Modernity and Postmodernity: Conflict and Compromise in the Global Economy." *International Journal of Sociology and Social Policy* 21(1/2): 29–52.

De Beauvoir, Simone. 1993. *The Second Sex.* Translated by H. M. Parshley. New York: Knopf.

Ditchev, Ivaylo. 2004. "The Forge of Consumers: An Essay on Communist Desire." Paper presented at the Russian, East European, and Eurasian Center at the University of Illinois, Urbana-Champaign.

Dunn, Elizabeth. 2003. "Trojan Pig: Paradoxes of Food Safety Regulation." *Environment and Planning A* 35:1493–1511.

——. 2004. *Privatizing Poland: Baby Food, Big Business, and the Remaking of Labor.* Ithaca, N.Y.: Cornell University Press.

——. 2005. "Standards and Person-making in East Central Europe." In *Global Assemblages: Technology, Politics, and Ethics as Anthropological Problems,* ed. Aihwa Ong and Stephen J. Collier, pp. 173–194. Malden, Mass.: Blackwell.

DuPuis, Melanie. 2000. "Not in My Body: rBGH and the Rise of Organic Milk." *Agriculture and Human Values* 17(3): 285–295.

——. 2002. *Nature's Perfect Food.* New York: New York University Press.

Epstein, Cynthia F. 1993. *Women in Law.* Urbana: University of Illinois Press.

Freidan, Betty. 2001. *The Feminine Mystique.* New York: W. W. Norton.

Foucault, Michel. 1979. *Discipline and Punish: The Birth of the Prison.* New York: Vintage.

Friedman, Harriet. 1978a. "Simple Commodity Production and Wage Labor in the American Plains." *Journal of Peasant Studies* 6:71–101.

——. 1978b. "World Market, State, and Family Farm: Social Bases of Household Production in the Era of Wage Labor." *Comparative Studies in Society and History* 20:545–584.

Gal, Susan, and Gail Kligman. 2000. *The Politics of Gender after Socialism: A Comparative-Historical Essay.* Princeton, N.J.: Princeton University Press.

Geertz, Clifford. 1968. *Peddlers and Princes: Social Change and Economic Modernization in Two Indonesian Towns.* Chicago: University of Chicago Press.

Gille, Zsuzsa. 2006. "The Tale of the Toxic Paprika: the Hungarian Taste of Euro-Globalization." Paper presented at the Post-socialist Reading Group at the University of Illinois, Urbana-Champaign.

Goodman, David, and Michael Redclift. 1985. "Capitalism, Petty Commodity Production and the Farm Enterprise." *Sociologia Ruralis* 25(3/4): 231–247.

Harcsa, Istvan, Imre Kovach, and Ivan Szelenyi. 1998. "The Post-Communist Transformational Crisis on the Hungarian Agrarian System." In *Privatizing the Land: Rural Political Economy in Post-Communist Societies,* ed. Ivan Szelenyi, pp. 214–245. London: Routledge.

Heller, Chaia. 2004. "Enjoyment and Choice in an Age of Risk: The Case of BSE in the

Czech Republic." In *The Politics of Food,* ed. Marianne E. Lien and Brigitte Nerlich, pp. Oxford: Berg.

Humphrey, Caroline. 2002. *The Unmaking of Soviet Life: Everyday Economies after Socialism.* Ithaca, N.Y.: Cornell University Press.

Keating, Michael. 1998. *The New Regionalism in Western Europe: Territorial Restructuring and Political Change.* London: Edward Elgar.

Kovach, Imre. 1994. "Privatization and Family Farms in Central and Eastern Europe." *Sociologia Ruralis* 34(4): 369–382.

Lampland, Martha. 2002. "Advantages of Being Collectivized: Comparative Farm Managers in the Postsocialist Economy." In *Postsocialism: Ideas, Ideologies and Practices in Eurasia,* ed. C. M. Hann, pp. 31–56. London: Routledge.

Latour, Bruno. 1998. *The Pasteurization of France.* Translated by Alan Sheridan and John Law. Cambridge, Mass.: Harvard University Press.

Ledeneva, Alena. 1998. *Russia's Economy of Favors: Blat, Networking and Informal Exchange.* Cambridge: Cambridge University Press.

Lien, Marianne, and Brigitte Nerlich. 2004. "Introduction." In *The Politics of Food,* ed. Marianne E. Lien and Brigitte Nerlich. Oxford: Berg.

Lind, David, and Elizabeth Barham. 2004. "The Social Life of the Tortilla: Food, Cultural Politics, and Contested Commodification." *Agriculture and Human Values* 21:47–60.

Mauss, Marcel. 1954. *The Gift: Forms and Functions of Exchange in Archaic Societies.* Translated by Ian Cunnison. New York: W.W. Norton.

Miller, Peter. 1994. "Accounting, 'Economic Citizenship,' and the Spatial Reordering of Manufacture." *Accounting, Organizations and Society* 17:178–206.

Morales, Alfonso. 2000. "Peddling Policy: Street Vending in Historical and Contemporary Perspective." *International Journal of Sociology and Social Policy* 21:3(4).

Nestle, Marion. 2003. *Food Politics: How the Food Industry Influences Nutrition and Health.* Berkeley: University of California Press.

Pipes, Richard. 1993. *Russia under the Bolshevik Regime.* New York: Knopf.

Rose, Nikolas. 1996. "Governing 'Advanced' Liberal Democracies." In *Foucault and Political Reason: Liberalism, Neo-liberalism and Rationalities of Government,* ed. Andrew Barry, Thomas Osborne, and Nikolas Rose, pp. 37–64. Chicago: University of Chicago Press.

Sassen, Saskia. 1995. "The State and the Global City: Notes Towards a Conception of Place-centered Governance." *Competition and Change* 1:31–50.

Shlapentokh, Vladimir. 1989. *Public and Private Life of the Soviet People: Changing Values in post-Stalin Russia.* New York: Oxford University Press.

Silvasti, Tiina. 2003. "The Cultural Model of 'the Good Farmer' and the Environmental Question in Finland." *Agriculture and Human Values* 20(2): 143–150.

Smollett, Eleanor Wenkart. 1989. "The Economy of Jars: Kindred Relationships in Bulgaria—An Exploration." *Ethnologia Europaea* 19:125–140.

Staudt, Kathleen. 1998. *Free Trade? Informal Economies at the U.S.-Mexico Border.* Philadelphia: Temple University Press.

Strathern, Marilyn. 2000. "Introduction." In *New Accountabilities to Audit Cultures: Anthropological Studies in Accountability, Ethics, and the Academy,* ed. Marilyn Strathern, pp. 1–18. London: Routledge.

Verdery, Katherine. 2003. *The Vanishing Hectare: Property and Value in Postsocialist Transylvania.* Ithaca, N.Y.: Cornell University Press.

Yurchak, Alexei. 2003. "Soviet Hegemony of Form: Everything Was Forever Until It Was No More." *Comparative Studies in Society and History* 45(3): 480–510.

——. 2006. *Everything Was Forever, Until It Was No More.* Princeton, N.J.: Princeton University Press.

Zbierski-Salameh, Suava. 1999. "Polish Peasants in the "Valley of Transition": Responses to Postsocialist Reforms." In *Uncertain Transitions: Ethnographies of Everyday Life in the Postsocialist World,* ed. Michael Burawoy and Katherine Verdery, pp. 189–222. Boulder, Colo.: Rowman & Littlefield.

FOUR

Tempest in a Coffee Pot

Brewing Incivility in Russia's Public Sphere

MELISSA L. CALDWELL

In the summer of 2005 I attended an afternoon church service in the center of Moscow with my elderly friend, Aleksandra. The day was exceptionally hot and muggy, even by Moscow standards. After sitting through a two-hour worship service in a church without air conditioning, we walked several long blocks to the main road toward the nearest metro station. By the time we reached the station we were both parched and tired, and Aleksandra suggested that we go somewhere to have a cool drink and rest for a few moments. We were just a short walk from one of Moscow's largest coffeehouses, a favorite of mine, and so I suggested we go there and my friend readily agreed. This particular coffeehouse was located on Tverskaia ulitsa, Moscow's central avenue and the home of the most exclusive and glamorous shops, in the first floor of a historic apartment building that still boasted prerevolutionary moldings and other decorations on the ceilings and walls. The coffeehouse had opened in the mid-1990s as part of the first wave of "Western" restaurants and cafés that arrived in Russia in the early postsocialist period. The coffeehouse offered an extensive selection of hot and cold coffee drinks, teas, milk shakes and other ice cream treats, desserts, and sandwiches, as well as roasted coffee beans, grinders, and coffee-making supplies. A wooden rack at the entrance contained an assortment of free Russian-, French-, and English-language newspapers. Equally important, especially on this particular day, was that the coffeehouse was air conditioned, and no matter the time of day or how busy it was, a seat at an intimate table or on one of the comfortable couches was always available.

As we strolled along the busy city sidewalk toward the coffeehouse, Aleksandra remarked that to be walking in the center of Moscow again was a special treat for her. Aleksandra's life is centered in the region where she lives, just south of the city center. Because of her health and her age, she rarely ventures far beyond her neighborhood. The last occasion that had drawn her outside this area was a concert in downtown Moscow many months earlier that she attended in the company of several longtime friends. Recalling that evening prompted her to reminisce fondly about other special nights she had spent in the city over the years, enjoying good food and drinks with friends.

We entered the coffeehouse to the cool and quiet peacefulness of the dark room, a startling contrast to the hot bustle of the street outside. To my surprise, just moments later, Aleksandra said she could not stay there; it was too expensive and she felt uncomfortable. Suspecting that she feared the prices would be significantly beyond her means, I reassured her that it was my treat, an invitation she had never refused in the past. In fact, several weeks earlier over lunch at Aleksandra's apartment, we had discussed dressing up and having coffee in downtown Moscow, a special "ladies' afternoon out" that would be my treat. Yet, despite my best efforts to encourage her to stay at the coffeehouse, she became increasingly agitated and adamant that we leave. As we resumed walking up the sweltering street in search of other options, Aleksandra complained fiercely about the coffeehouse: not only did she find the space uncomfortable, but the café was not an appropriate space for people like her. Eventually she found a place more to her liking: a pushcart on the sidewalk, manned by a uniformed young woman selling bottled water, juices, sodas, and ice cream. After purchasing a bottle of juice for Aleksandra and water for myself, we walked several more blocks until we found a bench, dirty but otherwise unoccupied, where we could sit for a while and enjoy the cold beverages, surrounded by the hustle and bustle of the city street.

Since that summer I have struggled to make sense of this encounter, particularly why Aleksandra so strongly resisted staying at the coffee-house because she found it "uncomfortable." By temperament, Aleksandra is a highly confident, adventurous, inquisitive woman who enjoys meeting new people, especially foreigners, and keeping up with the latest trends. Although her personal circumstances are limited by her tiny pension, Aleksandra still samples the latest trends. It was Aleksandra who bought a bottle of gin for her own birthday party simply because she had discovered it in a shop for the first time and wanted to try it. In the late 1990s, when mail-order catalogs, discount shopping cards, and new brands of coffee were only beginning to appear in Russia, it was Aleksandra who introduced them to me. She is also a social butterfly, and I had never seen her at a loss for words or self-assurance in public settings. In fact, she had facilitated several of my meetings with local political officials by telephoning them relentlessly or even storming their public offices and then charmingly convincing them to meet with me. For someone so comfortable experimenting with new consumption trends and performing in public settings, her behavior that afternoon was certainly puzzling.

Yet Aleksandra's actions may become more understandable when viewed in the larger context of postsocialist responses to new modes of consumption, particularly food practices. Like consumers throughout the post-socialist world, Russians have spent much of the last two decades not only trying to make sense of the new consumer products that have arrived in their midst but also attempting to figure out the larger implications and long-term consequences of those changes. Curiosity over the novelty and exotic nature of these new trends, particularly those associated with "the West," has been replaced by concerns with new socioeconomic hierarchies, taste preferences, the preservation of cultural traditions, and even the nature of choice as a performance of agency (Barker 1999; Patico 2008). Above all, Russian consumers have expressed strong sensitivity to issues relating to the moral inflections of consumption in the new Russia (Oushakine 2000; Patico 2005; Shevchenko 2002).

Russians' concerns with the morality of postsocialist consumption have not been confined to evaluations of particular consumer goods or practices but have also extended to debates about the moral inflections of the spaces of consumption. Over the past ten years attention to the proprieties of consumption spaces, particularly those of food and drink, have emerged repeatedly in conversations with Russian friends and acquaintances, as well as in larger public discussions in the Russian media and the political sphere. Embedded within these concerns are other, more complicated anxieties about safety, danger, intimacy, privacy, trust, and community.

The incident with Aleksandra and her avowal of discomfort in the coffeehouse, followed by the ease with which she settled on a public bench along a busy sidewalk, resonates with Russian interests in the moralities of consumer spaces. Although I cannot provide a definitive answer to the specific reasons motivating Aleksandra's reactions to the coffeehouse, the events that transpired that day offer a productive lens for examining the moral valences attached to particular consumer spaces in today's Russia. I suggest that the reorganization of certain consumption activities in new public settings is proving problematic for Russians like Aleksandra. By expressing her preference for drinking bottled juice on a public sidewalk bench rather than sitting in a coffeehouse, Aleksandra invoked a moral ideology of consumption in which certain spaces and practices were more appropriate—and comfortable—than others. Although the specific parameters of Aleksandra's opinions are certainly not representative of the views of all Russians, her concerns with comfort and propriety more generally are.

By exploring the anxieties provoked by new food settings such as cafés, restaurants, markets, and public sidewalks, I examine the moral ideologies that Russian consumers attach to public spaces of food consumption. These contestations, I suggest, reflect consumers' attempts to accommodate the new configurations of public and private that have been produced by dramatic changes in Russia's new food culture. In particular, Russia's new consumer realm, as it is manifested in a booming restaurant, café, and grocery store culture, has produced new forms of public space that, in turn, present opportunities for Russian consumers to generate new behaviors and new moral ideologies about these behaviors.

I begin with a brief overview of the spatial organization of eating and drinking, before moving on to a specific discussion of the architectures of food consumption in Russia. I contend that the themes of public and private evoked by the physical arrangements of the different processes of consumption—preparation, presentation, and consumption—belong to a larger set of public concerns with the emergence of a public sphere that is both civic and civilized in Russia. My discussion focuses primarily on three food settings: the market, coffeehouses, and public drinking spaces. My analysis draws on my ethnographic fieldwork in Russia, primarily in Moscow and Tver, since the mid-1990s.

Architectures of Propriety and Civility

Attention to the spatial arrangements in which food practices are situated offers insight not just into how consumers experience and navigate the profound changes wrought by the postsocialist consumption revolution but also into how consumers' everyday practices and beliefs are shaped in and through particular spatial formations (de Certeau 1984; Slater 1993; Zukin 1991). With regard to shopping practices, Don Slater (1993) argues that market activities do not exist in the abstract but rather take place in distinct physical spaces that are culturally and socially generated. As "both place and event" (ibid.:188), markets reveal particular configurations of social organization, power dynamics, cultural ideology, and even relationships of public and private. Sharon Zukin (1991) takes these ideas further, suggesting that taste preferences themselves are embedded within spatially articulated relationships of power, labor, demand, and choice.[1] Zukin's "landscape of cuisine" (ibid., 208) resonates with Ferrero's notion of the "foodscape" (2002:196) as ways of capturing the spatial aspects of food practices. Physically organized and managed spaces are also disciplinary spaces shaping the behaviors of people moving through them (McDonogh 1993). In turn, the practices of everyday life transform these spaces into meaningful "lived spaces" (de Certeau 1984:96), investing and embedding them within cultural and social elements.[2]

This argument that spatial arrangements reveal cultural and social ideologies intersects with current discussions among social and political analysts about the existence of civil society in socialist and postsocialist societies.[3] Current debates about the nature of civil society in Russia are infused with spatializing logics. Civil society advocates and implementers, mostly from the West, have drawn on sources such as Putnam's (2000) that locate civil society in distinct settings like city halls, public meeting halls, schools, churches, and even bowling alleys because of the presumed sense of community that emerges in these arenas.[4]

A shortcoming of postsocialist analyses of space and civil society is their predisposition to conclude that all public spaces are good, productive, and desirable. However, as George Ritzer (2004) and Gary McDonogh (1993) have suggested, from different perspectives and for other societies, not all public spaces are created equal nor do all members of society necessarily experience them positively—a perception certainly echoed by Aleksandra's discomfort at the coffeehouse. Both Ritzer and McDonogh identify the problem as one of defining meaningfulness for public spaces. McDonogh reminds us that many societies distinguish between spaces that are "empty" and those that are "filled," whereby "emptiness" is often represented as socially disruptive, even dangerous. This emptiness does not necessarily require the absence of social life but rather the absence of culturally appropriate life (McDonogh 1993), an idea Katz (1993) also suggests in her work on the dangers of public spaces. Ritzer (2004), meanwhile, argues that it is "filled" spaces that become problematic. Specifically the homogenizing trends of the culture of contemporary global capitalism create generic cultural forms that lose any sense of meaningfulness to local cultures (ibid.). Ritzer pays particular attention to the consequences of these homogenizing trends on the spaces of food consumption, including restaurants, cafés, and markets.

Taken together, both Ritzer's and McDonogh's approaches underscore the importance of seeking a diversity of cultural values as they are evoked and enacted in the spaces of public life, a perspective that intersects with Chris Hann's (1996) critique of postsocialist paradigms of civil society. Hann argues that it is imperative to consider cultural and moral issues, especially "the fusion of the moral, the social and the political," in order to understand civil society and how ordinary people experience it (Hann 1996:3). Hence, recasting the spaces of public life as *moral* spaces is productive for understanding the implications of how the architectures and topographies of food culture have changed over the past twenty years in Russia (see also Shectman, this volume), as well as in other postsocialist societies (see also Mincyte, this volume). In the following section I describe the spatial features of Russia's food culture and trace recent changes in this domain, before moving on to a discussion of the new behaviors and moral codes of behavior enacted by and in these spaces.

Managing the Spaces of Russian Food Consumption

The physical organization and management of everyday life acquired special significance in Russia during the socialist period, when space became a key locus for the formal and informal enactment of state policies and ideologies. Soviet officials promoted socialism as a totalizing social project that included the remodeling and reorganization of multiple spatial orders and dimensions. Socialist planners reworked public spaces in cities, towns, villages, and the countryside across the USSR through the implementation of distinctive architectural styles; the redirection and renaming of streets and sidewalks; the institution of massive public squares that could be used as parade grounds; and even the deliberate cultivation of thick public parks and forests in the middle of large cities (Boym 2001:96; Crowley and Reid 2002). One consequence of the standardizing aspects of socialist space was a homogenization of daily life, so that physical spaces—and the everyday life taking shape within them— acquired a generic feeling (Humphrey 1995).[5]

At the more intimate and mundane levels of everyday life, the socialist project entailed the deliberate recalibration of public and private spheres. As Victor Buchli (1999:41) notes in his study of Soviet architecture, Soviet officials targeted the sphere of the private or the domestic as "the locus of the battle against petit-bourgeois values inhibiting the establishment of socialism." One solution to this problem was transforming the domestic sphere into public or shared space. Communal housing and other ideologies of communal living represented one physical manifestation of these projects (Boym 1994; Buchli 1999).

Food practices were a second, and perhaps in some ways more profound, sphere in which these private/public transformations played out. Reconfigurations of private and public took shape in the architectures of food shops, particularly in terms of what was visible versus invisible. Socialist-era shopping systems that structured customers' access to goods through queues and counters also controlled the visibility, and availability, of those goods. In principle, this was a system of transparency in which goods were publicly displayed and customers knew what was available. In practice, however, socialist consumers knew that this visibility was a mere illusion.[6] Customers were not generally allowed to touch the goods until after they had paid for them, preventing customers from ensuring that the food items were fresh before purchasing them. At the same time customers were not surprised by unscrupulous shop clerks who might put a thumb on the scale to add weight or substitute inferior meat for good cuts. Moreover, the recurring shortages that plagued the socialist period ensured the flourishing of a parallel system of invisible food shopping in which shop clerks saved goods for themselves and their friends behind the counter, and special stores maintained special stocks of foods for elites (e.g., Young 1989).

Spaces of food preparation and consumption were similarly affected by these ideological changes. In some cases, socialist reformers advocated eliminating private kitchens and having food prepared in public spaces such as workplace canteens and public dining rooms (Borrero 1997, 2002; Rothstein and Rothstein 1997). In other instances, the realities of communal housing forced residents to compete for scarce kitchen resources, resulting in distinctive behaviors of secrecy, competition, and denial (Boym 1994:147; Gerasimova 2002).[7] The typically cramped nature of Soviet housing meant, more generally, that living spaces served multiple purposes; a bedroom, for example, might also operate as the family's dining room. In homes with private kitchens, the kitchen space was rarely large enough for more than a tiny table and a few stools.

This reworking of private eating spaces was mirrored by changes in public dining. Although the Soviet Union continued its culture of restaurants and canteens, the dynamics of these spaces changed as they were used primarily for formal, public activities such as workplace parties or wedding banquets rather than as places where individuals could engage in truly private activities. As Svetlana Boym points out, Walter Benjamin, in his reflections on his trip to Moscow in the 1920s, observed that the disappearance of private life in Russia included the loss of café culture (Benjamin 1978:109; cited in Boym 1994:126). Boym argues that the eradication of café culture came about because "café relationships are too intimate and too accidental, collective in an ideologically incorrect manner, eccentric but in a wrong style, not classless but déclassé (if not bourgeois)" (1994:126). In short, the intimacy and privacy associated with café culture was not appropriate for the new revolutionary objectives of socialist reformers. Where cafés did exist, they were often small, modest spaces. Yet these spaces were still largely outside the scope or concern of the state, particularly since the purpose of these spaces was for socializing among apolitical young people. As Yurchak notes, it is misleading to interpret these spaces as part of a "public sphere," because if anything they distanced themselves from politics (Yurchak 2006:141–146).

Ultimately the consequences of spatial design and organization extend beyond their visual and material appearances and into the realm of how they are experienced, what McDonogh (1993:5) calls "spatial conscious-ness." In the postsocialist period, changes in Russians' "spatial conscious-ness" have coincided with the transformation of consumption practices. Specifically changes in the content and style of Russian food practices have necessitated modifications of the very spaces in which these food cultures are situated and enacted. As a result, not simply are Russians' consumption preferences changing, but so, too, are the ways in which they inhabit and move through spaces of food consumption.

For instance, although fast-food restaurants such as McDonald's are perhaps most recognized for the types of food they introduced into Russia in the early 1990s, these restaurants also established new designs for the organization of public dining. In the case of McDonald's, the company introduced large, seating areas where customers seated them-selves, carried their own food, and at times even cleared their own tables. That McDonald's offered sit-down dining was a departure from the more customary Russian fast-food venues: typically small street-side kiosks from which customers could either walk away with their food or stand for a moment at a tiny counter or tall table.

Similarly the Western-style supermarkets that began appearing in the early 1990s introduced new spatial layouts that, in turn, induced new customer behaviors. Socialist-era grocery stores had typically been orga-nized around the physical separation of customers from food products by counters and discrete sections for different types of foods. For instance, fresh produce, meat, dairy, canned goods, staples, and beverages were all placed in different sections, accessible by different counters and served by different clerks. Customers were further separated from the business of shopping by the placement of separate counters for ordering, paying, and then receiving their purchases. By contrast, the open floor plans of post-socialist supermarkets allow customers to move freely along aisles of shelves or around open bins from which they can select items to place in a basket or buggy, before moving to a check-out stand located at the exit of the store. Even Moscow's famed prerevolutionary Eliseevskii grocery store made the transition to a Western-style supermarket system with self-serve aisles and checkout stands. It is noteworthy that the freedom of movement facilitated by these new layouts are also challenging customers to rethink the boundaries of personal space as they become accustomed to using shopping carts in ways that do not encroach on others' abilities to shop.

The consequences of this reorganization of Russian food spaces are also evident in the architectural and design styles it has inspired. Kitchen design is a lucrative industry, evident in the focus on home decorating and entertaining articles in popular magazines, the tremendous popularity of Ikea and other commercial retailers of home furnishings, and the growing market for more exclusive, high-end kitchen and dining room designers.[8] In the commercial sphere, the institutionally generic blandness that characterized color schemes and furniture in Soviet-era restaurants and cafés is being replaced by vibrant color schemes, unique decorations, and comfortable furniture all geared to create distinct ambiances and experiences.[9]

As a result, consumption-inspired spatial reorganization extends beyond home kitchens, restaurants, and supermarkets, and appears in the ways in which Russian consumers organize the commercial terrain of their cities and nation.[10] At the same time this reinvention and rearrangement of food spaces affects consumers' experiences as they inhabit and move through these spaces. Of particular significance is how Russian consumers interpret and evaluate the new configurations of public space that have emerged in these new food settings. As we will see, pleasure and anxiety are both common responses to these changes. But whereas the presumed pleasures, or at least advantages, of these changes are perhaps most easily explained, the anxieties they provoke are more revealing of the issues facing postsocialist consumers. After identifying a few features of Russia's new consumer public, I turn to three different, but related, manifestations of new food spaces, the anxieties they provoke among Russian consumers, and what these anxieties reveal about public life in Russia today.

Russia's New Consumer Public

During my fieldwork in Moscow in the mid- and late 1990s, finding public places to meet with informants and conduct interviews was often difficult. Restaurants and cafés with comfortable seating and affordable menus were in short supply. Most common were Soviet-era snack bars or cafeterias with limited seating and often located in out-of-the-way places in office buildings or schools. Moreover, access to these snack bars and cafeterias in office buildings was generally restricted to employees. Although Moscow was witnessing the emergence of a few restaurants and cafés, the prices at these establishments were out of reach for all but the most financially privileged—typically businesspeople with expense accounts and members of Russia's new economic elite. A dinner meeting for members of a professional women's networking organization, in 1995, illustrates these complications well. The meeting took place in a restaurant located in a remote district on the edge of the city. Access to the entrance of the restaurant was through an overgrown empty lot in an abandoned industrial zone. At the dinner, the differences in the menu selections of my companions were noticeable. Whereas the North American expatriate women with Western salaries chose freely from the menu, the Russian women attending the meeting either ordered nothing at all or split an inexpensive entrée between several people. Their discomfort with the prices of the dishes was evident in their body language and the horrified whispers they exchanged. My own awareness that appropriate public meeting places were in short supply was echoed by Russian friends and colleagues, who similarly complained that they had few options for meeting friends for a casual visit.

If public meeting spaces were limited, so, too, were possibilities for meeting with friends at home. During the Soviet period, the scarcity of private space in apartments, as well as the reality of surveillance, made socializing in one's home difficult. Only in the 1960s did a "kitchen culture" emerge among Russians, especially members of the intelligentsia, who lived in non-communal apartments with their own kitchens (Boym 1994:147–148). As Boym records for the experiences of Russian intellectuals, these kitchens acquired importance as sites of informality and intimacy "where people 'really talked,' flirted, and occasionally ate"

(1994:149), an experience that Ries (1997:21) has similarly described.[11] Yet even though meeting friends at home in one's kitchen was a practical choice, Russian friends did not always find this a satisfactory option. Short visits to friends' homes were not always feasible, as distances across the city could mean several hours spent on public transportation. Even a short visit might require a hostess to spend valuable time shopping for a few snacks to have with tea. Hence visits to friends' homes were more typically reserved for special occasions that would entail extensive dinner preparations and an expectation of spending many hours at the table, rather than the more informal cup of tea and pastries for a brief visit. Instead, Russians like my acquaintances visited with friends in other ways, most often by walking around the city, through shopping centers, or in public parks. Snacks such as a bag of potato chips, a chocolate bar, or a bottled beverage were most typically brought from home or purchased from a kiosk and enjoyed while sitting or standing nearby.[12]

When McDonald's opened its doors in the then Soviet Union in 1990, it heralded a significant achievement in public eating and drinking in terms of both spatial reorganization and public accessibility. By the late 1990s McDonald's restaurants had become one of the most common destinations for friends who wanted to visit with one another and for colleagues to engage in working lunches.[13] McDonald's was the site for one of my early interviews with Viktor, a university student who had moved to Moscow from a small town several hours outside the city, as it was the only place where we were sure to find a table and because Viktor, having not yet visited McDonald's, was curious to see it. Several months later Viktor confessed that he had become a "regular" at McDonald's, often visiting several times a week, and that he had also introduced the restaurant to his friends, with similar results. It was not the food that appealed to Viktor and his friends but rather the setting: for college students with few options for getting together outside an overcrowded and unpleasant room in the university dormitory, McDonald's represented a vibrant public space where they could meet and talk for long hours and at very little expense. Notably some visitors to McDonald's did not actually buy food there but brought in their own or merely sat at a table to read. Moreover, McDonald's does not, as a rule, enforce time limits, thereby enabling customers to remain at a table for extended periods.

McDonald's value as a public meeting space was mirrored in the other

Figure 4.1. Pedestrians and motorists stop at a roadside stand to buy and drink a glass of cold kvass, a fermented summer beverage. Photograph by Melissa L. Caldwell.

fast-food restaurants and coffeehouses slowly emerging in Moscow in the late 1990s. Despite the need and desire for public spaces, however, a recognizable "café culture" did not truly appear in Russia until the early 2000s, when it took off with a veritable explosion of coffeehouses. By the spring of 2008 the Coffee House and Shokoladnitsa coffeehouse chains together boasted more than 340 locations in Russia (Antonova 2008). The expansion of the Shokoladnitsa chain is particularly intriguing, as the restaurant was originally a Soviet restaurant featuring a chocolate-themed

Figure 4.2. Brightly lit coffeehouses like this one compete for space in Moscow's commercial and residential districts alike. Photograph by Melissa L. Caldwell.

menu, Soviet-style décor, and Soviet-style service at its location near the *Oktiabrskaia* metro station in downtown Moscow.[14] Other popular chains include Coffee Town and Zen Café. Each of these cafés is similar in style: small tables, comfortable chairs, racks of free English-language newspapers, and music. Many also have a sidewalk section during the summer months. Even McDonald's has tapped into the coffeehouse phenomenon by redesigning its restaurants to include a separate section for the McCafé, a coffeehouse concept that the company has successfully used else-

Figure 4.3. McDonald's McCafés are popular throughout the city. Photograph by Michael Herzfeld.

where in Europe. In the McCafé section of the restaurant, customers can purchase a wide variety of hot and cold coffee drinks and pastries, and enjoy the free newspapers provided on racks and stands. Customers in all these cafés represent a similarly diverse slice of the Russian population: teenagers, students, young professionals, middle-aged workers, and older persons.

It is important to note that in Russian coffeehouses, coffee drinks are not necessarily the only or even the preferred beverage of choice. Teas, soft drinks, milkshakes, and most notably beer and alcoholic cocktails are typically included on the menu. (In some coffeehouses the menu section for alcoholic drinks is longer than that for coffee drinks.) Coffeehouses generally offer extensive menus of food items such as soups, salads, sandwiches, and pastas in addition to pastries and ice cream.[15] A few chains, such as Shokoladnitsa, have begun offering American-style breakfasts with bacon and eggs. Breakfast options at restaurants only appeared relatively recently, inspired primarily by McDonald's and the American-themed restaurant Starlite Diner. For most Russians, breakfast is a meal eaten at home.

The effects of Russia's new café culture are appearing in my relationships with friends as well as in the ways I conduct fieldwork. Increasingly friends no longer suggest that our get-togethers take place in public parks or in their homes but rather in a café. My arrival often seems to be an excuse to try a newly opened café. Informants are also more likely to suggest that we meet in a café for interviews rather than in an office or on a public bench. When interviews take place in people's homes, the obligatory offer of a cup of tea just as often includes a cup of brewed coffee as well. Although instant coffee, which became popular in the 1990s, has not disappeared entirely from home kitchens, coffee grinders, drip coffee makers, French Presses, and even espresso machines have become noticeably more common.

The scope of this new café culture is particularly evident in Tver, where the opening of the city's first official coffeehouse in the early 2000s was greeted joyfully by members of the town's university population, especially faculty members with fond memories of European coffeehouses from their travels abroad. Humanities and social sciences faculty from the city's largest university, conveniently located just a short walk from the coffeehouse, found the venue valuable for meeting with colleagues and students. Comfortable armchairs and small couches provided cozy, intimate places for customers to sit and talk with one another or for individuals to read or work on projects. Magazines and newspapers were available in racks or on end tables conveniently placed throughout the main room. By 2007 wireless Internet was available and offered Web surfers a more appealing alternative to the grungy Internet gaming/video lounges populated by adolescent boys or to the Internet department at the local post office, where there was always a wait for the few terminals and a strict time limit when one became available.

Although the Tver coffeehouse opens in the morning, business typically does not pick up until mid-afternoon when customers begin arriving for a late lunch or an afternoon snack. For customers who want to enjoy a coffee and pastry, the menu at the coffeehouse offers numerous coffee drinks and slices of pre-made cakes, pies, and other desserts. Customers who want something more savory or substantial can choose from a list of soups and salads, and even order a drink from the African university student who is the bartender at the well-stocked bar.[16] The coffeehouse stays open late into the evening for patrons to gather with friends and colleagues. Over the past several years similar cafés and restaurants have appeared in Tver, primarily in the central square area of the historic downtown district.

Although Tver's first coffeehouse is noteworthy for introducing a new beverage culture to the city, it has acquired a secondary, perhaps more important significance as a public space, particularly as a public space for community life. In the late 1990s several friends and colleagues in Tver often lamented the dearth of public spaces in the community. One friend, a university professor, expressed this criticism in terms of an absence of community life. Since the coffeehouse opened, it has acquired a reputation as an art gallery featuring the work of local artists and as a meeting place for community organizations to hold discussions, parties, and other events. Departments and research groups at the local universities use the space, for example, for public lectures and discussion groups rather than meeting in campus facilities. The public, community aspect of the café is also popular among students and other local community members. Bulletin boards allow visitors to post messages about community events, housing opportunities, and items for sale. Other coffeehouses that have opened in Tver have emulated the style of this coffeehouse by promoting similar uses for their own spaces. These trends are mirrored in Moscow and elsewhere in Russia, as coffeehouses diversify by holding musical performances, public lectures, and special-interest enrichment events.

Increasingly coffeehouses serve multiple purposes as deliberately organized community spaces, and thus they contribute to new forms of social organization and, by extension, to a new vision of public life in Russia. It is the new public life afforded by the café culture that Russian consumers find most appealing. That the phenomenon of take-away coffee has not yet found its niche in Russia testifies to the suggestion that once Russian consumers enter a coffeehouse, they prefer staying there to enjoy their drinks.

More than simply providing new venues for citizens to engage in publicly oriented activities, however, Russia's café culture is part of a larger cultural movement characterized by the reorientation of public and private. Even as cafés acquire greater visibility as spaces for the performance of public life, Russian consumers continue to treat them as intimate spaces for personal, private activities. And it is this quality of addressing both the public and the private simultaneously that makes customers

Figure 4.4. Starbucks is a relative latecomer to Moscow, with the opening of its first store in the fall of 2007. Photograph by Melissa L. Caldwell.

feel uncomfortable and renders spaces like coffeehouses problematic. In the following section I turn to the issue of what makes certain public food spaces discomforting, even hazardous in some cases, for Russian consumers.

Incivility and the Hazards of Public Food Spaces

Despite the benefits of cafés, restaurants, and even supermarkets in Russia, many consumers view these as hazardous food spaces. Sometimes the hazards are social, as diners realize that restaurants and cafés may in fact be too public. In small cities like Tver, where there are still very few restaurants, there is the danger of running into one's colleagues at dinner. One night in the summer of 2007 my friends, Volodya and Masha, excitedly took me to a newly opened restaurant that they had been waiting to try. As we walked in, they joked about looking forward to enjoying a night out without having to think about work. To their dismay, however,

Volodya's supervisor was sitting at the bar near our table, and, later, the hostess seated another colleague at a table nearby.

During dinner, Volodya and Masha voiced their frustrations not only at having to be circumspect in our conversation but also at not knowing the proper etiquette when meeting a coworker in a restaurant. They discussed whether it was more courteous to greet their colleague, even if it meant disturbing the person's meal, or not to acknowledge the person at all. The issue was most serious concerning Volodya's supervisor, who was sitting at the bar with his back to us and so had not seen us entering the restaurant. In the end, when the man turned around to talk to the waitress, he spotted us just as Volodya looked up. The two men acknowledged each other with a nod. Because of the spontaneous nature of the encounter, Volodya was able to act as if he had only just seen his boss. In the case of the coworker, we passed him on our way out of the restaurant, which allowed my friends to greeted him cordially but briefly.

Although my friends were able to resolve the issue of social etiquette, the knowledge that their colleagues were nearby hampered my friends' comfort at talking freely. In a similarly revealing instance, an acquaintance in Moscow was so concerned about running into his coworkers at a café near his workplace that he insisted on walking through the entire space to see if he recognized anyone before he agreed to speak freely during our conversations.

Another hazard in food spaces is that of dishonesty. My friend, Ksenia, was a physical education teacher at an elementary school in Tver, and so our visits typically took place either in a sports setting (Ksenia seemed to have an endless supply of ping pong and badminton equipment in her handbag) or in her kitchen. Shortly before I returned to the States in the fall of 2005, Ksenia and I went to a café that had just opened on her side of the city. When we first sat down at our table, Ksenia confessed that she rarely visited cafés, primarily because as a single mother of a teenage son, the cost of a beverage in a café was a luxury she could hardly justify. She had also heard that one had to be careful when eating in cafés, because the employees were dishonest and tried to cheat customers. When we finished our snack and the waitress brought the bill, Ksenia, though amenable to my offer to pay, insisted on reviewing the check. On doing so, she discovered that the waitress had charged us for items we had not ordered. Calling the waitress over, Ksenia sharply berated her before demanding a new check, which she also carefully scrutinized before allowing me to pay. On leaving the café, Ksenia told me that her concerns about dishonesty had been justified and that this experience had dissuaded her from visiting another café.

Fears that food spaces are places of danger and fraud have also materialized in Russian attitudes and policies toward food markets. Conversations with Muscovite and Tver informants about their shopping practices reveal recurring concerns with deception in markets. Some informants recommended carrying a personal scale to verify that the weights of items sold by vendors are accurate. In the summer months television news programs frequently aired articles about fraud in food markets and the efforts by officials from the department of weights and measures to regulate the scales used by vendors. These concerns about the morality of the marketplace were manifested in a popular critique of capitalism, in which Russian consumers correlated capitalist market practices with deception, inferior-quality goods, and lack of safety (Gabriel 2005; Kaneff 2002; Patico 2001; see also the chapters by Jung and Klumbytė, this volume).

Yet at the same time that deception was framed in economic terms, consumers' views reveal deeper concerns with the consequences of demographic change on national identity and heritage in Russia. Consumers who were the most troubled by market fraud described their perspectives in reference to the presumed honesty of vendors, with outsiders classified as inherently less trustworthy and their food as being of low quality. Muscovite informants, in particular, preferred not to buy food from sellers who were from Central Asia, the Caucasus, and Africa, because these individuals, in their view, were more likely to sell substandard products and engage in other types of consumer fraud.[17]

Attitudes about the dangerous qualities of markets also inform beautification and gentrification initiatives in Moscow and other cities. Over the past several years Moscow's mayor Yuri Luzhkov has implemented aggressive initiatives to clean up and beautify the city. In addition to planting trees and flowers, updating building façades and metro stations, and installing refuse and recycling bins throughout the city, city authorities have also forcefully relocated aesthetically unappetizing food sites to less visible places. Sidewalk kiosks have been closed and the structures removed from city streets and underground passageways. Even the city's food markets are being closed and relocated to indoor, enclosed spaces with clearly defined stalls, departments, and aisles. In many respects, enclosing markets in indoor spaces suggests it is the openness of food markets—and all that openness symbolizes for the disorder of economic transactions in today's Russia—that city officials find most hazardous. By installing vendors in enclosed spaces with clearly defined aisles and departments, circumscribing the movement of shoppers through these spaces, and enforcing the visibility of the goods for sale, authorities can manage the physical, economic, and even nutritional safety of these settings and the foods sold there.[18]

Most revealing, however, is how Muscovite consumers and vendors interpret these changes. Russia has a long history of "spatial cleansing" (Herzfeld 2006) in which state authorities control the morality of public spaces through the removal of unsightly elements, notably people (see Stephenson 2006). During the summer of 2007 acquaintances in Moscow repeatedly voiced their suspicions that the closure and relocation of outdoor markets was the latest tactic in the state's efforts to eliminate "foreigners," notably people from the former Soviet republics of Central Asia and the Caucasus. Market closures were accompanied by police "sweeps" of markets in which unregistered foreigners were arrested. Market vendors were forced to obtain official permits, a requirement further allowing the state to control who could enter and work in these spaces. Informants also observed that by relocating markets far outside the city's regular transportation routes, city authorities marginalized unregistered foreigners whose movements through the city were already severely curtailed by the very real fear that they would be apprehended by the local police. Several acquaintances suspected that this was a deliberate tactic by city authorities to exacerbate the anxieties of these individuals and force them to leave the city altogether.[19]

Finally, issues of anxiety, discomfort, danger, and safety are perhaps most visible in the changing sphere of alcohol consumption. The development of Russia's beverage market has encompassed soft drinks, juice, and bottled water, as well as beer, spirits, wine, and "weak" alcoholic drinks such as energy drinks and malted beverages.[20] The growth of this market, however, has not necessarily been matched by the expansion of settings for their consumption. Despite high rates of alcohol consumption in Russia, as well as high rates of alcoholism, a topic Katherine Metzo addresses in this volume, few public spaces are sanctioned for the consumption of alcohol. "Bar culture" is only starting to emerge in Russia, primarily among young professionals with disposable income. More common is the practice of ordering beer or increasingly a glass of wine with a meal in a restaurant or café. The Riumochnaia, the traditional, small "by-the-shot" bar (*riumchiki* are shot glasses) where customers (usually middle-aged, working-class men) can stop in after work to enjoy a 50-ml or 100-ml shot of vodka, have been disappearing in recent years.

Instead, social drinkers are increasingly colonizing public parks and sidewalks as spaces to drink and visit with friends. Particularly noticeable is that these spaces are being appropriated primarily by teenagers and young adults—in other words, individuals who live with family or in dormitories and so do not have private spaces of their own. (Although most are males, females are increasingly joining their male companions to drink.) This appropriation of public spaces for drinking by young people has escalated over the past ten years. Whereas in the late 1990s, two or three small groups may have been seen sitting on the benches or fences lining shady sidewalks, today entire sidewalks and park areas are commonly taken over by some one hundred to two hundred young people. A particularly popular area is that surrounding the Novokuznetskaia metro station. The sidewalks around this station are a prime gathering place for social drinkers, beginning in late afternoon and continuing well into late evening. Several hundred people might be seen gathered in small groups and spread out throughout the area. In the summer of 2007 the city demolished a cluster of nearby buildings and created a park with benches and sidewalks. When I visited the area in the fall of 2008 the number of people gathering to drink and socialize there seemed to have increased dramatically.

These changes have elicited discomfort and criticism from many Russians who despise having to walk through crowds of inebriated people and around the debris of bottles, cigarettes, and empty chips packets. Informants repeatedly described these young people as "hooligans" and stated that they did not feel safe walking near these spaces. Some informants reported that they had changed their walking routes altogether to avoid spaces where young people gathered.

Although alcohol consumption is clearly not new in Russia, its movement from private, discrete, and relatively invisible spaces into public view is a noticeable departure from previous practices. The discomfort evoked by the movement of drinking behavior into public view illuminates persistent cultural ideals about the correlation between particular spaces and the socially appropriate behavior that goes on in those spaces. Loud, boisterous behavior that is inappropriate—and unsafe—on public park benches is acceptable in spaces outside the immediate public view, such as in a private home or at a private function such as a party. This distinction emerged clearly when I visited a Riumochnaia with an American male colleague (and fellow Russia scholar) in the summer of 2007. During our visit we stood at a small table, enjoying our vodka and the action around us. Because it was early evening, the room was filled with middle-aged men who had gathered to meet friends on their way home from work. The atmosphere was lively with the sound of laughter and conversation. When my colleague stepped over to talk briefly with several men at a nearby table, the two men standing at the table immediately next to ours leaned over to talk with me. They both apologized for their behavior, explaining that I had to understand that men behave "like men" in these spaces. With that apology, they sent a clear message that certain behaviors were permissible in spaces like this one, as well as the implication that it was I, as one of only two women and obviously dressed as a professional, who was disrupting the norms of the space.

The discomforting aspects of public drinking were further illuminated in comments by a colleague who had, in the late 1990s and early 2000s, complained repeatedly about the lack of a public sphere in Tver and then celebrated the arrival of the first coffeehouse. This colleague was particularly troubled by the dramatic surge in public drinking by young people who congregated in the pedestrian zone and yard area outside her apartment.[21] Although sympathetic to the fact that these young people probably had no other place where they could gather, she strongly opposed their appropriation of this particular public space.

As these examples reveal, there are limits to the public sphere in terms of who can use it and for what purpose. Norms of propriety are ultimately discourses of civility. When understood through the realm of space, ethics of propriety operate as moralizing systems that classify public spaces into settings for both civil and uncivil society.

Living Private Lives in the Public Eye

By way of conclusion, I return to the vignette that began this chapter: Aleksandra's refusal to visit the coffeehouse in downtown Moscow. When considered in the context of concerns about the hazards and anxieties provoked by public spaces of consumption, Aleksandra's actions can be reinterpreted as a commentary on the delineation between public and private space and the propriety of public and private behavior. For people like Aleksandra, one can be most casual and open with friends and family only in truly private spaces such as at home. In contrast, in public spaces such as on a bench located on a bustling city sidewalk, there is no presumption of privacy but only anonymity produced by being within a crowd, which, paradoxically, produces its own form of privacy. The coffeehouse disrupted this distinction by confusing the anonymity of a public space with the intimacy of a private space. Because the coffeehouse was a public space for private activities, Aleksandra was uncomfortable sharing that intimate space with strangers. Her concerns with this confusion of public and private mirrored the discomfort of my friends, Volodya and Masha, when they tried to determine the proper etiquette of acknowledging coworkers who, like themselves, were enjoying a private meal.

The experiences of Aleksandra, Volodya, Masha, Ksenia, and other Russians described in this essay reveal that the reorganization of space in Russia's postsocialist food sphere complicates how consumers understand, interpret, and experience these new settings as simultaneously public and private spaces. Consequently they are confronted with having to renegotiate the norms of socially legitimate food experiences that are permissible in those spaces. As seating arrangements, décor, and spatial layouts change, Russian consumers must rethink relationships between transparency and secrecy, and between trust and fraud.

Even as the creation of spaces for public, perhaps even civic, life in these new food settings fills a critical gap in previous social arrangements in Russia, consumers are discovering that the benefits of these spaces are often accompanied by significant risks. On the one hand, concerns with surveillance, a hallmark of the Soviet period, are returning in new guises as diners realize that their actions in public spaces are monitored, even regulated, by the presence of other customers. On the other hand, the very openness of these settings may in fact be an illusion that obscures more than it reveals.

Ultimately these negotiations over the proprieties of public spaces tap into ongoing discussions in Russia about the nature of a civilized life in today's Russia. Being civilized means not simply participating in Russia's new consumer world but also enjoying it. Enjoyment, essentially, means feeling comfortable in particular settings, and comfort is as much about knowing the rules for engaging those settings as it is about feeling safe in the social worlds those spaces generate. As an expression of safety, comfort is the experiential quality of intimacy, regardless of whether that intimacy exists in a private kitchen, a public café, a neighborhood Riumochnaia, or a public park bench.

ACKNOWLEDGMENTS

This chapter is based on materials gathered in Moscow between 1995 and 2008. Funding for this research was generously provided by the Davis Center for Russian and Eurasian Studies, Department of Anthropology, and the Committee on Degrees in Social Studies at Harvard University, the Mellon Foundation, a Foreign Language Area Studies Fellowship, and the University of California, Santa Cruz. I thank my fellow foodie colleagues in the Food and Body Multi-Campus Research Group of the University of California, who generously and thoughtfully read and commented on an earlier draft of this chapter. I particularly thank Carolyn de la Peña, Julie Guthman, Melanie Dupuis, Charlotte Biltekoff, Alison Alkon, Kim Nettles, and Erika Rappaport.

NOTES

1. See, especially, Zukin's observations about the particular spatial arrangements of sociopolitical power informing gourmet food cultures (Zukin 1991:206–208).

2. For an extended discussion of the disciplinary aspects of space and spatial formations, see Herzfeld 2006.

3. In the early days of the postsocialist period, the most prominent question in these discussions centered around whether socialist societies possessed a "civil society," with many analysts concluding that they did not (e.g., Wedel 1994). By the 2000s the rhetoric of this debate had shifted so that questions of whether a civil society existed were replaced by

discussions over the nature and location of civil society. See Hann and Dunn 1996 for accounts and critiques of civil society in the postsocialist world.

4. Efforts to create postsocialist civil societies have also drawn on neoliberal theories that emphasize the creation of private spheres through privatization measures (Hann 1996:9). Yet even these "private spheres" are not fully private, as these spaces are in fact designed to support and benefit the public. Food spaces, particularly transnational restaurant chains and food manufacturing corporations, have proved to be fundamental partners not only in introducing the values of Western models of "civil society"—specifically privatization and market capitalism in Russia but also in introducing private spheres as public spaces. Thus these privatizing measures also support the creation of new publics and new public consumers.

5. This generic feeling and sense of homogeneity were captured brilliantly in the Soviet film *The Irony of Fate* (*Ironiia sud'by*).

6. Yuson Jung (this volume) makes a similar point for the case of Bulgaria.

7. Svetlana Boym (1994:147) cites an informant who described kitchens in communal apartments as a "domestic Nagorno-Karabakh."

8. See also Krisztina Fehérváry's (2002) fascinating article on the rise of kitchen remodeling in Hungary.

9. This diversification of design and experience is especially noticeable in the styles used by restaurants and cafés offering "ethnic" and "foreign" food experiences (see Caldwell 2006).

10. Another space-related trend is apparent in the rise of "culinary tourism" in which Russian landscapes are mapped through restaurants, grocery stores, and other food spaces (Caldwell 2006), a phenomenon that a writer for a Russian cooking magazine called "Geo-gastronomia" (Anonymous 1998:8).

11. See also Nancy Ries's (1997:10) description of the related rituals of intimacy and tea drinking in the workplace.

12. During my preliminary fieldwork in Moscow in 1995, my landlady was so concerned that I would not find anything to eat during the day that she packed *buterbrody* (open-faced sandwiches) every day for me to take and eat on a park bench. It was not an unwarranted fear, I discovered.

13. This use of McDonald's spaces is discussed more extensively in Caldwell 2004. More generally, the phenomenon of "business lunch" in Russia is fascinating. Although "business lunch" originated in the mid-1990s largely in response to new business practices in Russia, particularly the Western tradition of conducting business with customers over a mid-day meal, it has since evolved into a special menu typically less expensive than the dinner menu, perhaps akin to the "Early Bird Special" in American culture.

14. In 1998, before Shokoladnitsa made the transition from a sit-down restaurant to a coffeehouse, a friend and I ate there for lunch. Reminiscent of "Soviet-style" service, the waitress alternately ignored and berated us, most items on the menu were not available, and the drab ambiance was the epitome of institutional formalism. Today the Shokoladnitsa cafés are bright, cheery places offering wireless Internet, magazines and newspapers to read, and an extensive menu of always available hot and cold beverages, pastries, salads, sandwiches, soups, and cocktails. The clientele ranges from "hip" high school students to middle-aged workers and retirees.

15. In discussions about the potential successes of Starbucks, which finally opened its first store in Russia in the fall of 2007, observers suggested that, if the company hopes to be competitive in Russia, it may have to include alcohol on its menu. During a visit to a Moscow Starbucks in October 2008, however, alcoholic beverages were not listed on the menu. A few Moscow residents commented that Starbucks was very expensive—far more expensive than

the other coffeehouses, where the price of a cup of coffee was already seen as verging on the unrealistic.

16. A sense of mystery surrounds the bartender's origin. Vague stories have variously suggested that he is an African student at the local university, that he is a Russian of African descent, and even that he is the owner of the coffee shop. Regardless, from my visits there, he was clearly a popular bartender and enjoyed good relationships with his regular customers.

17. A recurring theme in informants' comments was the distinction between "ours" (*nash*) and "not ours" (*ne nash*), a distinction that acquired racializing qualities when also coupled with descriptors such as "black" (*chernyi*) to describe people presumed to be less trustworthy. For a discussion of these racialized market discourses, see Caldwell 2003. See also Patico 2001 for a discussion of St. Petersburg consumers' hierarchies of value for foreign consumer goods.

18. In his article comparing "spatial cleansing" projects in Italy to those in Thailand, Herzfeld (2006) notes that the worldwide trend has been to remove markets from public view.

19. These changes had obvious consequences for one of the aid programs I have been study-ing since 1997. This program provides monthly bags of supplemental food supplies to refugees, asylum seekers, and other low-income people from Africa and the Middle East. Previously program staff and volunteers purchased staples of rice, flour, sugar, and oil at a nearby market and then transported the goods back to the program's office by metro. Now, however, the logistics of reaching the relocated market (several metro and bus lines away) require finding a volunteer who can donate the use of an automobile, a significantly limiting factor.

20. On "weak" alcoholic drinks, see Shectman 2008:24–26. For the case of Poland's growing juice market, see Dunn 2004.

21. Young people urinating on the walls and in the stairwells of her building and leaving piles of bottles and other refuse in the area, as well as the tremendous noise generated from this socializing, were problems.

REFERENCES CITED

Anonymous. 1998. "*Moskva na ostrie shampura* (Moscow on a sharp skewer)." *Restorannye vedemosti*, February 1:4–10.

Antonova, Maria. 2008. "Crazy for Coffee." *The Moscow Times*, April 23.

Barker, Adele Marie, ed. 1999. *Consuming Russia: Popular Culture, Sex, and Society since Gor-bachev.* Durham, N.C.: Duke University Press.

Borrero, Mauricio. 1997. "Communal Dining and State Cafeterias in Moscow and Petrograd, 1917–1921." In *Food in Russian History and Culture*, ed. Musya Glants and Joyce Toomre, pp. 162–176. Bloomington: Indiana University Press.

———. 2002. "Food and the Politics of Scarcity in Urban Soviet Russia, 1917–1941." In *Food Nations: Selling Taste in Consumer Societies*, ed. Warren Belasco and Phillip Scranton, pp. 258–276. New York: Routledge.

Boym, Svetlana. 1994. *Common Places: Mythologies of Everyday Life in Russia.* Cambridge, Mass.: Harvard University Press.

———. 2001. *The Future of Nostalgia.* New York: Basic Books.

Buchli, Victor. 1999. *An Archaeology of Socialism.* Oxford: Berg.

Caldwell, Melissa L. 2003. "Race and Social Relations: Crossing Borders in a Moscow Food Aid Program." In *Social Networks in Movement. Time, Interaction and Interethnic Spaces in Central Eastern Eruasia*, ed. Davide G. Torsello and Maria Pappova, pp. 255–273. Dunajksa Streda (SK): Lilium Aurum.

———. 2004. "Domesticating the French Fry: McDonald's and Consumerism in Moscow." *Journal of Consumer Culture* 4(1): 5–26.

———. 2006. "Tasting the Worlds of Yesterday and Today: Culinary Tourism and Nostalgia Foods in Post-Soviet Russia." In *Fast Food/Slow Food: The Cultural Economy of the Global Food System*, ed. Richard Wilk, pp. 97–112. Lanham, Md.: AltaMira.

Crowley, David, and Susan E. Reid. 2002. "Socialist Spaces: Sites of Everyday Life in the Eastern Bloc." In *Socialist Spaces: Sites of Everyday Life in the Eastern Bloc*, ed. David Crowley and Susan E. Reid, pp. 1–22. Oxford: Berg.

De Certeau, Michel. 1984. *The Practice of Everyday Life*. Translated by Steven Rendall. Berkeley: University of California Press.

Dunn, Elizabeth C. 2004. *Privatizing Poland: Baby Food, Big Business, and the Remaking of Labor*. Ithaca, N.Y.: Cornell University Press.

Fehérváry, Krisztina. 2002. "American Kitchens, Luxury Bathrooms, and the Search for a 'Normal' Life in Postsocialist Hungary." *Ethnos* 67(3): 369–400.

Gabriel, Cynthia. 2005. "Healthy Russian Food Is Not-for-Profit." *Subsistence and Sustenance*, Special Issue of *Michigan Discussions in Anthropology* 15:183–222.

Gerasimova, Katerina. 2002. "Public Privacy in the Soviet Communal Apartment." In *Socialist Spaces: Sites of Everyday Life in the Eastern Bloc*, ed. David Crowley and Susan E. Reid, pp. 207–230. Oxford: Berg.

Hann, Chris. 1996. "Introduction: Political Society and Civil Anthropology." In *Civil Society: Challenging Western Models*, ed. Chris Hann and Elizabeth Dunn, pp. 1–26. London: Routledge.

Hann, Chris, and Elizabeth Dunn, eds. 1996. *Civil Society: Challenging Western Models*. London: Routledge.

Herzfeld, Michael. 2006. "Spatial Cleansing: Monumental Vacuity and the Idea of the West." *Journal of Material Culture* 11(1/2): 127–149.

Humphrey, Caroline. 1995. "Creating a Culture of Disillusionment: Consumption in Moscow, a Chronicle of Changing Times." In *Worlds Apart: Modernity through the Prism of the Local*, ed. Daniel Miller, pp. 43–68. London: Routledge.

Kaneff, Deema. 2002. "The Shame and Pride of Market Activity: Morality, Identity and Trading in Postsocialist Rural Bulgaria." In *Markets & Moralities: Ethnographies of Postsocialism*, ed. Ruth Mandel and Caroline Humphrey, pp. 33–51. Oxford: Berg.

Katz, Cindi. 1993. "Power, Space, and Terror: Social Reproduction and the Public Environment." In *The Cultural Meaning of Urban Space*, ed. Robert Rotenberg and Gary McDonogh, pp. 105–121. Westport, Conn.: Bergin and Garvey.

McDonogh, Gary. 1993. "The Geography of Emptiness." In *The Cultural Meaning of Urban Space*, ed. Robert Rotenberg and Gary McDonogh, pp. 3–15. Westport, Conn.: Bergin and Garvey.

Oushakine, Sergeui. 2000. "The Quantity of Style: Imaginary Consumption in the New Russia." *Theory, Culture & Society* 17(5): 97–120.

Patico, Jennifer. 2001. "Globalization in the Postsocialist Marketplace: Consumer Readings of Difference and Development in Urban Russia." *Kroeber Anthropological Society Papers* 86:1127–1142.

———. 2005. "To Be Happy in a Mercedes: Tropes of Value and Ambivalent Visions of Marketization." *American Ethnologist* 32(3): 479–496.

———. 2008. *Consumption and Social Change in a Post-Soviet Middle Class*. Stanford, Calif.: Stanford University Press and Woodrow Wilson Center Press.

Ries, Nancy. 1997. *Russian Talk: Culture and Conversation during Perestroika*. Ithaca, N.Y.: Cornell University Press.

Ritzer, George. 2004. *The Globalization of Nothing*. Thousand Oaks, Calif.: Pine Forge.

Rothstein, Halina, and Robert A. Rothstein. 1997. "The Beginnings of Soviet Culinary Arts." In *Food in Russian History and Culture,* ed. Musya Glants and Joyce Toomre, pp. 177–194. Bloomington: Indiana University Press.

Shectman, Stas. 2008. "Juiced." *The Moscow Times Moscow Guide* (summer): 24–26.

Shevchenko, Olga. 2002. " 'Between the Holes': Emerging Identities and Hybrid Patterns of Consumption in Post-Socialist Russia." *Europe-Asia Studies* 54(6): 841–866.

Slater, Don. 1993. "Going Shopping: Markets, Crowds and Consumption." In *Cultural Reproduction,* ed. Chris Jenks, pp. 188–209. New York: Routledge.

Stephenson, Svetlana. 2006. *Crossing the Line: Vagrancy, Homelessness and Social Displacement in Russia*. Aldershot, England: Ashgate.

Wedel, Janine R. 1998. *Collision and Collusion: The Strange Case of Western Aid to Eastern Europe, 1989–1998*. New York: St. Martin's.

Young, Cathy. 1989. *Growing Up in Moscow: Memories of a Soviet Girlhood*. New York: Ticknor & Fields.

Yurchak, Alexei. 2006. *Everything Was Forever, Until It Was No More: The Last Soviet Generation*. Princeton, N.J.: Princeton University Press.

Zukin, Sharon. 1991. *Landscapes of Power: From Detroit to Disney World*. Berkeley: University of California Press.

FIVE

The Geopolitics of Taste

The "Euro" and "Soviet" Sausage
Industries in Lithuania

NERINGA KLUMBYTĖ

The "Euro" and "Soviet" (*Tarybinis*) sausage industries were started by two Lithuanian food-processing companies: Biovela and Samsonas, respectively. Samsonas began producing "Soviet" sausages in 1998, and Biovela launched its "Euro" sausage brands prior to the referendum for the European Union (EU) in 2003. Samsonas's profits skyrocketed after it began to produce "Soviet" sausages (LAFPMRA 2005).[1] In 2005 all "Soviet" meat brands comprised more than 50 percent of all Samsonas's meat production.[2] In the mid-2000s these "Soviet" brands constituted about one-fifth of the meat product market in Lithuania. Of these brands, various "Soviet" sausages were among the most popular. "Euro" sausage brands, in contrast, did not yield similar profits nor achieve the same popularity as the "Soviet" brands. The production of "Euro" sausages neither increased nor diminished by 2007.[3] The producers themselves referred to "Euro" sausages as an "uninteresting brand." Although consumers rewarded these two brands differently, both sausage brands gained recognition in a number of national competitions and fairs, and were awarded diplomas and medals for safety, quality, reliability, and other characteristics.[4]

The "Euro" brand joined the large family of already existing "Euro" and "Europe" trademarks, amounting to three hundred in Lithuania.[5] These trademarks have consistently proliferated during the postsocialist period, marking the new Lithuanian-European space.[6] Among many others are the shopping mall Europa (Europe); the Europos parkas (Europe park), where the center of Europe is presumably located; the restaurants Europa and Europica; the autoservices company Euro auto; the playground Euroopa; one of the most popular pharmacy chains Euro vaistinė (Euro pharmacy); and the cleaning chain Euro švara skalbykla-valykla (Euro cleaning services). For "Euro" sausages, the innovation was in the unprecedented move of assigning the "Euro" symbol to food.[7] For "Soviet" sausage brands, the Soviet (*Tarybinis*) symbol was used publicly as a trademark for the first time.[8]

"Soviet," on the one hand, and "Euro" or "Europe," on the other, are antithetical geopolitical codes and symbolic orders that became routine during the Cold War.[9] In public and official space in Lithuania, "Soviet" refers to the former Soviet Empire and thus is identified with the past and with the East. Consequently the label "Soviet" is often associated with backwardness, totalitarianism, and failure (see also Klumbytė 2003). "Euro" or "Europe," on the other hand, invokes Lithuania's post-Soviet history epitomized by Lithuania's integration into the EU in 2004. Unlike the word "Soviet," the words "Euro" and "Europe" are associated with the present, the future, and the West and simultaneously signify success, prosperity, and democracy. Thus the "Euro" brands connect products to the semiotic space of European modernity, quality, and prosperity, thereby linking them to what Böröcz (2006) has named "European goodness"—a European normative superiority that is unambiguously benign (Böröcz 2006:125). By naming a product "Soviet" producers invoke past oppression and colonization, and so the victory of "Soviet" over "Euro" brands in the food market is counterintuitive.

In Lithuania's food market the "Soviet" and "Euro" brands reproduce and contest the symbolic regimes of the Cold War. Both "Soviet" and

"Euro" sausages are marketed as "European" and are thus connected to values of safety, progress, and success. Taste, however, is related to Lithuanian tradition and authenticity, disconnected from both ideals of European modernity and EU food ideologies about nutrition and health. The popularity of "Soviet" sausage brands is related to successful marketing strategies that associate "Soviet" sausages with natural food and Lithuanian taste traditions. For consumers, "Euro" sausages stand for European food styles and ideologies that tend to be perceived as alien. In this essay I argue that the marketing and consumption of "Soviet" and "Euro" brands exemplifies the geopolitics of taste in which food-related practices and sentiments are embedded in trans/national geographical, political, and gustatory orders. By focusing on how taste is embedded and integrated in Lithuania's geopolitical and national history and identity, I show how taste is primarily a social phenomenon.

My analysis is based on ethnographic research in Lithuania in 2003 and 2004 and on follow-up research in the summers of 2005 through 2008. During 2003–4, I conducted research in the villages of Panevėžiukas, Braziūkai, and Maksimonys, and in the cities of Vilnius and Kaunas, where I collected more than two hundred interviews and life histories focusing on political identities, citizenship, nationalism, and the post-Soviet state. In the summers of 2005 through 2008 I conducted research on "Soviet" and "Euro" brand marketing and consumption. I interviewed former interviewees in villages as well as thirty new people in Kaunas and several individuals in Vilnius. All the interviews were unstructured and focused on people's food preferences, nutrition ideologies, and opinions about "Soviet," "Euro," or other brands in the food market. Almost two-thirds of the interviewees were women. These individuals were older than thirty-five, which meant that they had come of age in Soviet Lithuania. I also interviewed the directors for commerce and marketing of Samsonas, Vilniaus mėsa, and Biovela, the companies that produce "Soviet" or "Euro" sausages, as well as Soviet-era Kaunas and Šiauliai meat-packing plant employees. I also carried out interviews with marketing specialists and conducted research in the Vilnius District Court on the "Soviet" trademark infringement case. Media and archive analysis concluded my research.

My discussion starts with Lithuania's sausage history. I then analyze Lithuanian consumption and marketing trends for "Soviet" and "Euro" brands, focusing specifically on different ideologies and ideas about natural food. Although the tendency among my interviewees to choose "Soviet" over "Euro" sausages was visible—and usually those who bought "Euro" did not buy "Soviet," and vice versa—other consumers tried both. The following discussion primarily revolves around Lithuanians' preference for "Soviet" sausage over "Euro" and other brands. "Sausage" here largely refers to small- and large-diameter, emulsion-type sausages (wieners, frankfurters, and bolognas), as these sausages were at the center of most conversations.[10]

Sausage History

Athenaeus (ca. 170–ca. 230 CE), a Greek of Naucratis in Egypt mentioned sausages in *Deipnosophists* ("Sophists at Dinner") in AD 228. Sausages were popular among ancient Greeks and Romans (Smith 1870; Gozzini Giacosa 1992). Sausage making originally was a method used to preserve meats, and the name "sausage" derives from the Latin word *salsus*, "salted." Although there is no exact documentation of where the first wiener-type sausage was produced, some indications are that Johann Georg Lahner from Frankfurt produced it in 1805 in Vienna. Frankfurters, derived from the German model, were a kind of sausage that was new to Russians when Anastas Mikoyan, the Communist Party leader in charge of provisioning throughout the 1930s, introduced them to the mass urban consumer population (Fitzpatrick 1999:90–91). Mikoyan used the imagery of pleasure, plenty, and modernity in order to promote them, arguing that frankfurters, "a sign of bourgeois abundance and well-being," had to be available to the masses (ibid.). As products mass-produced on machines, they were superior to food produced in the old-fashioned ways by hand (ibid.:91). The Soviet Stalinist experience with sausage production was introduced to Lithuania after the country's incorporation into the USSR in 1940.

Some companies produced sausages industrially in Lithuania before that country became a Soviet Republic. A well-known, joint-stock company is Maistas ("The Food"), founded in Kaunas in 1923 and later expanded to the cities of Klaipėda, Šiauliai, Tauragė, and Panevėžys.[11] In pre-Soviet Lithuania in 1926, 200 small sausage companies produced 100–400 kg of sausage per day. Unable to compete with industrial sausage companies, small companies began disappearing. In 1938 only 117 companies were left.[12]

In Soviet Lithuania huge meat-packing plants were erected in Kaunas, Vilnius, and Klaipėda, starting with the Vilniaus mėsos kombinatas (Vilnius Meat Packing Plant) built in 1958. Meat-packing plants in Panevėžys, Tauragė, and Šiauliai were reconstructed and expanded, and by the late 1960s there were a total of six meat-packing plants. This expansion of meat production reflected Lithuania's agricultural policy to specialize in meat and milk production.[13] In 1985 Lithuania produced more meat than the Soviet Union on average and more than any other Soviet Republic. For the entire USSR during this period, the average production of meat was 62 kg per person per year, whereas in Lithuania the average was 141 kg per person per year (Anušauskas et al. 2005:538). Although this production output was high, it does not tell us the quantities of meat products or sausage that were available for Lithuanian consumers as sausages were exported to other USSR republics. In the USSR the 1970s and 1980s were marked by a stagnant food situation as food production and per capita consumption deteriorated.[14]

After 1989 the decentralization of the Soviet economy shaped the post-Soviet meat industry: Soviet-era, meat-packing plants shrunk into smaller private companies or went out of business. In 2007 Lithuania had 199 meat-packing plants and slaughterhouses, many of which sold their products to the national market.[15] In small village stores today customers can choose between several brands, and large supermarkets offer a wide variety of sausages, most of them produced in Lithuania.

In Soviet times and into the early 1990s public fascination with Western (European) goods and food was prominent. However, although sausage was an important symbol in political history, it was never an object of similar geopolitical discrimination like jeans or rock music (cf. Caldwell 2002; Zhuk 2008). Unlike jeans or Western records, sausage from the West has not been superior to Lithuanian sausage. In the post-Soviet period consumers' fondness for Lithuanian sausage coexists with the preference for Western (European) goods among the young and the business class (cf. Caldwell 2002; Lankauskas 2002). Many people from the last Soviet generation—those who were born and came of age in Soviet times and who constituted the majority of my interviewees—tend to buy locally produced food and do not share the fascination with Western goods expressed by Lithuania's young people and elites.

Many consumers associate sausages primarily with Soviet times rather than with Europe because of their experiences with industrialized Soviet-era sausages in Soviet Lithuania. In Soviet times these sausages did not carry the label "Soviet." Instead, sausages were often perceived as "ours" (*mūsų*), since they were produced in Lithuania by Lithuanians, and one would commonly hear that "our sausage" travels to Moscow or the USSR or that Lithuania feeds the Soviet empire.[16] Thus, already in the Soviet era, sausage was a site of political emotions expressing sentiments about the national community and the geopolitical order.

European Quality, Lithuanian Taste

Producers of "Euro" and "Soviet" sausages invoke themes of European modernity to advertise their companies and products. According to Bio-vela's Web page, the company's production and control of quality correspond to EU requirements.[17] Artūras Skairys, Biovela's marketing director, claimed that "Euro" sausages expressed Biovela's image of a "European meat packing plant."[18] He maintained that "European" refers to new technologies, innovations, a new perspective, trust, high quality, and expensive products. Biovela also emphasizes that "Euro" sausages respond to the model of contemporary good nutrition popularly associated with Europe: sausages contain little fat and many proteins.

Similarly Samsonas represents itself as a "European and modern company," which implies that it produces healthy and safe products of good quality, and that the company meets EU sanitary and hygienic requirements, uses new production and packaging methods, and conducts effective quality and production control.[19] Samsonas also takes pride in producing sausages using "mature Western technologies,"[20] which associates their sausages with progress, prestige, and success.

In both "Euro" and "Soviet" sausage marketing, taste is disconnected from European modernity and considered to be non-European or non-Western. The label on "Euro" sausages reads *"Kokybė europietiška, skonis lietuviškas!"* (European quality, Lithuanian taste!) (Figure 5.1). Skairys claimed that Lithuanian food is much more delicious than European.

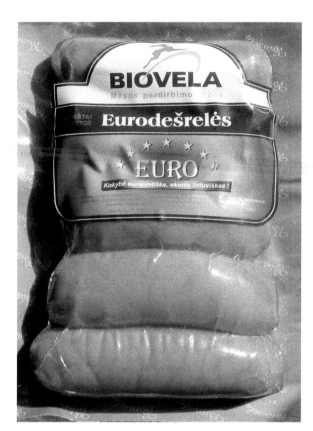

Figure 5.1. A package of "Euro" sausages, July 2007. Below the "EURO" sign is the statement *"Kokybė europietiška, skonis lietuviškas!"* (European quality, Lithuanian taste!). Photograph by Neringa Klumbytė.

According to laboratory taste experiments requested by Biovela and conducted by Kaunas University of Technology Food Institute, like in Soviet times Lithuanians like garlic and also love to see fat in sausage, something one rarely finds in the West where ingredients are mixed well to make sausages resembling salami. Further, fatty food is generally appreciated by Lithuanians. Based on these findings, Biovela developed a brand named "Lithuanian standard" to appeal to "Lithuanian taste." "Lithuanian standard" became a much more successful group of sausages than "Euro." Indeed, it is the second most popular brand in Lithuania, and in the mid-2000s constituted about 5 percent of Lithuania's entire meat-product market. There are, as Skairys inferred, people of the "Lithuanian standard" who like a "live [*gyvas*] and true product."

In the case of "Soviet" brands, "Soviet" sausages represent the Soviet-Lithuanian tradition of good taste. Rimgailė Vaitkienė, the former marketing director of Samsonas, claimed that in Soviet times sausages were made without meat substitutes (*mėsos pakaitalai*),[21] and were therefore more natural and more delicious.[22] Samsonas claims to continue this tradition, although neither the technology nor the recipes used to produce "Soviet" sausages derive from Soviet times. Some consumers contest the Soviet-era tradition of good taste, pointing out that sausages at that time were of poor quality (see below);[23] others claim that "Soviet" sausages indeed resemble sausages in Soviet times—very delicious, good quality, and healthy; and still others contend that even if they are not the same, they are reminiscent of the sausages and traditional tastes of Soviet times.[24] But these traditional tastes are now "our" or "Lithuanian" tastes and thereby disconnected from the USSR and its political history.

Sausages reproduce and contest geopolitical orders routinized during the Cold War that juxtaposed the superiority of "Europe" and the "West" to the inferior status of "Soviet" and the "East." Western associations enhance sausages with technological superiority that in turn reproduces Cold War imagery and is accepted by most consumers. At the same time Western or European goodness is rejected by giving preference to the presumably distinct Lithuanian taste. During my research I encountered a few people who purchased "Euro" sausages and presented them as examples of Lithuanian good taste, defining this taste according to pan-European values of quality, nutrition, and health. In many other cases, however, Lithuanian taste was bound to Soviet-era gastronomic traditions and values of quality that contradicted EU-wide food quality standards.

Synthetic and Natural Modernity and Competing Quality Regimes

In the Soviet period the state's emphasis on food safety along with its inability to maintain safety standards fostered a widespread awareness about food quality (Caldwell 2007; cf. Rothstein and Rothstein 1997). In post-Soviet Lithuania consumers' concerns and distrust of industrial foods were primarily promoted by EU standards for quality, safety, and nutrition, as well as negative experiences with the capitalist food market (cf. Buechler and Buechler 1999). Many interviewees claimed that there was nothing to eat, since post-Soviet food was neither delicious nor of good quality. To illustrate their arguments they drew on their personal experiences: some sausages tasted bad and had to be thrown out; others smelled up the kitchen when cooked and were even refused by cats and dogs; still other sausages discolored the water during cooking or dissolved and became shapeless masses in the cooking pot. Sausage producers were blamed for not caring about people's health and for maximizing their profits by adding all kinds of "things" to sausages. Some people concluded that sausages were "pure synthetics."

The image of "synthetics" was applied to both post-Soviet food and "Euro" sausages. People who liked "Soviet" sausages tended to exclude them from other post-Soviet brands by describing them as "natural" and "good." "Soviet" sausages came to stand for Lithuanian tradition, authentic food, and good taste, whereas "Euro" sausages and other post-Soviet brands were disregarded because of their ostensibly lower quality and foreignness. Rimas Frizinskas, the commerce director of Samsonas, claimed that, unlike today, in the Soviet era synthetic substitutes were not used for sausage production.[25] An anonymous person who responded on the Internet to an article about "Soviet" and "Euro" brands agreed with Frizinskas that "food really tasted better 'under the Russians.' Now it is some kind of hopeless synthetics. Yuck." (Well but, 07/19/2006 1:56 PM).[26] Regina, a woman in her early seventies from Kaunas, maintained:

> Earlier food was natural. My relatives from Germany used to ask me to bring butter and cheese from [Soviet] Lithuania because they did not have good food. And Lithuanian food was delicious and natural. Now, when they [the producers in Lithuania] started to copy everything from the West, all food got much worse . . . Sausage was also good [in Soviet times]. Now bologna is simply starch and hemaplasma [kraujo plazma].

Unlike in the Cold War discourses and post-Soviet modernization narratives that privilege Europe, Regina's reflections portray the Soviet-era Lithuanian tradition as the source of goodness: Soviet-era food is good, and post-Soviet Western "copies" are not. Germany, in particular, is claimed to lack natural and delicious foods.

Like Regina's commentary, in discussions with many other interviewees the quality of sausages was often communicated through the idiom of "naturalness." "Naturalness," which is exclusively attributed to "Soviet" sausages, is among the major food-quality categories throughout the former Soviet space. Melissa Caldwell, in her study of Russian consumption practices, shows how domestically grown foods, and those procured from personal agriculture or windowsill gardens, are valued for their perceived purity and naturalness. Russians maintain, moreover, that Russian soil itself is cleaner and healthier than non-Russian soil and that food taken directly from the ground does not need to be washed (Caldwell 2002, 2007). Diana Mincyte, in her work on unpasteurized milk in Lithuania, discusses how social relations and trust rather than licenses and certificates are essential in assigning a value to raw milk and in perceiving it as safe. Mincyte argues that, for raw milk consumers in Lithuania, safety and quality—as defined in terms of Western industrialized foods—are irrelevant (Mincyte 2006).

During my research, interviewees perceived natural food as coming from nature, as unindustrialized and self-made. Raw milk from the countryside or sausage produced at home from meat acquired from a trusted farmer represented the ultimate natural products. In Internet discussions, disagreements about "Euro" and "Soviet" sausages are often interrupted by home-made food advocates. Commentators suggest that sausages can be made at home and that these are the most delicious and healthful. Iks maintains:

> *When I spend some time in the village during holiday and eat natural cucumbers, meat, milk, eggs, then after my return to the city it takes me a month to accommodate to all kinds of trash from the store, everything stinks and has no taste. . . . Thanks God, I am a woman from Soviet times. I have [special] culinary skills because they were forced on us then [in the Soviet era], thus I can make more natural food at home. (Iks, 07/20/2006 12:32 PM).*[27]

Another person on the Internet responded similarly to the discussion about "Soviet" and "Euro" brands by expressing distrust of Soviet and post-Soviet sausage and by comparing it to a natural sausage:

> *You can buy natural sausage in special small stores, in the farmers' market (with some exceptions). Milk sausages always include variety meats, that's why you always find all kind of trash there. Earlier—toilet paper, now—E and skin. (about natural, 07/20/2006 6:51 AM).*[28]

In her commentary Iks connects her culinary skills with Soviet times, indicating that not only does food become corrupted but so, too, do people who no longer can produce quality food. Corruption indexes the post-Soviet decline, a narrative common in various other post-Soviet spaces (see Petrović 2006; Sliavaite 2006; Kideckel 2008). The person in the second commentary speaks of milk sausages sold in the stores and supermarkets as containing trash. Toilet paper marks the poor quality of Soviet-era sausage. Similarly food additives and meat substitutes used in post-Soviet products are also signs of the poor quality of post-Soviet sausage.[29] Both observers reproduce the hierarchies of natural and industrialized, and of Soviet and post-Soviet, food.

As the above examples indicate, "natural" implies that sausages have no meat substitutes such as soy and starch, a notion popularized through the advertising of "Soviet" sausages. Moreover, consumers also believe that natural foods have no preservatives and chemicals. The use of antibiotics and growth hormones in animal fodder also makes food unnatural. Kristina, a woman in her early fifties from Vilnius, stated that "buttermilk, milk, and sour cream remained as they were, good, but meat got much worse." For her, even "the 'Soviet' sausages are not as good as they were in those [Soviet] times." Still, she buys "Soviet" sausages since they are "the best of all available, delicious, and without meat substitutes like soy, hemaplasma, skin, and starch." Kristina claimed to be a "pure food enthusiast." "Soviet" sausage presumably made of "pure" meat was congruent with her ideology of nutrition. Kristina remembered that earlier:

> We used to buy sausages and wieners, they were very delicious. [They tasted delicious] not because we were more hungry. The "Doctor's" sausage [a type of bologna] was superb, now it is hard, you do not know what they put in there. No brand can equal sausages of the Soviet period. I am telling you this not because I feel some kind of sentiments to that order.

Unlike Kristina, however, many other interviewees claimed that "Soviet" sausages were as good as sausages in Soviet times. A doctor in her early fifties from Kaunas maintained that she buys "Soviet" sausages "because they are without meat substitutes. Like earlier [in Soviet times]. Without chemicals, soy. They are the best of all. Very delicious."

The producers of "Soviet" and "Euro" sausages respond to and reinforce consumers' understanding of quality. Samsonas claims that "Soviet" meat products mean a resolute search for quality and a return to the natural.[30] The quality and naturalness of "Soviet" sausages are primarily

Figure 5.2. The faces of "Soviet" sausages on a billboard in Aleksotas, Kaunas. The words *Tarybinė* (sing. fem.), *Tarybinės* (plural fem.), and *Tarybiniai* (plural masc.) mean "Soviet" in Lithuanian. These labels are on the "Soviet" sausage packages. Every package also contains the logo *"Mėsos pakaitalams ne!"* (No for meat substitutes!). August 2006. Photograph by Neringa Klumbytė.

communicated through the advertising logo "no for meat substitutes," which is printed on the label of every package of "Soviet" sausages (Figure 5.2). According to Samsonas, because of the "naturalness" of these products, they have become very popular among advocates who enjoy healthy lives as well as those who have hardships adjusting to today's "synthetics."[31] Biovela also presents its production as "natural," claiming that its sausages and meat products contain "natural seasoning" or are themselves "natural." However, because the "naturalness" of Biovela's sausages is discussed only on their Web site, it does not reach many consumers.

The packaging on "Soviet" sausages is also designed to reflect producers' attitudes toward quality and naturalness. The background of most images includes smiling and happy young people, as well as cultivated and uncultivated fields (Figure 5.2); nature, of course, invokes freshness and purity. The images are the icons of a simple life rather than the social and political realities of Soviet times. Even if some of the images are from the Stalinist period, they do not bring to mind the Stalinist horrors but refer instead to Soviet-fashioned happiness and optimism (see Gronow 2003; Fitzpatrick 1999; Kotkin 1995). People pictured on the packaging exude youth, beauty, energy, fitness, romance, and enjoyment. They promise pleasurable positive involvement in an aesthetic post-Soviet community.

"Euro" sausages are less popular not only because of their association with synthetic modernity but also as a result of the common meanings of the terms "Europe" and "Euro." At the time of my research, interviewees said that labeling the sausages as "Euro" was nonsensical, since they identified words such as "Euro" and "Europe" with geography and politics, not food. Moreover, in Lithuania, "Europe" is increasingly seen as a marker of high class. It designates a post-Soviet modernity from which many of my interviewees feel excluded. Businesses that use "Euro" or "Europe" in their company names are primarily in the capital or in other large cities, and the prestige signified by "Euro" or "Europe" also usually implies high prices.

Companies like Biovela try to rearticulate and benefit from "European" prestige by dissociating it from high prices and making it more egalitarian. By introducing "Euro" sausages prior to the referendum for Lithuania to become a member of the EU, Biovela intended to benefit from the heightened interest in the EU. Because many people were worried that prices would rise after joining the EU, producers made "Euro" sausages cheaper and of poorer quality.[32] Unlike "Euro" sausages, the "Soviet" sausages are the highest-quality brands and among the most expensive on the market.[33] Other companies use similar strategies. Lanlita, for example, advertises its windows as "European windows" but at "Lithuanian prices." Political parties and candidates also draw on European prestige and contribute

Figure 5.3. The prestigious shopping center "Europe" in Vilnius, July 2008. Photograph by Neringa Klumbytė.

to European egalitarianism. In the 2004 elections Lithuania's president, Valdas Adamkus, promised to bring "European well-being to every household!" Adamkus claimed to have achieved the goals of his last term: Lithuania had become a member of both the North Atlantic Treaty Organization (NATO) and the European Union. The present goal was to take advantage of EU membership to become a European welfare state by using EU assistance and funds (see Klumbytė 2006a).[34]

As the above discussion shows, perceptions of sausage quality primarily depend on whether they are seen to be "natural" and not on EU quality standards such as the product's safety, nutritional value, and hygienic requirements. In valorizing natural food, consumers challenge normalizing hierarchies of expert scientific knowledge, including those of European health authorities. The ideology of natural food presupposes the alternative modernity that prioritizes self-made and trustworthy foods as well as Soviet-era Lithuanian industrial traditions.

The Geopolitics of Taste

Vignette: Commentaries on the Internet to the article "The Cold War in the Food Industry" by Džina Donauskaitė. Atgimimas, 07/19/2006.[35]

To Džina [the author], 07/19/2006 1:00 PM

In Soviet times producers used more water [to make sausages], and now they bring all kind of shit from the EU and poison our people.

The Eater, 07/19/2006 1:16 PM

Well, Samsonas's "Soviet" sausages are truly the best. My grandchildren acknowledge this. When I ask them what kind of sausages they want, they all start crying: only Samsonas's.

Cuba to the Eater, 07/19/2007 1:31 PM

Just don't say that grandchildren aren't crying "*Čili pica*" and "Coca-Cola." Children are the most susceptible to advertising and the first to consume synthetic good taste. They will grow up like real Americans!

Unsigned, 07/19/2006 1:36 PM

The real Soviet sausages [sausages in Soviet times] were always putrid. I associate this brand only with putridity and muck, because food in Soviet times was DISGUSTING [capitalized in original].

Damaged memory, 07/19/2006 1:48 PM

There was an anecdote in Soviet times, maybe from the Armenian radio: why is toilet paper in shortage? Because they mince it and put it in wieners, this was the explanation. The similar explanation was for why cats turn away from "Doctor's" sausage. Then such anecdotes seemed accurate for those who ate wieners or other sausages that were hard to get. Thus, you can only guess that because they ate that sausage their memory is damaged.

Blue chicken, 07/19/2006 3:21 PM

Oh, even if the bluest, but real [chicken], with unmodified genes, clean of antibiotics and hormones . . . [Imagine that] yellow fat from the chicken going up, uuuuuch . . . [she craves for Soviet time chicken which was known for its bluish legs].[36]

Nobody died from hunger [in Soviet times] and there were as many fatties as there are now.

Darius, 07/19/2006 3:36 PM

I am 31. I lived in Soviet times and worked in Sigma factory. I received education, graduated from college. For me Soviet times are like the lost paradise. It is much better than present-day America. In Soviet times . . . food was without chemicals and food supplements, it was very delicious, very natural and healthy, it cost little.

The Soviet, 07/19/2006 4:20 PM

For Darius—indeed, I also remember how good it was to live in Soviet times—in the morning you eat natural bread with natural sausage "Doggy's delight" [Russ. *sobaciaja radost*, the derogatory metaphor for Soviet-era sausages], at work for lunch you get a dirty aluminum bowl of unidentifiable soup, not only without preservatives, but also without fresh ingredients, in the evening you make noodles *po flotski* [pasta, cooked and then fried, often mixed with minced meat, onions, and the like].

Kaunas resident, 07/19/2006 6:08 PM

What kind of nonsense is it—good quality Soviet time sausages. Real rubbish. Half of Lithuania ate stolen meat. Sausages were made of lignin, water, blood, and all kind of other handy things. . . . Once I ate a stolen "Doctor's" sausage which was made for the All-Union Exhibition of People's Economic Achievements in Moscow. Oh, this was so good! Meat packing plant workers did not advise eating sausage from shops. Don't make fun of people, there are also older people who read these commentaries and who remember those times well . . . It [the "Soviet" label] helped Samsonasto export its sausages to Russia. They sold out themselves, *svolačiai* [Russ. *svolachi*, "rascals"].

Meat, 07/19/21 9:36 PM

I do not remember that it [food] would have stunk. Milk sometimes got spoiled and . . . But what does it mean? It means that it was real. Now you can keep it for weeks and it is still good. Oh, I would like to get a sausage with mustard so badly, in a station buffet—these are such romantic memories.

Pardon, 07/20/2006 12:29 PM

The best food was around 1993–1996 when "Soviet" quality wasn't gone and when "euroquality" was not there yet. Ziggy, when did you eat dumplings from the store last time? What concerns Soviet [dumplings]—these were quite good—"Vilniaus," "Ekstra." Now you cannot try any brand . . . Well.

Cat's spokesman, 2006/07/19 2:43 PM

Today I had to throw out a big piece of Biovela's "Doctor's Euro" sausage. It was spoiled. Disgusting, as a matter of fact. Well, this does not happen with Samsonas's "Soviet" sausage. Let's don't search for any ideologies here. The stomach and taste receptors can tell it well. You can call sausage the way you want. It has to be edible. Now a cat eats Kitekat'ą [cat food], but try to force it to eat "Euro" sausages. That's how it is.

The Eurooptimist to Soviet idealists, 2006/07/19 0.06 PM

Let's eat Euro food and there is a 30 year guarantee. We will be like embalmed in coffins, like great V. I. Lenin in Kremlin.

These judgments about "Soviet" and "Euro" brands or, more generally, about Soviet and post-Soviet/European food, indicate that European food and sausages can almost never be good. Out of 531 commentators, only a few individuals agreed that post-Soviet brands were safe and of good quality since they met EU food-safety standards and regulations. In many other cases either Soviet and post-Soviet/European food was defined as bad, or Soviet food was claimed to be good and post-Soviet/ European to be bad. The picture that emerges from the commentaries above, and from my interviews, shows the pervasive belief that European or post-Soviet food is dangerous, unhealthy, and of poor quality. Opinions diverge regarding Soviet food. Some commentators spoke of Soviet food as poor in quality, unsafe, and unhealthy, whereas others claimed that it was of good quality, tasty, and desirable. "Soviet sausage," for most consumers, was synonymous with "good-quality" sausage even if it was not associated with Soviet times.

In many discussions about "Soviet" and "Euro" sausages, taste was linked to sentiments about social and political history and the geopolitical order. In most commentaries and interviews, positive memories about Soviet sausage (to which post-Soviet "Soviet" brands were often related) correlated with positive reminiscences about Soviet times and nostalgia for the socialist era (see Klumbytė forthcoming). In these cases a good-quality "Soviet" sausage was a metonym for the superior Soviet past. It was also a way to criticize current social and political history. On the other hand, those who spoke negatively about Soviet times either consumed post-Soviet "Soviet" brands as ostensibly apolitical or refused to buy them. In the few cases where individuals chose "Euro" over "Soviet" or other brands, they did view Soviet times in a negative light and supported the EU and European modernity. Thus a sausage, at least in its "Euro" and "Soviet" variety, has a place in political history and in expressing and fashioning identities, belongings, and national and geopolitical orders.

Producers advertise both post-Soviet "Soviet" and "Euro" sausages as European and link them to safety, progress, and success. Both brands also invoke Lithuanian traditions of taste, familiarity, and authenticity. The popularity of "Soviet" brands over "Euro" and other brands is related to successful marketing strategies that appeal to sentiments about natural food and Soviet-era taste traditions. "Euro" sausages, even if marketed as embodying Lithuanian tastes, stand for relative gustatory indistinction as well as European foodways and ideologies of quality that consumers tend to perceive as alien. Moreover, in Lithuania "Europe" becomes increasingly a high-class marker. It designates a post-Soviet modernity from which many people feel excluded, and which in turn also contributes to the relatively lesser popularity of "Euro" brands.

By articulating taste and contextualizing it within political and social history, and by decontextualizing "Soviet" and "Euro" sausages from Cold War discourses, whether in stores, at dinner discussions, or on Internet sites, individuals reproduce symbolic geopolitical and trans/national orders. Those who prefer "Soviet" sausages over other brands, including "Euro," relate them to natural food and "our" Soviet-era Lithuanian tradition. In these cases "Soviet" refers to the simple and good life rather than to totalitarian order, backwardness, and oppression. Those who refuse "Soviet" sausages usually perceive "Soviet" in congruence with Cold War narratives.

These sentiments are amplified in public spaces. Managers of companies that produce "Soviet" sausages are sometimes labeled cynics who, as claimed by journalist Audrius Matonis, call high-quality products "Soviet" without considering that the "Soviet" system and "Soviet" ideology crippled Lithuania and its people.[37] Some people consider producers or consumers of "Soviet" brands pro-Soviet.[38] Certain intellectuals and politicians believe that consumers of "Soviet" sausages vote populist and think communist.[39] They call those who are nostalgic for the "Soviet" past "victims" who long for the "torturer," the backward people delaying social and political projects of the future and modernity, or the turnips (*runkeliai*, derogatory, literally "sugar beets") who may stop the country's way to Europe.[40] In this context the production, marketing, and consumption of "Soviet" sausages redefines the boundaries of society and reproduces alterity (cf. Boyer 2001). Taste in this case is an important criterion for inclusion or exclusion as well as reiteration of post-Soviet hegemonies and ideologies.

ACKNOWLEDGMENTS

I am very thankful to Zsuzsa Gille, Melissa Caldwell, and Venelin Ganev for their comments and suggestions on earlier versions of this chapter.

NOTES

1. Personal communication with Rimas Frizinskas, the director of commerce for Samsonas, August 2005.

2. Ibid.

3. Personal communication with Artūras Skairys, the director of marketing for Biovela, August 2007.

4. See http://www.compiler.fi/tradestation/baltics/lithuania/lt-archive/lt-archive2004/lt.week24.html (accessed June 13, 2006). Seven "Soviet" sausage brands were recognized as "Product of the Year" by the Lithuanian Confederation of Industrialists. "Euro" sausages were awarded a gold medal as "Product of the Year 2004." The Lithuanian Confederation of Industrialists arranges the competition "Lithuanian Product of the Year" annually. Various products are nominated "Product of the Year" if they meet criteria of quality, safety, and reliability, among others. For evaluation criteria, regulations, and rules, see http://www.gaminys.lt/eng/evaluation.phtml; see also http://www.lpk.lt/default.asp?DL=E&TopicID=87; and Samsonas Web page http://www.tm-lt.lt/main.php?action=main::article.show&article_id=564 (accessed May 29, 2006).

5. Patent Bureau of the Republic of Lithuania 2006. See www.vpb.lt (accessed May 29, 2006).

6. "Euro" refers to the EU currency; as a brand name it often stands for "Europe."

7. "Euro" beer emerged in the market before the referendum for the European Union around the same time as "Euro" sausages appeared in 2003. "Euro" beer was produced on the initiative of the Ministry for Foreign Affairs of Lithuania.

8. The borrowed term *sovietinis* ("Soviet") was used widely (although not on brand names) throughout the 1990s, and the native form *tarybinis* ("Soviet") regained public presence mainly with "Soviet" sausage brands. The use of the borrowed term *sovietinis* was encouraged by linguists, who tactically decided to promote the borrowing rather than the Lithuanian derivative *tarybinis* for communication in public spaces. In this way they emphasized the foreignness of objects, practices, and the regime. On the other hand, many other borrowings were discouraged as part of an effort to purify the Lithuanian language. Additional food products labeled "Soviet" (*Tarybinis, Tarybinė*) emerged in the early 2000s, including "Soviet" bread, "Soviet" dumplings, "Soviet" calzone, and "Soviet" root beer. Before "Soviet"

sausages appeared in the market, some brands invoked the realities of Soviet times (e.g., the "Three kopeiks" brand of buns, referring to the price of these buns in Soviet times), but the term "Soviet" was not used. Preceding "Soviet sausages" were "Soviet chronicles," TV reportages from Soviet times broadcast by LNK television.

9. On symbolic geographies in Eurasia see Bakić-Hayden and Hayden 1992; Böröcz 2006; Davidson 2007; Todorova 1994; and Wolff 1994.

10. Frankfurters and wieners are called emulsion-type sausages because of the mixture of protein, fat, and water. Emulsion-type sausages are subdivided into small-diameter and large-diameter sausages, and frankfurters and wieners are examples of the former. Originally wieners were stuffed in sheep casings and frankfurters in pig casings. Bolognas, examples of large-diameter sausages, are stuffed in large casings. See http://www.fao.org/docrep/003/x6556e/X6556E07.htm (accessed May 29, 2006).

11. See *Panevėžio mėsos fabrikas* (1992) (Vilnius: Aušra).

12. See *Mažoji Lietuviškoji Tarybinė Enciklopedija* (1966), pp. 390–391.

13. See the speech by Ringaudas Songaila, the secretary of the Lithuanian Communist Party Central Committee, "Mūsų kryptis—pienas ir mėsa" ("Our Objective Is Milk and Meat"). R. Songaila, *Valstiečių laikraštis*, no. 115 (3156) (September 25, 1966): 2. On meat production in Lithuania, see also Anušauskas et al. 2005:538; and Bernatonis 1970

14. On the deterioration of the food situation in the late Soviet period see, e.g., Kenneth Gray, *National Food Review*, October–December 1989, http://ww.findarticles.com/p/articles/mi_m3284/is_n4_v12/ai_8274317/pg_3 (accessed October 20, 2005). On the varieties of sausages produced using the standards of the USSR and Lithuania in the late 1980s, see Paškonienė 1992. On Panevėžys meat-packing plant output in the 1990s, see *Panevėžio mėsos fabrikas* 1992.

15. Available at http://www.vic.lt/ris?id=8327&action=more. Žemės ūkio informacijos ir kaimo verslo centras (accessed May 17, 2007).

16. Melissa Caldwell (2002), in her discussion of nationalism and food consumption in post-Soviet Moscow, shows how domestic food producers, store clerks, and customers collaborate to classify foods and other products as either "ours" (*nash*) or "not ours" (*ne nash*) and describe local goods as superior to foreign goods in terms of taste, quality, and healthfulness. Similar tendencies are apparent in post-Soviet Lithuania where the distinction "ours"/"not ours" coexists and is modified by other categories, such as "Soviet"/"post-Soviet." As the discussion in this chapter shows, Soviet-era food is often perceived as "ours"—traditional, delicious, and healthful—whereas post-Soviet food is seen as inferior in terms of quality, taste, and healthfulness and is rarely labeled "ours." On "our" foods in Lithuania, see also Lankauskas 2002. For preference of foreign to "our" food in post-Chernobyl Ukraine, see Phillips 2002.

17. See http://www.biovela.lt/index.php?s_id=2&lang=lt (accessed June 13, 2006).

18. Personal communication with Artūras Skairys, Biovela's marketing director, August 2007.

19. Samsonas production catalog.

20. See http://www.litfood-fair.com/samsonas/index.php?page=3 (accessed June 13, 2006).

21. According to Jolita Martutaitytė, a chief specialist in the Quality Branch of the Food Safety and Quality Department (Saugos ir kokybės departamento Kokybės skyrius), the highest-quality meat products have to be produced from meat. Plant and animal proteins, food fillings (*maisto užpildai*), and mechanically separated meat cannot be used. The highest-quality products have to contain the established minimal amount of meat, represented by the quantity of meat proteins, and fat (Vilma Kavaliauskienė, spokesperson for the Ministry of

Agriculture, "The meat quality was defined more clearly," January 6, 2004). See http://www.zum.lt/min/Atstovas/dsp_news.cfm?NewsID=1634&langparam=LT&Title= &From= &To=&Page=1&list=10 (accessed July 5, 2007). According to Lithuania's Department of Standardization, protein meat substitute (*baltyminis mėsos pakaitalas*) is a food substance (*maisto medžiaga*) consisting of proteins that constitute the greatest part of the functional food substance (for example, egg powder, blood plazma, milk powder, wheat protein concentrate, and others). Protein meat substitutes replace meat in order to replace proteins in a meat product (Lietuvos Standardizacijos Departamentas 2003; Lietuvos standartas LST 1919, 2003 December).

22. See http://www.takas.lt/pr/archyvas/?st-1&msg_id=440 (accessed February 13, 2005). See http://www.litfood-fair.com/samsonas/index.php?page=3 (accessed June 13, 2006).

23. Elsewhere I argue that memories about Soviet times and Soviet-era food situations express people's political subjectivities (see Klumbytė, forthcoming).

24. Many consumers associate post-Soviet "Soviet" sausages with Soviet-era sausages. This association is confirmed not only by my own research but also by other sources. Linguists who conducted evaluations of the term *Tarybinis* (Soviet) argued that the term "Soviet" could invoke associations with products of the Soviet period, with recipes or technologies used in Soviet times. Various surveys also confirmed that many people associated Samsonas's "Soviet" brands with Soviet times. According to the advertisement and image company "Serna" survey of June 20–25, 2003, in the five biggest cities of Lithuania (people interviewed were between twenty-five and fifty years of age), 45.6 percent of respondents associated "Soviet Milk Sausages" and "Soviet Doctor's Sausage" with Soviet-era products, and 35.2 percent had no associations. According to the "Sprinter" representative survey of November 24–29, 2003, consumers of the "Soviet" brands associated the name *Tarybiniai* ("Soviet") with Soviet times (20 percent), quality products (16 percent), and delicious sausages (14 percent). See Vilnius District Court, Case No. 3K-3-461. See also the program on sausages on Lithuanian Television, http://www.lrt.lt/media.php?strid=2961828&id=4031891 (accessed September 30, 2007).

25. See http://www.delfi.lt/archive/article.php?id=10151615 (accessed July 22, 2006).

26. Ibid.

27. A commentary on the article "Šaltasis karas maisto pramonėje" ("The Cold War in the Food Industry") by Džina Donauskaitė. *Atgimimas*, July 19, 2006. See http://www.delfi.lt/archive/article.php?id=10151615 (accessed August 20, 2006).

28. E numbers are number codes for food additives, such as colors, preservatives, antioxidants, stabilizers, flavor enhancers, and so on, and are usually found on food labels throughout the European Union.

29. One food technologist and food-quality inspector who worked in Šiauliai meat-packing plant in late-Soviet times assured me that wrapping paper similar to brown paper bags in the United States was used for the production of bologna.

30. See http://www.litfood-fair.com/samsonas/index.php?page=3 (accessed on June 13, 2006).

31. See Samsonas's official Web site: http://www.samsonas.lt/?galery;67;group;43 (accessed May 13, 2007).

32. "Euro" sausages are classified as "first-quality" products, whereas "Soviet" sausages are classified as "highest-quality" products. In Lithuania the meat-product quality is classified into the highest, the first, and the second quality. The highest quality brands cannot contain meat substitutes, fillings such as starch, and mechanically separated meat. In the first-

quality meat products, substitutes and fillings are limited and soy is not allowed (Lithuanian Standard LST 1919).

33. "Soviet" sausage producers claimed that when producing "Soviet" sausages they responded to the emerging niche in the food market—a request for a high-quality product. Although the high quality of "Soviet" sausages significantly contributes to their success, it does not explain why "Soviet" sausages take such a large share of the meat-product market and distinguish themselves from other high-quality and cheaper sausages. I argue elsewhere that the brand name "Soviet" is very important for "Soviet" brand success (see Klumbytė 2006).

34. See "*Europos gerovė turi ateiti į kiekvienus namus: Nesitraukiantis iš rinkimų V. Adamkus žada būti vienijančiu moraliniu autoritetu*" ("European Well-being Has to Come to Every Household: V. Adamkus Doesn't Retreat from Elections and Promises to Be a Uniting Moral Authority"). *Lietuvos rytas*, May 26, 2004, No. 120.

35. The article was republished by *Delfi*, Internet news portal, July 19, 2006, at http://www.delfi.lt/archive/article.php?id=10151615 (accessed on May 17, 2007).

36. In Wolfgang Becker's film *Good Bye, Lenin!* (2003), a sign of the East German food consumption experience is one chicken in the store fridge beside a puddle of blood. The oft-mentioned chicken as well as sausage were common idioms when consumers spoke of the Soviet food situation. In Lithuania a blue chicken means that it is skinny, with bluish legs; a "blue chicken," therefore, always infers a negative comment.

37. See the discussion by journalist Audrius Matonis, in the program *Be pykčio* (Without Anger), Lithuanian Television (LTV), July 2005.

38. Erdvilas Jakulis, a linguist from Vilnius University, stated that *Tarybinis, Tarybinė* (Soviet) may invoke associations that products are made in the nonexistent state or that producers and consumers of these products are pro-Soviet (Vilnius District Court, Case No. 3K-3-461).

39. See Laimantas Jonušys, "*Sovietinės dešrelės ilgesys*" ("The Longing for a Soviet Sausage"). Lithuanian writers' weekly *Literatūra ir menas*, 12/10/2004, No.3027. See http://www.culture.lt/lmenas/?leid—id=3027&kas=straipsnis&st—id=5860 (accessed on May 12, 2006).

40. See Leonidas Donskis, "*Aukos meilė budeliui, arba už ką lietuviai taip myli Rusiją?*" ("The Victim's Love for His Torturer, or Why Do Lithuanians Love Russia So Much?"), *Klaipėda*, February 28, 2005. Available at http://www.delfi.lt/archive/index.php?id=6138259 (accessed on March 12, 2005). The name "turnips" emerged in early 2000 after the strikes of sugar beet farmers in Suvalkija, the southern region of Lithuania, and was soon extended to include many of the resentful, the poor, the rural and other *others*. During the strikes the farmers blocked the highway connecting all Baltic countries to Poland, or, as one political science professor put it, "our way to Europe." A poster in Vilnius in 2003 stated: "We are for Europe! The turnips are not going to stop us!" The billboard advertised drinks. For a discussion of this subject, see Klumbytė (2006:57–61).

REFERENCES CITED

Anušauskas, Arvydas, et al., eds. 2005. *Lietuva 1940–1990: Okupuotos Lietuvos istorija. Lietuvos gyventojų genocido ir rezistencijos tyrimo centras*. Vilnius: Spindulys.

Bakić-Hayden, Milica, and Robert Hayden. 1992. "Orientalistic Variations on the Theme

'Balkans': Symbolic Geography in Recent Yugoslav Cultural Politics." *Slavic Review* 51(1): 1–15.

Bernatonis Juozas. 1970. *Maisto pramonė ir jos vystymosi perspektyvos.* Vilnius: Žinija.

Böröcz, József. 2006. "Goodness Is Elsewhere: The Rule of European Difference." *Comparative Studies in Society and History* 48(1): 110–137.

Boyer, Dominic. 2001. "Media Markets, Mediating Labors, and the Branding of East German Culture at Super Illu." *Social Text* 19(3): 9–33.

Buechler, Hans, and Judith-Maria Buechler. 1999. "The Bakers of Bernburg and the Logics of Communism and Capitalism." *American Ethnologist* 26(4): 799–821.

Caldwell, Melissa L. 2002. "The Taste of Nationalism: Food Politics in Postsocialist Moscow." *Ethnos* 67(3): 295–319.

———. 2007. "Feeding the Body and Nourishing the Soul: Natural Foods in Postsocialist Russia." *Food, Culture, and Society* 10(1): 44–71.

Davidson, Deanna. 2007. "East Spaces in West Times: Deictic Reference and Political Self-Positioning in a Post-socialist East German Chronotope." *Language and Communication* 27:212–226.

Fitzpatrick, Sheila. 1999. *Everyday Stalinism: Ordinary Life in Extraordinary Times: Soviet Russia in the 1930s.* New York: Oxford University Press.

Gozzini Giacosa, Ilaria. 1992. *A Taste of Ancient Rome.* Translated by Anna Herklotz. Chicago: University of Chicago Press.

Gronow, Jukka. 2003. *Caviar with Champagne: Common Luxury and the Ideals of the Good Life in Stalin's Russia.* Oxford: Berg.

Kideckel, David. 2008. *Getting by in Postsocialist Romania: Labor, the Body, and Working-Class Culture.* Bloomington: Indiana University Press.

Klumbytė, Neringa. 2003. "Ethnographic Note on Nation: Narratives and Symbols of the Early Post-Socialist Nationalism in Lithuania." *Dialectical Anthropology* 27(3–4): 279–295.

———. 2006. "Deterritorializing Post-Socialist Nostalgia: Tradition, Memory, and the Global Market of 'Soviet' Food Products." Paper presented at the Thirteenth Annual Symposium of Soyuz, the Post-Communist Cultural Studies Interest Group. Bryant University, Smithfield, Rhode Island, March 3–5.

———. 2006a. "Ethnography of Voting: Nostalgia, Subjectivity, and Popular Politics in Post-Socialist Lithuania." Ph.D. diss., Department of Anthropology, University of Pittsburgh.

———. Forthcoming. "The Soviet Sausage Renaissance." *American Anthropologist.*

Kotkin, Stephen. 1995. *Magnetic Mountain: Stalinism as a Civilization.* Berkeley: University of California Press.

Lankauskas, Gediminas. 2002. "On 'Modern' Christians, Consumption, and the Value of National Identity in Post-Soviet Lithuania." *Ethnos* 67(3): 320–344.

LAFPMRA (Lithuanian Agricultural and Food Products Market Regulation Agency). 2005. Available at http://www.litfood-fair.com/samsonas, electronic document (accessed October 13).

Leitch, Alison. 2003. "Slow Food and the Politics of Pork Fat: Italian Food and European Identity." *Ethnos* 68(4): 437–462.

Mincyte, Diana. 2006. "The Pasteurization of Lithuania: Informal Dairy Markets and Globalization." Paper presented at the Thirteenth Annual Symposium of SOYUZ, the Post-Communist Cultural Studies Interest Group, Bryant University, Smithfield, March 3–5.

Panevėžio mėsos fabrikas. 1992. Vilnius: Aušra.

Paškonienė, Asta Dalia. 1992. *Dešros ir rūkyti mėsos gaminiai.* Vilnius: Vilniaus Universitetas.

Petrović, Tanja. 2006. "'When We Were Europe': Socialist Workers in Serbia and Their

Nostalgic Narratives. The Case of the Cables Factory Workers in Jagodina (Serbia)." Paper presented at the International Conference on "Post-Communist Nostalgia," University of Illinois at Urbana-Champaign, Urbana, April 7–8.

Phillips, Sarah. 2002. "Half-Lives and Healthy Bodies: Discourses on 'Contaminated' Food and Healing in Post-Chernobyl Ukraine." *Food & Foodways* 10:27–53.

Rothstein, Halina, and Robert Rothstein. 1997. "The Beginnings of Soviet Culinary Arts." In *Food in Russian History and Culture*, ed. Musya Glants and Joyce Toomre, pp. 177–194. Bloomington: Indiana University Press.

Sliavaite [Šliavaitė], Kristina. 2005. "From Pioneers to Target Group: Social Change, Ethnicity and Memory in a Lithuanian Nuclear Power Plant Community." Lund Monographs in Social Anthropology 16. Lund, Sweden: Department of Sociology, Lund University.

Smith, William, ed. 1870. *A Dictionary of Greek and Roman Antiquities.* 3rd American edition by Charles Anthon. New York: Harper and Brothers.

Todorova, Maria. 1994. "The Balkans: From Discovery to Invention." *Slavic Review* 53(2): 453–482.

Wolff, Larry. 1994. *Inventing Eastern Europe: The Map of Civilization on the Mind of the Enlightenment.* Stanford, Calif.: Stanford University Press.

Zhuk, Sergei. 2008. Popular Culture, Identity, and Soviet Youth in Dniepropetrovsk, 1959–84. Carl Beck Papers. University of Pittsburgh.

SIX

A Celebration of *Masterstvo*

Professional Cooking, Culinary Art, and Cultural Production in Russia

STAS SHECTMAN

"The work of the professional cook is a special kind of work"—that is what the deputy director of the Moscow City Consumer Market and Services Department told the audience at the Eleventh Moscow Open Youth Championship in the Culinary Arts and Service. "We need to remember that we, with our work, with our profession, are needed everywhere by everyone. We bring happiness, *blagopoluchie* (well-being). We foster and protect our country and our Russian national culture." Congratulating the students and their teachers for their participation in this "celebration of professional *masterstvo* (skill, craftsmanship)," the city official encouraged the young competitors to "let your imaginations run free and, through the work of your hands, be realized." She closed her address with a final entreaty, made on behalf of "all [us] veterans" of the culinary field: "Enrich the glory of Russia's national cuisine, the most interesting and richest in the world. . . . Safeguard it, develop it, honor it, and let it prosper."

Since 2002, aspiring young culinary students from cities and regions across Russia have gathered in the nation's capital to participate in this cooking competition. Organized and run by the Moscow Culinary Association (MCA), the Championship is a day-long, juried competition showcasing the culinary skills and talents of Russia's "rising young culinary stars." Representing their respective schools, colleges, and universities, the students compete in cooking, baking, confectionery art, bartending, and restaurant service. Throughout the event they prepare multicourse dinners, banquet meals, and desserts, all of which are rated on technique, complexity, presentation, and taste. Luxurious cakes and pastries and elaborate sculptures of sugar and caramel decorate the showroom's tables. In the bartending competitions, judges watch contestants spin bottles, flip shakers, and pour cocktails, scoring them on individual style and flair, mixing technique, and recipe originality. Although all the competitors receive honorary diplomas and medals, the champions are awarded special prizes. From there they advance to participate in larger national and international contests, ultimately competing for a prestigious place on the national team that will represent Russia in the Internationale Kochkunst Austeeling, the World Culinary Olympics, which take place every four years in Germany.

Culinary competitions and exhibitions belong to a world of cooking far removed, although not completely disconnected, from the home kitchen, where food is, before anything else, made to be eaten. Cooking competitions tend toward the culinary ideal, privileging the technical standards and formal aesthetics of cuisine and its production over the subjective, sensual experience or primal urgency of its consumption. As spectacles of gastronomy, culinary competitions push cooking to its performative extremes, elaborating the symbolic dimensions of food and amplifying its capacity to bear cultural and social meanings. Yet, for all its "semiotic virtuosity," in its tangible and material forms food is also a social, economic, and political product, presupposing and reifying "technological arrangements, relations of production and exchange, conditions of field and market, and realities of plenty and want" (Appadurai 1981:494). Food is an interface between "the material and the imaginary, the corporeal and the social" (Liechty 2005:5) and one of the most powerful domains for the production, reproduction, and transformation of culture and society.

If we are what we eat, then what and how we cook play significant roles in the creation and expression of identity. The Moscow Youth Culinary Championship exemplifies ways in which professional cookery influences culture, the communication of identity, and the construction of community in contemporary Russia. With its appeals to national culinary heritage, its focus on the elaboration and display of professional skills, and its invocation of a global gastronomic field, the youth contest in Moscow also condenses and refracts larger trends in the post-Soviet and international food-service industries. Contemporary debates about national identity and the cultural meanings of food and eating are also shaped by the contest. Food, in this analysis, plays the role of both cultural product and social process. It is at once the tangible evidence of the larger material and discursive practices shaping Russia's contemporary culinary landscape and a site where social actors struggle over and transform the meanings of food's relation to self, identity, nation, and world.

Three aspects of the Championship are particularly significant. Several competing notions of group identity and community are communicated in and emerge from the event's public performance of professional culinary work. In gathering students, educators, and culinary professionals from across Russia, the competition mobilizes a sense of common interest and occupational identity among its participants. At the same time, references to the Soviet public-catering profession imagine a historical continuity, linking the Soviet and post-Soviet culinary professions and invoking shared cultural values and social roles. In drawing these connections, the MCA lays historical claim to the post-Soviet food-service profession, imbuing it with specific cultural distinction and national significance.

As an "exhibition of culinary art" and a competition in culinary production, the Championship is also implicated in the construction of Russia's, and particularly Moscow's, contemporary restaurant industry and food culture. By spotlighting cooking as a skilled craft and cuisine as an object of art, the competition is a site for the cultural, social, and industrial elaborations of food that often gain special significance as "cuisine." Examining the competitive categories in the Championship, as well as the actual objects produced and displayed and the criteria by which they are

evaluated, highlights the ways that aesthetic choices communicate changing notions of taste and cuisine. Through these aesthetic and social practices, local social actors engage with and transform transnational circulations of people, images, ideas, objects, and capital. Focusing on the
discourses and practices through which "cuisine" gains meaning as a
cultural category and value as a material object provides insights into the
processes through which food becomes a marker of culture and culture is
commodified as food.

Finally, it is important to consider the role of the Championship within
Russia's postsocialist culinary landscape. Although the Championship
cannot be divorced from market demands and ideologies of the country's
rapidly growing hospitality and food-service industries, it is also not re-
ducible to them. Rather, the event suggests the contradictions and tensions involved in the emergence and development of these industries in
postsocialist Russia. Culinary spectacles such as this one—along with
other exhibitions, salons, and classes—are part of how ideologies of class
and markers of social stratification are enacted, but they are also sites for
struggles over symbolic power. Through the production and display of
cuisine, certain social groups and actors in Russia assert claims on new
market forms and relations, endowing them with national distinction and
redeploying them as representations of culture on local, national, and
global scales.

The examples discussed in this essay are from fieldwork conducted in
Moscow between 2006 and 2008. During that period I attended two of
the Moscow Open Youth Championships, in 2006 and 2007. My personal
observations and descriptions all come from those two events, but data
on past competitions were also collected through archival research and
interviews.

Reintroducing Production

The study of consumption and commodities has played a key role in
anthropological debates about the processes and consequences of globalization. Daniel Miller (1995a:141) has argued that this "recent turn . . .
represents a major transformation in anthropological theory, method, and
perspective." "Very little of what we possess is made by us in the first

instance," writes Miller (1995b:1), emphasizing that it is as "consumers," aware of living through objects and images created by others, that most people engage with the institutions and relations of modernity. In recognizing the fundamental place of commodities and consumer culture in modern life, anthropologists have explicitly argued against fears that the spread of consumer culture and globalization *necessarily* threatens cultural diversity and specificity. Grappling with the question of how transnational processes shape and penetrate local worlds, scholars have argued that objects, ideas, and images "do not just float ethereally across the globe. . . . They are all, instead, localized in very specific time-space contexts" (Inda and Rosaldo 2002:11–12). These studies have explored the complex dialectics through which consumers appropriate, negotiate, or reject new cultural forms and practices, occasionally in potentially subversive ways. Consumption becomes a form of cultural production, offering, as Arjun Appadurai (1996:3) has pointed out, "new resources and new disciplines for the construction of imagined selves and imagined worlds."

Given the jarring juxtapositions of state socialism with the emergence of new consumer markets in Russia and East Europe, perhaps it is no surprise that anthropologists have found consumer behavior and consumption practices particularly rich sites for examining the ways in which postsocialist citizens have struggled with large-scale social, economic, and political change. Under state socialism, consumption played a highly circumscribed and politicized role in citizens' relations to one another, to the economy, and to the state. These were "economies of shortage," where the state focused its energies more on the production and distribution of goods than on the satisfaction of consumer desires (Verdery 1996). Consumerism, at least as envisioned by the Soviet state, was a key element in the efforts to cultivate Soviet values and construct ideal Soviet subjects rather than the leisure pursuit and expressive activity of the Western shopper (Patico and Caldwell 2002:287).

In the postsocialist context, then, consumer adjustments and responses to new market relations "represent the most tangible manifestations of more extensive societal upheavals" (Patico and Caldwell 2002:287; see also Verdery 1996). Ethnographic research has proven particularly well equipped to explore the complexities and consequences of these engagements, tracing the ways that people draw on historically produced value systems in making sense of and appropriating the rapid influx of global commodities and consumer trends (Barker 1999; Berdahl et al. 2000; Burawoy and Verdery 1998; Caldwell 2002, 2004; Humphrey 1995, 2002; Mandel and Humphrey 2002; Patico 2001; Patico and Caldwell 2002). Certainly, these studies have also provided important correctives to over-generalized claims about the market's penetration into socialist societies, cultural imperialism, or the "triumph" of capitalism.

Yet all the anthropological attention lavished on consumers seems to have come at the cost of studying the people and practices that produce the cultural forms and objects that others consume (Mahon 2000). Media and popular cultural forms such as film, video, music, visual arts, and theater, argues Maureen Mahon, are "anthropologically significant sites of the production and transformation of culture" (2000:469). Viewing these forms as both cultural product and social process, Mahon points out that the processes and practices of producing these forms are part of the ways in which social actors create, negotiate, and articulate identity, community, difference, and nation. These processes, however, display a fundamental asymmetry. Access to the tools through which the global is translated into and legitimized as "the local" is unevenly distributed, an inequity deeply enmeshed in struggles over symbolic, social, and economic capital. Analyzing the ways that social actors understand and negotiate the material constraints and discursive frameworks within which they operate, as well as the relationships between the particular content of these forms and their institutional and ideological contexts, can yield important insights into processes of social and cultural reproduction and transformation.

In the Soviet Union these same forms were central to the state's efforts to cultivate social, moral, and aesthetic ideals (Boym 1994:31). Beginning with Stalin's regime, ideas of *kul'tura* (culture) and *kul'turnost'* (culturedness) were mobilized by the state in its project of creating ideal Soviet citizens (Kelly et al. 1998:9). Cultural production played a key role in these efforts, exercised through various cultural forms and avenues, including the production of literature, performance, cinema, art, parades, festivals, and celebrations (Barker 1995:25).

In the anthropology of post-Soviet Russia, studies of cultural production and producers are relatively rare. This is all the more disappointing for the ways in which studies of post-Soviet modes, forms, and practices of cultural production could, as with studies of consumption, yield important insights into "shifting structures of authority, responsibility, privilege, and personhood" (Patico and Caldwell 2002:287). Perhaps this relative quiet has something to do with a (well-founded) concern for writing against the ideological legacies of the Cold War and neoliberal assumptions about the "legitimate" form that a postsocialist "transition" should take (see, for example, Bordahl 2000; Burawoy and Verdery 1999). These cultural forms, after all, with their associations with "propaganda," carry heavy ideological baggage, making studies of consumption all the more attractive in their capacity to challenge these top-down models of power.

Yet examples exist of ethnographic studies that are concerned with the complex ways in which cultural producers produce without presuming the ways in which consumers consume (Mandel 2002; Olson 2003; Urban 2004; Yurchak 1999, 2000). These studies have examined diverse cultural forms and practices, from the post-Soviet revival and reinvention of Russian folk music (Olson 2003) and the formation of a community of blues musicians and fans (Urban 2004) to the throwing of underground rave parties in St. Petersburg and Moscow (Yurchak 1999) and the production of soap operas in Kazakhstan (Mandel 2002). In doing so, they have shown how post-Soviet citizens, some of whom occupy different social positions than many consumers, have used these (sometimes foreign) cultural forms and technologies to construct and disseminate ideologies about identity, community, tradition, and nation, as well as to shape social relations, cultural meanings, political ideologies, and social space.

Thus the need to nudge social actors involved in the production of cultural forms into ethnographic view, for they deserve attention, too. In this essay the focus is on the contemporary community of culinary professionals in Russia—or at least the community as it is imagined by and in the MCA's Open Youth Championship in the Culinary Arts and Service—and their agency as producers of the symbolic and material elaborations of food that we grace with the term "cuisine" (Appadurai 1988). An examination of their culinary production provides insights into how these cultural forms and practices mediate identity, culture, and community while taming and employing new market forms and relations.

The Moscow Culinary Association: From
Veterans to Young Specialists

One cannot help but note that one of the constitutive parts of
human life, which even in the face of radical transformation
remains rather conservative and is less amenable to change, has
always been food. Over the course of the centuries, humanity
methodically perfects the production and preservation
of food and the organization of its consumption.

—*Nikolai Zavyalov,* Istoriia obshchestvennogo pitaniia
Moskvy [*The history of public catering in Moscow*]

The "transition" from the state-run to the market-based food-service industry displaced the relatively stable institutional structures, social relations, and cultural fields within which Soviet culinary professionals worked. From the very beginning of the Soviet Union, food and eating were seen as key elements in the project of building Soviet society. As early as 1917 the Bolshevik government set in motion its project of developing a large-scale system of *obshchestvennoe pitanie* (public catering or food service) with a decree from Lenin reorganizing the infrastructure of food production and supply (Rothstein and Rothstein 1997; see also Zavyalov 2006). These early reforms were steeped in ideology, reflecting the state's ideals about the new Soviet society and values. Some of the first targets for the Bolsheviks' reforms were restaurants and, especially, private kitchens, which were seen as wasteful and inefficient vestiges of bourgeois society and a "yoke holding back the moral, ethical, and political development of the female" and the family (Rothstein and Rothstein 1997:178; Borrero 1997). The establishment of communal kitchens and cafeterias figured prominently in "the fight against the private kitchen." These new spaces were envisioned as playing a key role in reshaping citizens' eating habits and, in turn, their relations to one another and to the state.

Central to the state's commitment to public catering was the development of an industrial infrastructure and technological basis for the production and delivery of food, as well as scientific approaches to nutrition, food preparation, and delivery. In a 1931 Communist Party resolution "On the Measures for the Improvement of Public Catering," the Central Committee began outlining plans for "raising the quality and variety of dishes, improving sanitary standards, strengthening the technological foundations of industry, and raising workers' interest and enthusiasm in the outcomes of their work."[1] Research institutes were established to conduct studies in nutrition and food science, develop new technologies and processes of food production and preparation, and even experiment with synthetic food surrogates (Rothstein and Rothstein 1997:181). Culinary schools and technical colleges were established, providing an array of courses for cooks, confectioners, administrators, and servers.

By the beginning of the 1980s many aspects of Moscow's public catering industry had, as one veteran of the industry put it, exhausted the momentum of their earlier achievements (Zavyalov 2006:131). Although a number of cafés and restaurants were already operating as "cooperatives" toward the end of the 1980s, most of the public catering establishments were still organized under Soviet codes and regulations that controlled everything from location, size, seating capacity, and types of equipment allowed to the delivery of supplies and ingredients, standards and recipes for dishes, and prices. Many of these establishments were "working on outdated technologies, poorly functioning equipment, and were unable to meet the growing demands of the population" (Zavyalov 2006:132). To this list of complaints, the observer added the problem of a shortage of young workers ready to enter the food-service industry (Zavyalov 2006:131).

Thus, in this context of "exiting socialism," the Moscow Culinary Association was established. Founded in 1991, the MCA was Russia's first post-Soviet professional culinary association, a distinction that some of the association's members still note with pride. Their pride, however, is not so much for being first among the network of culinary associations connecting members of Russia's rapidly growing hospitality and food-service industries and institutions. Rather, it comes from a collective sense of having weathered the storms of post-Soviet transformation and having "preserved" the cultural values and traditions of their craft in the face of tumultuous change. In *Moscow: 850 Years of Trade and Service* (1997), a survey of the capital's retail and consumer services landscape published by the city government in commemoration of Moscow's 850th anniversary,[2] the MCA's president, Tamara Nikolaevna Sharova, describes the Association's founding:

The economic transformations of the 90s had serious repercussions for public food service. All those years of work and the seemingly unbreakable ties within the system of public catering . . . were abruptly broken. Many restaurants and cafés found themselves on the verge of bankruptcy and closure. In order to help the system adapt to the demands of the market, to safeguard those rich traditions, and to not lose decades of accumulated experience, the directors of the city's largest establishments, along with specialists and veterans of the field, decided to join forces and found the Association. (Varfolomeyeva 1997:168)

Indeed, the aim of "safeguarding" the achievements of decades of service in the Soviet public catering industry is written directly into the Association's mission statement. "The MCA sees the culinary arts as a valuable part of national culture, and emphasizes that the folk traditions of Moscow *zastolia* [commensality] and *gostipriimstvo* [hospitality] must be preserved and developed on a contemporary world level," reads one Association brochures (*Moskovskaia assotsiatsiia kulinarov*, n.d.). Perhaps the best example of the Association's espoused role as "guardian of culinary heritage" was its stewardship of the Museum of Public Catering.[3] Founded in 1977 by "leading specialists in the public catering industry," the museum is dedicated to preserving the history of Russia's, and specifically Moscow's, culinary culture and food-service industry, while honoring the "heroic" men and women who worked in the field in the Soviet Union. Through its display of images, artifacts, and key figures from Russia's culinary and public catering history, the museum tells the story of the country's culinary development, tracing a straight line from prerevolutionary times through the Soviet era to Moscow's post-Soviet present.

In addition to its work as a cultural institution, the Association has, from its inception, been very much focused on professional and industrial development. Its top priorities include:

Promotion of the prestige of the cooking and confectionery professions, advancement of the professional skill of Moscow's culinarians, introduction of modern technologies into the capital's food-service establishments, strengthening of interregional and international relations, cooperation with professional training institutions, and the provision of full support for young specialists. (*Moskovskaia assotsiatsiia kulinarov*, n.d.)

As an *obshchestvennaia organizatsiia* (a nonprofit social organization), the MCA receives support from and is counted among a range of local institutions and offices—the most important one is the Moscow City Consumer Market and Services Department—that are part of the infrastructure of the capital's post-Soviet consumer market and economy. The Association's board of directors occupy various positions within Moscow's contemporary culinary community, including chefs, confectioners, and educators. Its acting and honorary members extend even further into the capital's restaurant and food-service industry to include restaurateurs and restaurant employees, food and equipment suppliers, and retired veterans of the Soviet public catering industry. In 1993 the Association was admitted into the World Association of Cooks Societies (WACS). Because WACS members join as countries rather than as individual associations or members, the MCA became Russia's representative in this "global community of culinarians comprised of over 70 countries with a membership estimated in excess of eight million cooks and chefs" (World Association of Cooks Societies 2008).

Most interesting here are the particular ways in which the culinary past is drawn into the present. Despite the structural break with the Soviet Union's system of public catering, the Association does not necessarily imagine it as a rupture in the meanings and values that characterized the profession in Soviet times. Just as the museum narrates the history of professional cooking and food service as a unilinear progression from tsarist feast and humble *traktiry* (taverns) to post-Soviet, fine-dining restaurants and fast-food chains, so, too, does the MCA align itself closely with and valorize the culture and traditions of Russia's public catering and culinary past. And just as the museum celebrates the roles of culinary professionals, such as chefs, cooks, servers, scientists, and nutritionists, in their service and contributions to (Soviet) society and Russian culture, so, too, does the Association strive to instill and nurture these values in the "young specialists" charged with carrying the field into the future. Yet, although distant echoes may be heard of the Soviet public catering project in the MCA's objectives of continuing to modernize the food-service industry and develop the country's system of culinary education, these strategies now play themselves out within different social, cultural, and economic fields. In its efforts to promote and raise the prestige of Russia's (specifically Moscow's) culinary profession, the MCA is also attempting to negotiate new forms of cultural and social capital within the post-Soviet and globally inflected field of culinary production (cf. Bourdieu 1993).

A Celebration of *Masterstvo*

> There is no doubt that the training of young cooks, confectioners, and waiters who will be able to demonstrate their achievements in the culinary craft and display their creativity in the application of new technological skills in the capital's food industry is not only the main objective of professional teaching establishments, but also one of the priorities of the Moscow government.
>
> —*Vladimir Ivanovich Malyshkov, Director of the Moscow City Consumer Market and Services Department*

"Working in the restaurant industry not only productively but also creatively, making cuisine into a real art, requires serious knowledge and a professional approach to the business," explained MCA's president Tamara Nikolaevna. "The task of our youth is not to blindly follow new, ultramodern trends, but rather to receive reliable information about the development of the restaurant business and world culinary practices, while at the same time preserving Russian culinary and hospitality traditions" (interview, March 12, 2008).

Of all the Association's objectives, working to develop young specialists in the culinary profession may be the Association's most highly valued activity. Throughout the year the Association organizes and attends master classes, culinary salons, competitions, lectures, and international field trips, all related to the art or industry of food service. These activities, in addition to justifying the bureaucratic and (relatively small) material support the Association receives from the municipal government, is also one of the ways that new culinary trends and practices filter through to educational establishments and students. Its position within the social network of Moscow's educational establishments and culinary professionals enables the MCA to mediate between an emerging generation of workers and broader local, national, and international trends and developments in the industry. Tamara Nikolaevna explained that it was "after we attended the World Culinary Congress [a biennial international meeting of culinary professionals organized by the WACS] [that] for the first time we saw the kind of serious attention given to the youth entering the field, and so in 1996 we decided to organize the Championship" (interview, March 12, 2008).

Although the Championship is neither the only youth culinary competition in Russia nor the only event the MCA organizes, it holds particular significance as the first event to focus specifically on students and young workers. The Association organized the first Championship as a way to bring together the capital's schools, colleges, and universities in order to build networks, exchange ideas, and inspire students. Held in 1996, the first Championship was relatively small, attended by only seventy participants and limited to educational establishments in Moscow. Not until 2002 was the event opened to regions and schools outside Moscow. The move to the Open Championship marked an important moment for the MCA, for it signaled both the health of Russia's developing food-service industry and the success of the Association's work. Now, not only did Moscow stand at the forefront of the nation's culinary profession, but the MCA could also position itself as the organizational "center" of the growing network of culinary associations and schools throughout the country. In line with the MCA's larger organizational goals, one of the Championship's aims is to foster cooperation and strengthen relationships with Russia's regions. Although some of the Association's educational and developmental activities involve bringing Moscow professionals to conduct master classes in other cities, the Championship marks the close of the MCA's work year and an opportunity for all the establishments with which the Association has worked to meet in the capital and celebrate their cooperation.

The 2006 Championship was an especially significant event. That year the Association celebrated its fifteenth anniversary and the Championship marked its tenth. Having outgrown its prior accommodations in a corner of the annual Moscow Hotel Business Expo, the Championship was now regularly held at the Kosmos Hotel, perhaps a more fitting space for its landmark status in the capital's cultural and urban landscape. As in previous years, the opening ceremonies found the competitors, their teacher-coaches, and supporters collected in the auditorium, where they sat with their respective team- and schoolmates and proudly cheered their support whenever someone from their school or city was called to the stage. That year more than two hundred teams from ten cities participated, some from as far away as Ekaterinburg. A professional master of ceremonies orchestrated the proceedings, introducing special guests and sponsors and waxing poetic about the event's significance and the achievements of its student participants. Between speeches, students from local schools and colleges performed songs and dances, many of them set to American pop music and modeled on music video choreography. The first several years that the Championship was held, these performances were part of the competition. Students were awarded prizes for their displays of talent and musicianship. Recent Championships have retained these performances but as entertainment rather than competition. Still, the musical portions of the opening ceremonies add energy and excitement to the proceedings, engaging the audience, drawing them into the experience, and heightening the shared sense of celebration.

Anthropologists have written extensively about the roles of rituals and celebrations in producing, negotiating, and contesting group identity and community (Schieffelin 1985; Turner 1967, 1969; Van Gennep 1960). This work has explored the various ways in which the symbols, values, and boundaries of community are enacted and given social reality through rhetorical and embodied performances (Schieffelin 1985; Kruckemeyer 2002). The opening ceremonies of the Championship reveal much about the ways that the MCA and its supporters understand the values and ideals of their work, as well as the historical and contemporary boundaries and meanings of the "culinary community." A significant portion of the ceremonies is given over to speeches by various government officials, representatives of the hospitality and food industries, and members of the MCA. Tamara Nikolaevna expressed many of the event's most salient themes and sentiments when she took to the stage:

> I'm very happy to welcome you all, colleagues from Moscow and from all the regions. Today, we meet for the tenth time, and I'm truly very grateful to all the educational establishments and their directors for your annual participation in this wonderful competition. This event provides us with an opportunity for developing professional skill and for the growth of our educational establishments. You understand, when you look out into this hall, a hall full of our future, with shining, wonderful eyes, that our future is in reliable hands. And we, in our turn, will help you, my friends. Help you and teach you to bring *dobro* [good] to people, because, really, our profession is the most generous, the kindest profession. So I thank all of you for your participation and all of the cities that have come to us today, I wish you luck, happiness, and success.

Similarly, the president of another culinary association noted that at "today's tenth anniversary, we celebrate not only with Moscow culinarians and not only with young Moscow culinarians, but in the circle of our colleagues from the regions." Addressing the audience as "colleagues," these speakers called attention to the shared occupational identity of the event's participants, linking Moscow and "the regions" in their common goal of developing professional skills. This image of commonality is underscored by the honorary diplomas and medals awarded to every school and participant simply for attending the event. Amid loud applause and cheers from home-team supporters, schools are called to the stage one by one to receive these awards, providing each establishment and student with the experience of belonging to the larger community, and presenting each of them to the audience as members of Russia's culinary community.

Throughout the Championship, repeated emphases on "skill," "creativity," and "imagination" highlight particular dimensions of culinary work as an artistic craft. In his research on restaurant cooks in Chicago, Gary Alan Fine noted that professional cooking occupies an "ambiguous position within the world of work, linked to production, service, and management" (1996a:93). These positions reflect competing "demands for aesthetic choices, consistency, efficiency, autonomy, and highly skilled technical work" (Fine 1992:1271). To help them navigate these sometimes contradictory positions and demands, workers draw on a range of "occupational rhetorics," through which they "justify their work and explain to themselves and their public why what they do is admirable and/or necessary" (Fine 1996a:90). The MCA does not mask the idea that the competition is, at some level, about "work," but it does de-emphasize its connections to industry and the labor market in favor of a more socially oriented and culturally valued image.

Thus, at the same time that these discursive strategies help shape the meanings of culinary work, they also infuse them with culturally specific values. In the language of the Championship's opening ceremony speeches and dedications (and to a slightly lesser extent, the closing ceremonies as well), the culinary profession is conceived of in terms of its significance to society and culture. With its connections to proper eating practices and nutritional knowledge, the work of cooking is constructed as a vital aspect in physical and spiritual *zdorov'e* (health) and students are imagined as "young specialists" possessing expert knowledge. "Your work touches on every aspect of people's lives," explained one speaker; "it is important for the health of the individual and of the nation." These speeches conjure not only an individual body but the greater "social body," recalling aspects of the ideological construction of food service in the Soviet Union.

The president of the Russian Interregional Association of Culinarians, an association closely related to and sharing some of the same board members as the MCA, underscored the dimensions of social service when he told the students that, although "it is a great thing to receive a medal, wonderful to win prizes, that is not the most important thing. The most important thing is your desire to become great masters who are needed not only by our city, not only by our country, but by the entire culinary world." Another speaker drew these cultural connections in more detail by describing the event as a "celebration of the creativity of young hands, of the youth who are our replacements" and enjoined the students to "protect that which we have received from our older generation—the traditions of Russian national cuisine and Moscow *khlebosol'stvo* [hospitality]."

These links to a historical community are illustrated with references to and invocations of "veterans of the field," the Soviet generation of culinary professionals. Rhetorically these "veterans" serve as temporal anchors and historical sources that are mobilized to construct the current meaning of culinary work. Of course, an important element in drawing these connections comes from the many MCA members, as well as people who teach and coach the students, who were themselves part of the Soviet public catering industry. While discourse plays a significant role in invoking a shared occupational identity, these ties are given social reality through the nondiscursive, performative dimensions of the Championship and the opening ceremonies. In this sense, the relationship between the Soviet and post-Soviet culinary professions is literally embodied on stage by the veterans, who are living proof of this historical continuity.

In 2001 the MCA created the *znak priznaniia* (sign of recognition), its "highest honor" bestowed upon "our colleagues for their personal contribution to the development of the culinary arts and service, the capital's hospitality industry, and, of course, the preparation of our young, talented specialists." Awarded during the opening ceremonies of the Championship, the *znak priznaniia* is more than symbolic recognition and invocation of the values of culinary work and service. It is also a ritual, a public performance of historical ties and continuity with the past. Referring to the recipients as *"novye kavalery obshchestvennogo pitaniia"* ("new knights of public catering"), "veterans of the field," and "highly qualified specialists," the MCA calls each one to the stage individually, announcing their years of service in the field, the restaurants, kitchen-factories, or schools where they worked, and any other honors they have received. For some awardees, the *znak priznaniia* acknowledged more than thirty years of service. One veteran, for example, was announced as "a Master of professional training, having taught in the Moscow College of Hotel Management, Tsaritsina, since 1982." Another "has more than twenty-five years of experience in international events and competitions. She has worked in the Kosmos kitchen-factory for fifteen years. Her teams have competed in many local and national competitions and have often brought back medals." Still another veteran was announced as "one of Moscow's best confectioners. He has worked in the Hotel Metropol, El Dorado restaurant, Alexandria Café. He is the Russian champion in confectionary art and has served as representative of our country in the World Culinary Olympics in Luxembourg." Students were encouraged to view these figures as role models. A restaurant chef offered them "one piece of practical advice." Noting that, although "you can do things in different ways, tradition is the foundation of everything. Everything new is something old that has been forgotten. I encourage you to talk to your mentors, because, always, tradition is the basis of our work."

In 2007 this history extended even further. That year the event was honored by the attendance of some of the last surviving generation of "Hero Chefs," who had "served their country with distinction during World War II" and throughout the Soviet Union. No speaker during the opening ceremonies failed to express his or her thanks and appreciation to these "true veterans" for their service. Many people exemplified the sense of respect and awe evoked by these honored guests by referring to them as *"nashi legendy"* (our legends). One highly successful and well-known contemporary Moscow restaurateur, who is also the president and founder of the Russian Federation of Hoteliers and Restaurateurs, encouraged the students to take pictures with them, "because these are our legends, our past, people who started in the field as far back as the beginning of the last century! In the twenties! Can you imagine what that means?" In valorizing these older chefs as legends, the speakers not only emphasize the historical continuity and sense of community, but they further underscore the idea that the contemporary culinary profession shares a culture and value system with the profession in the past. These performances present the construction of the culinary community as a historical reality, offering living proof of these links.

These discursive and performative practices are significant not just because they establish shared professional interests and occupational identities among the Championship's participants. They also imbue culinary work with special meaning as a "craft" and connect this craft to a historical community with common cultural values and ideals. In shifting attention from cooking as an occupation to cooking (and restaurant work in general) as a cultural and social service, the opening ceremonies suggest avenues through which social actors tame and employ particular forms and practices in the production of identity and community. In this instance, the MCA constructs alternative cultural values and meanings for contemporary work practices, which in turn are celebrated as symbols of local and national culture (Terrio 1996). Cooking becomes not only a vehicle for extending, preserving, and strengthening culinary heritage; it becomes the very manifestation of it.

Performing Skill, Exhibiting Taste

During the 19th century, culinary art exhibitions were a forum for reformers of the culinary art, like Marie Antoine Carême, Posper Montagne, Joseph Favre and Auguste Escoffier. Even today, in our fast-moving time, the function of culinary art exhibitions is to provide models, as well as a podium for the international development of the culinary art [*sic*].

—*World Association of Chefs Societies*, WACS Culinary Guideline 2008

Let us consider this waiter in the cafe. His movement is quick and forward, a little too precise, a little too rapid. . . . All his behavior seems to us a game. . . . He is playing, he is amusing himself. But what is he playing? We need not watch long before we can explain it: he is playing at being a waiter in a cafe. There is nothing there to surprise us.

—*Jean-Paul Sartre*, Being and Nothingness

Where the Championship's ceremonies emphasize solidarity and community, the competitive events focus on distinction and individual expression. As an "exhibition of culinary art," the Championship combines aspects of sport and museum, providing an arena for the performance, display, and evaluation of professional skill and artistic talent. These displays and performances in turn represent broader ideologies of taste, class, and labor, as well as tradition, national identity, and cosmopolitanism. The intersection of art, economics, and ideology underscores the idea that cuisine is the edible product and "transformed expression" of the social relations and material conditions surrounding its production (Bourdieu 1993:32).

For all the MCA's appeals to culinary tradition and heritage, the Association's members and veterans of the public catering industry readily admit that Russia's cooks work under very different circumstances than they did in the past. In my conversations with cooks and chefs working in Moscow, as well as in the discourse of the Championship's opening ceremonies, few aspects of contemporary cooking signal these differences more than the idea of creativity. Soviet cuisine, as it was explained to me, was often the product of the limitations of kitchen technology, cooking technique, product availability, and ideological and bureaucratic controls. The ultimate symbol of these limitations was the *Sbornik retseptur* (Recipe Collection), the culinary authority for the Soviet public catering industry. Its recipes and techniques formed the backbone for the food served everywhere from *stolovye* (cafeterias) to elite restaurants and hotels. In retrospect, for many current chefs and cooks who worked in the Soviet Union, the *Sbornik* (along with the system of *tekhnologicheskye karty* [recipe cards] which documented all the ingredients, their raw and cooked weights and portions, and cooking techniques of every dish) represents a bureaucratic burden on culinary creativity that has since been lifted.[4] During the opening ceremonies of the 2007 Championship, one chef told the students, "We envy you. You live in a time of creativity. In our day we had the *Sbornik* and harsh technological demands and limitations. So we envy you that you have the freedom and room to play with your ideas."

This freedom is limited, however. In the context of the Championship, rules govern both the products produced and the practices that produce them. From its very inception, the Championship has been closely modeled on regulations developed and set by the WACS, the committee that regulates all culinary exhibitions seeking WACS approval and status. Moreover, the WACS considers it "vitally important" for all member nations to adhere to its guidelines in order "to make culinary competitions fair to all competitors" (World Association of Chefs Societies 2008:5). These regulations are published and made available to all member nations with the intent of creating "a standard-level playing field" and "universally acceptable guidelines for fair assessment" (2008:6). The booklet covers the accepted competitive categories and rules for these events, adjudication criteria, the obligations of judges, and the process for attaining approval from WACS for a culinary competition. The criteria are specific, regulating the time contestants have for particular events, the range of ingredients and dishes from which they can choose, the percentage of ingredients that can be cleaned or prepared beforehand, and the portion size, nutritional balance, and number of courses and servings that should be prepared.

These regulations, to some extent, gloss over the economic differences between member nations and the cultural differences within them. Embedded within the ideas of "universal acceptability" and a "standard playing field" are assumptions about the definitions of "cuisine," "proper service and presentation," and even the relationship between national culture and cuisine. Regulations that stipulate the creation and serving of three- or four-course meals, for example, presume particular eating practices and traditions. Even in the one section specifically addressing competition in "Asian" countries and allowing for the use of woks, criteria state that "a three-course meal is expected" and "courses must be individually plated" (World Association of Chefs Societies 2008:16). Notably WACS accepts applications from one society of chefs per country, which then represents the entire nation and its cuisine. Individual culinary differences and traditions within a country are thus filtered through the society of its representative chefs, which in the course of international competitions is enjoined to create dishes that "reflect the traditional cuisine of the country" (2008:16). Although there are certainly practical reasons for these decisions, they presume the practice of restaurant work and professional cooking. The culture and practices of the professional restaurant kitchen, then, become the organizing logic for culinary competitions.

However, the relationship between these guidelines, the MCA, and its culinary competitions is more complex and ambivalent. In discussions

with Association members, no one expressed concern about the obligation to conform to the WACS guidelines or the possible consequences for
preparing and presenting traditional Russian cuisine according to contemporary European standards. Nor did anyone question the assumptions underlying the ideas of universal guidelines or a level playing field.
Rather, for the Association, the adoption of these guidelines is a strategic
decision, designed to provide Russian competitors with the knowledge,
skills, and experience they would need to participate in international
competitions. There is little doubt among the MCA that Russian chefs
have the talent and that Russian cuisine has the heritage to compete
internationally, but there is also a sense that "we have some catching up to
do." Thus the Championship, along with other local and national competitions, are important training grounds, where Russian cooks and confectioners can experiment with and develop the skills they will "need" to
compete internationally. After all, the Association sees as its own goals
the simultaneous preservation and advancement of the Russian culinary
tradition.

The Championship itself represents a local adaptation of the international model. The event is open to students, as well as youths who have
already entered the workforce. The accepted age range is from sixteen to
twenty-three years of age and up to twenty-five for the "art-class events,"
which are competitions in food and confectionery art. In developing the
particular repertoire of events comprising the competition, the MCA
takes into account its own assessment of the capabilities and limitations of
the Russian culinary profession and the students who are training to enter
it. Time limits are increased while the number of courses, dishes, and
servings is decreased. More significant, changes in the repertoire reflect
the particular priorities and needs of the local and national culinary field
and industry. In 2006, for example, the MCA introduced the bartending
and art-class competitions in response to, and in acknowledgment of, new
occupational identities and specialties in the industry and educational/
establishments. These additions suggest that the event crosses various
levels including the local, national, and international.

As of 2007 the Championship consisted of seven general competitive
categories, some including multiple events such as team and individual
competitions, bartending contests, themed table design and service, and
the art-class competitions. The artistic, thematic, and performative range

of these events is impressive and beyond the scope of this essay. However, several examples from the two competitions I attended illustrate the ways in which culinary aesthetics and practice come to represent and mediate class, culture, and national identity.

One of the most fascinating events in the Championship is the *domashnoe zadanie* (homework) competition, a team event where four students collectively represent their school, restaurant, or food-service establishment. Teams consist of a manager of operations, two cooks, and a pastry chef. Their entries are prepared ahead of time according to a pre-approved theme and must consist of one banquet dish of fish and one of meat for six people, two types of cold appetizers served in individual portions, two *goriachie* (hot) dishes or entrees in individual portions, three different desserts, and one cake. According to the Championship's guidelines, students are evaluated based on their ability to demonstrate that they have "acquired new culinary techniques and can produce new combinations of ingredients," and that they can "represent contemporary trends in the creation of banquet meals and individual dishes." Competitors are also required to submit detailed recipes for their dishes.

Each table differed in the dishes it presented, although the entries fell roughly into two stylistic categories. One was representational aesthetics, where food was designed in "recognizable" forms such as animals, trees, flowers, people, and small houses. These were almost all representations of Russian cuisine and were described to me as "traditional" dishes. Plates of whole sturgeon steamed or baked were garnished by jellied pictures of birds and nature scenes. They were accompanied by and set with traditional folk crafts such as *Gzhel,* a unique type of Russian porcelain, and *khokhloma,* a folk pattern often used to decorate wooden spoons, plates, bowls, and other tableware. One student called his dish *"ryba po-tsarski"* (tsarist-style fish) and presented it on top of a Russian flag and crest made of meat jelly (Figure 6.1); another student formed the Tsar Cannon and Bell out of meat; and a third submitted a table representing the traditional foods of his city, Smolensk. He described the table in this way:

E very people's culture is reflected in their cuisine. Here we have an old Smolensky table, and on it are represented all our national dishes. We have salted fish served with a special mead, chicken baked in dough in a Russian pechka [oven], Smolensky pirogi, and quail. For drinks, we have mead, kvas [made from fermented black bread], and cranberry mors *[a type of juice], and to accompany them, traditional Russian* pirogi *that guests are always treated to as part of Russian hospitality [*khlebosol'stvo*].*

The second presentational style was decidedly more abstract. These tables presented food in the aesthetic language of international cuisine, with abstract designs emphasizing color combinations and patterns. The cuisine on these tables did not index specific objects or images but instead reflected the sensibilities of modern art. In contrast to the traditional recipes described above, the cuisine visually masked rather than called attention to its ingredients. One table that particularly caught my eye was covered in a satiny white tablecloth, beneath which different sized plat-forms created a mountainous landscape (Figure 6.2). Cocktail glasses and test tubes filled with multicolored liquids, gels, and layers sat on top of the platforms. The aesthetic was a direct reference to one of the current "hot" international culinary trends and symbols of "high cuisine" called "mo-lecular gastronomy," where chefs employ scientific methods and their knowledge of food chemistry and physics to create dishes with unusual and novel combinations of flavor, texture, and color. The students de-scribed their entries as follows:

We decided to focus on European style because right now it's more contemporary, more progressive, and like in many restaurants, they're cooking in rather minimalistic, minimum ways, that is, to show the minimum amount of production but to make it memorable. We've presented several variations. Here is a Japanese wakame salad layered with cherry fried in a deep fryer so that it's pretty. The dish is made of Chilean sea bass and beans, layered and with food coloring added. We made these all so that you get a full range of colors and patterns. It's all modeled on this famous restaurant in Spain and is made to be contemporary, original, and stylish.

When I told the students that I was familiar with the restaurant, which is called El Bulli, one of them expressed surprise and asked me how I knew about it. In their response to my familiarity with molecular gastronomy and El Bulli, where this style of cooking was developed, the students were astonished that a layperson was familiar with what they considered spe-cialized knowledge. In this way they were negotiating their own positions as cooks versed in a form of high culinary culture that was not widely known. Although many of them were unlikely to be able to afford to eat in

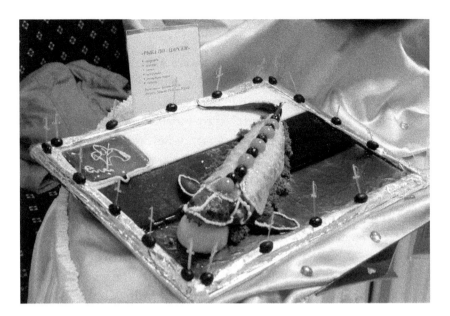

Figure 6.1. An entry of whole sterlet atop a jellied Russian flag, called *"ryba po tsarski* (tsarist-style fish), represents traditional Russian culture and national heritage. Photograph by Stas Shectman.

Figure 6.2. Abstracted ingredients, multicolored layers, and test-tube presentations signal the aesthetics of contemporary international cuisine. Photograph by Stas Shectman.

the kinds of restaurants on which they were modeling their food, their work signified a different kind of capital as knowledgeable culinary cosmopolitans and professionals within the local field.

In these examples, culture and class are variably represented in terms of aesthetic style and choices. Contemporary dishes presented in the style of international cuisine differed visibly from the aesthetics that marked and signified traditional culture. It is significant that Russian cuisine was imagined in terms of traditional presentational styles, whereas the more abstract and modern aesthetics were referred to as "European." Regardless of these differences, however, these tables suggest the ways in which larger culinary and cultural trends are expressed in and mediated by the aesthetics, naming practices, and techniques employed by the students. These stylistic differences, moreover, are not limited to the aesthetics of the food. Choices in tableware such as stylish, "designer" plates or more traditional handicrafts enter into the visual communication of class, style, and "Russian" versus "international."

Another fascinating example of the ways in which these performances enacted broader notions of class can be found in the "thematic table" competition. Here contestants have to set and decorate a table for two to four "VIP" guests according to a theme of their choosing. The tables were evaluated based on their creativity, style, and originality, as well as the use of contemporary elements of dining, including choices of plates, glasses, and cuisine. During the competition, each team presented its table to the panel of judges, explaining the overall theme, the relations between the disparate elements, and the three-course menu that, hypothetically, would be served on this occasion. One table I observed was organized under a seasonal theme representing fall. The students presented a small skit with a poetic text set to a light jazz soundtrack. One student played the role of waiter, the other two were guests. Dressed in a black vest and crisp white shirt, the student playing the part of the waiter recited a poem about fall, romance, and a trip to Paris, the "city of love." As he described the various elements of the table, which included creative square glass plates framing dried leaves, a centerpiece of orange and brown flowers, designer silverware, and elegant wine glasses, a young man dressed in a stylish white suit and black tie approached the table.

"What would our guest like?" inquired the waiter, handing the young man a menu.

"I have a date with a young lady," replied the guest, at which point he was joined by a "young lady" in a striking white evening gown. Kissing her hand, he showed her to a chair.

"You're enchanting, my princess," said the young man.

"It's you that I'm enchanted by," replied the young woman.

Here the performance of fine-dining service merges with the display of etiquette and manners that signify high culture (infused with a little romance). The students are not only playing at being in a restaurant, they are learning the language of restaurant culture and the practices of class distinction. It is perhaps telling in this case that the location chosen was Paris, the city not only of love but of haute cuisine and restaurants.

The jury for the Championship consists of chefs and confectioners who work in Moscow's contemporary restaurant industry. During the opening ceremonies, the year's jury is introduced on stage to the competitors. The introductions list the judges' credentials, including where they have worked and in what local, national, and international competitions they have participated and won awards. This listing of judges' qualifications both legitimates their roles as evaluators and demonstrates their expertise in the field. Thus they evaluate the competitors not only on the basis of the presentations but on the students' ability to show mastery of culinary techniques and terminology. Participants are required to explain their decisions and demonstrate an awareness of "proper" cutting and cooking techniques and flavor combinations. As I followed the jury through its rounds, I watched the interactions between the judges and the competitors. The former questioned the latter about the types of ingredients they used and the preparation of the dishes, noting the proper use of culinary techniques and language (Figure 6.3). In these exchanges the judges sometimes criticized students' entries, pointing out mistakes in presentation, cooking, or aesthetics. In other cases I saw participants approach other competitors and engage in discussions about their entries, offering and seeking constructive criticism.

Fine (1992) reminds us that, in spite of the rhetorics of artistry and craftsmanship surrounding certain notions of cuisine, "restaurants are industrial organizations operated for profit by capitalists. Although food must look, smell, taste, and feel good to maintain an audience, that is not sufficient" (1271). In pointing out these tensions between the artistic aspirations and market demands of professional cooking, Fine calls

Figure 6.3. Chef-judges observe and score a competitor in the individual art-class competition. Photograph by Stas Shectman.

attention to the ways in which aesthetics are closely intertwined with and reflective of larger structures of power, ideology, history, and economics. In these examples, we see the production of representations of culture, class, and industry as they draw on local, national, and transnational styles and practices. Focusing on the production of cuisine as both a material and symbolic product provides insights into the ways in which food, at least within the food-service industry, is marked as traditional or contemporary, ethnic or international, as well as the ways that food products attain value as art.

Culinary Strategies

In the introduction to his sociological study of the culture of restaurant work, Fine (1996b:8–9) argues that "restaurants are so linked to free-market capitalism that socialist nations quickly become known for the poor quality of food they present to diners. When a socialist country begins to move from a planned economy, the restaurant is one of the first arenas in which the development of an entrepreneurial market economy is noted." This is an apt observation, especially for Moscow, where public catering was among the first and most important municipal sectors to be privatized in the early Yeltsin years (Bater 1994:206). By 1993 public catering, along with retail and consumer services, accounted for 98 percent of all municipal establishments that were privatized (1994:206). In those years approximately 250,000 Muscovites joined the ranks of the new class of private business owners and an estimated one million of the city's residents worked in the nascent private sector.

The emergence and growth of the post-Soviet restaurant and food industries signal transformations that far transcend the relatively intimate space of the table and the performances that take place around it. These transformations include changes in the structure of ownership that radically alter the logic of urban development and social space; the increased penetration of Russia by the global agricultural system and transnational food industries, and the emergence of new spaces of sociality, practices of leisure, and markers of class. As "specialized sites of consumption" and "delectation," restaurants also play significant roles within the symbolic economy of cities (Zukin 1995). They are spaces through which global circulations of people, images, objects, and ideas enter into and are mediated by local practices, which in turn produce the meanings and experiences of locality. In an example closely echoing Moscow's post-Soviet culinary development, Laurier Turgeon and Madelein Pastinelli (2002) explore the emergence of an international and ethnic restaurant scene in Quebec. Noting that the "sharp decline of traditional restaurants versus the proliferation of fast food, ethnic, and gourmet restaurants is surprising in Quebec with its strong nationalist bent" (248), they inquire whether these tendencies are signs of the disappearance of traditional culture as Quebec is "absorbed into the new global order," or of Quebecois "changing their cultural activities and strategies to be better recognized in an increasingly global modern world?" (ibid.).

Returning to Moscow, the answer seems to tend toward the latter. Fine's point, which is that restaurants are one of the first arenas where societal change is "noted," suggests that restaurants and other market forms and cultural practices embedded in local contexts are condensed representations of "other" societies and cultures. This underscores the ways that foreign observers read these forms as shorthand for the social and cultural development of postsocialist countries. I argue, however, that it also points to the *conscious* awareness of postsocialist citizens of how their own market forms and cultural practices are viewed and (mis)understood by outside observers. Such awareness suggests the strategic uses of restaurants and cuisine. Annexing and domesticating global market practices, local social actors actively use these signs and practices, redeploying them as representations of culture, identity, community, and nation on both local and global stages. These practices "allow modernity to be rewritten more as vernacular globalization and less as a concession to large-scale national and international policies" (Appadurai 1996:17).

In January 2008 Russian star chef and restaurateur Anatoly Komm opened his long-awaited restaurant Varvary. Use of the Russian word *varvary,* meaning "barbarians," as the name, according to Komm, is a deliberate jab at Europe for ostensibly thinking of Russians as barbarians. "Of course, we've done a lot to deserve it," he explained one evening in the luxurious lounge of his restaurant, which is decorated with a mix of Russian folk art rendered in ultra-modern, stylized designs or commissioned from local artisans.

> *After all, it was us who brewed mulled wine out of Petrus [one of the most expensive French wines]. It was us who ordered black caviar by the kilo, only to put out our cigarettes in it. Every country is judged first and foremost by its table, by its food. With my restaurant I just want to show that there's something in Russia besides oil and gas. I want people to come to my restaurant and see just what kind of barbarians we really are. (Interview, February 13, 2008)*

Like the decor, Komm's cuisine is an ultra-modern take on Russian tradition. Not coincidentally, Varvary serves Russian molecular cuisine, one of the current culinary trends that signify, among other things, high-culture and avant-garde culinary art. Long before the restaurant even opened, however, Moscow food writers and journalists were already shouldering it with the burden of being the great hope for Russian cuisine. One food critic from the newspaper *Vedomosti* wrote that if Varvary works out for Komm it will be a major step toward "incorporating contemporary Russian cuisine into the world culinary process" (Zimin 2007). After months of praise as "the first Russian haute cuisine restaurant," one restaurant reviewer wrote that Komm "has done for Russian cuisine what only Pushkin was able to do for the Russian language" (Tsivina 2008:39).

For all its connections to and place within the market demands and profit motives of the food-service industry, cuisine and the work of cooking cannot merely be reduced to another commodity and form of labor in the global capitalist system. In contrast to Marx's reductive view of labor as an "instrumental act of appropriating and transforming nature," these examples suggest that work may be alternatively understood as a form of cultural production, "a social process through which humanity creates durable objects and relations" with profound potential for producing and altering cultural and political formations (Ulin 2002:693). This view dovetails with Alfred Gell's (1998) notion of art as a vehicle for agency, a way of acting in and on the world that mediates social relationships. Local cultural producers employ global cultural forms to create new representations of culture and identity that are not only meaningful to local actors but that are also responses to new transnational social, cultural, and economic fields.

The examples discussed above suggest some of the tensions and contradictions at work in processes of cultural production. On the one hand, the Championship is deeply enmeshed in market relations and is a site for the ideological production of workers for the restaurant industry, but, for the participating students, the event provides an important opportunity to negotiate social and cultural capital. These practices suggest that, although the students may lack the economic resources to access and take part in the consumption of cuisine as a marker of class, participating in the production of these markers provides them with the symbolic capital to construct themselves as cosmopolitan post-Soviet subjects. At the same time these practices make it possible for them to contribute to and participate in the production of cuisine such as Komm's, laden with ideologies of art and notions of high and national culture. Given that the production of aesthetic objects and objects of aesthetic value is a fundamentally *social* process (Bourdieu 1993; Fine 1992), the Championship provides one path for students to enter into the world of culinary production. Further research would profit from examining the ways in which these practices of production in turn shape and inform the practices and meanings of consumption.

Appadurai (1996:17) has suggested that the history of cultural forms and practices differs from their genealogy in that their history is "about their ongoing domestication into local practice," whereas their genealogy is "about their circulation across regions." Through the simultaneously local and global forms and practices of food and cooking the MCA constructs community, negotiates its values, and produces representations of traditional and contemporary Russian culture. The Championship presents one example of the processes through which these global forms and practices are "domesticated," infused with local cultural meaning, and written into the history of national cultural forms. Yet the process does not end there. These cultural practices are part of the ways in which food is transformed into and elaborated as cuisine, but they are also the paths through which cuisine is packaged as representations of culture. In the Championship's role as a training ground for larger national and international competitions, the practice of cooking is aimed ultimately toward the strategic representation of Russia at major events such as the World Culinary Olympics and the Bocuse d'Or in France. Professional cooks and confectioners come to serve as culinary ambassadors, international representatives of the state of Russian culinary art. Whether in international competitions or in the local restaurant industry, these students are working in the production of post-Soviet culinary culture.

ACKNOWLEDGMENTS

A large portion of this research was made possible by a Fulbright-Hays Doctoral Dissertation Research Abroad grant. I would like to thank the Moscow Culinary Association for their generosity, openness, and cooperation throughout my research. I would also like to express special thanks to Melissa Caldwell for her encouragement and insight.

NOTES

1. *Iz istorii obshchestvennogo pitaniia* (www.pitanie2007.ru/history.materials_0005.html; accessed 2007).

2. While the book, published under the direction of the Moscow City Consumer Market and Services Department (Departament potrebitelskogo rinka i uslug), ostensibly commemorates the capital's 850th anniversary, it does so through the lens of its consumer services and retail trade sector, precisely the first components of the municipal economy to be privatized under the reforms of the early 1990s. Notably the book celebrates the city's contemporary retail and consumer services market, writing relatively new businesses such as Perekrestok and Sedmoi Kontinent grocery stores and restaurant chains like McDonald's and Rossinter into the same history as stores like Eliseevskii and TsUM and factory kitchens and food-processing plants that still existed in the Soviet era.

3. In 2007 the museum was transferred to the stewardship of the Moscow City Consumer Market and Services Department. That year, renovations on the museum were completed and it was renamed the Museum of Culinary Arts. The old, dusty halls and crowded, Soviet-era display cases received a complete makeover. This modernization, which touched not only the museum's displays but also its content, suggests larger changes in the city's culinary landscape. Along with the inclusion of contemporary restaurants and even fast-food chains such as McDonald's, Yolki-Palki, and Mu Mu, the change in the museum's name also implies a discursive shift away from the connotations and values of Soviet food service to the contemporary restaurant scene with its emphasis on cuisine as fashion, style, and art.

4. Although the system of *tekhnologicheskye karty* still exists in the contemporary restaurant industry, where failure to complete them may result in fines, chefs still refer to the Soviet system with its standardized recipes as significantly less culinary creative than the current industry.

REFERENCES CITED

Appadurai, Arjun. 1981. "Gastro-Politics in Hindu South Asia." *American Ethnologist* 8(3): 494–511.

——. 1988. "How to Make a National Cuisine: Cookbooks in Contemporary India." *Comparative Studies in Society and History* 30(1): 3–24.

——. 1996. *Modernity at Large: Cultural Dimensions of Globalization.* Minneapolis: University of Minnesota Press.

Baker, Adele Marie. 1999. "Re-reading Russia." In *Consuming Russia: Popular Culture, Sex, and Society since Gorbachev,* ed. Adele Marie Barker, pp. 3–11. Durham, N.C.: Duke University Press.

Bater, James. 1994. "Privatization in Moscow." *Geographical Review* 84(2): 201–215.

Berdahl, Daphne, Matti Bunzl, and Martha Lampland, eds. 2000. *Altering States: Ethnographies of Transition in Eastern Europe and the Former Soviet Union.* Ann Arbor: University of Michigan Press.

Borrero, Mauricio. 1997. "Communal Dining and State Cafeterias in Moscow and Petrograd, 1917–1921." In *Food in Russian History and Culture,* ed. Musya Glants and Joyce Toomre, pp. 162–176. Bloomington: Indiana University Press.

Bourdieu, Pierre. 1984. *Distinction: A Social Critique of the Judgment of Taste.* Translated by R Nice. Cambridge, Mass.: Harvard University Press.

——. 1993. *The Field of Cultural Production: Essays on Art and Literature.* New York: Columbia University Press.

Boym, Svetlana. 1994. *Commonplaces: Mythologies of Everyday Life in Russia.* Cambridge, Mass.: Harvard University Press.

Burawoy, Michael, and Katherine Verdery, eds. 1998. *Uncertain Transition: Ethnographies of Change in the Postsocialist World.* Maryland: Rowman & Littlefield.

Caldwell, Melissa L. 2002. "The Taste of Nationalism Food Politics in Postsocialist Moscow." *Ethnos* 67(3): 295–319.

——. 2004. "Domesticating the French Fry: McDonald's and Consumerism in Moscow." *Journal of Consumer Culture* 4(1): 5–26.

Fine, Gary Alan. 1992. "The Culture of Production: Aesthetic Choices and Constraints in Work." *American Journal of Sociology* 97(5): 1268–1294.

——. 1996a. "Justifying Work: Occupational Rhetorics as Resources in Restaurant Kitchens." *Administrative Science Quarterly* 41(1): 90–115.

———. 1996b. *Kitchens: The Culture of Restaurant Work.* Berkeley: University of California Press.

Gell, Alfred. 1998. *Art and Agency: An Anthropological Theory.* Oxford: Clarendon.

Humphrey, Caroline. 1995. "Creating a Culture of Disillusionment: Consumption in Moscow, a Chronicle of Changing Times." In *Worlds Apart: Modernity Through the Prism of the Local,* ed. Daniel Miller, pp. 43–68. London: Routledge.

———. 2002. *The Unmaking of Soviet Life: Everyday Economies after Socialism.* Ithaca, N.Y.: Cornell University Press.

Inda, J. X., and R. Rosaldo, eds. 2002. *The Anthropology of Globalization: A Reader.* Oxford: Blackwell.

Kelly, Catriona, Hilary Pilkington, David Shepherd, and Vadim Volkov. 1998. "Introduction: Why Cultural Studies?" In *Russian Cultural Studies: An Introduction,* ed. Catriona Kelly and David Shepherd, pp. 1–20. New York: Oxford University Press.

Kruckemeyer, Kate. 2002. " 'You Get Sawdust in Your Blood': 'Local' Values and the Performance of Community in an Occupational Sport." *Journal of American Folklore* 115(457/458): 301–331.

Liechty, Mark. 2005. "Carnal Economies: The Commodification of Food and Sex in Kathmandu." *Cultural Anthropology* 20(1): 1–38.

Mahon, Maureen. 2000. "The Visible Evidence of Cultural Producers." *Annual Review of Anthropology* 29:467–492.

Mandel, Ruth. 2002. "A Marshall Plan of the Mind: The Political Economy of a Kazakh Soap Opera." In *Media Worlds: Anthropology on New Terrain,* ed. Faye D. Ginsburg, Lila Abu-Lughod, and Brian Larkin, pp. 21–228. Berkeley: University of California Press.

Mandel, Ruth, and Caroline Humphrey, eds. 2002. *Markets and Moralities: Ethnographies of Postsocialism.* New York: Berg.

Miller, Daniel. 1995a. "Consumption and Commodities." *Annual Review of Anthropology* 24:141–161.

———. 1995b. *Worlds Apart: Modernity Through the Prism of the Local.* London: Routledge.

Moskovskaia assotsiatsiia kulinarov. n.d. *Voskhodiashie zvyozdy kulinaria xxi veka.* Moscow.

Olson, Laura J. 2003. *Performing Russia: Folk Revival and Russian Identity.* New York: Routledge.

Patico, Jennifer. 2001. "Globalization in the Postsocialist Marketplace: Consumer Readings of Difference and Development in Urban Russia." *Kroeber Anthropological Society Papers* 86:127–142.

Patico, Jennifer, and Melissa L. Caldwell. 2002. "Consumers Exiting Socialism: Ethnographic Perspectives on Daily Life in Post-Communist Europe." *Ethnos* 67(3): 285–294.

Rothstein, Halina, and Robert A. Rothstein. 1997. "The Beginnings of Soviet Culinary Arts." In *Food in Russian History and Culture,* ed. Musya Glants and Joyce Toomre, pp. 177–194. Bloomington: Indiana University Press.

Sartre, Jean-Paul. 2003 [1943]. *Being and Nothingness: An Essay on Phenomenological Ontology.* London: Routledge.

Schieffelin, Edward L. 1985. "Performance and the Cultural Construction of Reality." *American Ethnologist* 12(4): 707–724.

Terrio, Susan J. 1996. "Crafting Grand Cru Chocolates in Contemporary France." *American Anthropologist* 98(1): 67–79.

Tsivina, Daria. 2008. "Anatoly Komm." *Kommersant Weekend,* no. 3(49) (February 1): 39–41.

Turgeon, Larier, and Madelein Pastinelli. 2002. " 'Eat the World': Postcolonial Encounters in Quebec City's Ethnic Restaurants." *Journal of American Folklore* 115(456): 247–268.

Turner, Victor. 1967. *The Forest of Symbols: Aspects of Ndembu Ritual*. Ithaca, N.Y.: Cornell University Press.

———. 1969. *The Ritual Process: Structure and Anti-Structure*. Piscataway, N.J.: Aldine Transaction.

Ulin, Robert C. 2002. "Work as Cultural Production: Labour and Self-Identity among Southwest French Winegrowers." *Journal of the Royal Anthropological Institute* 8(4): 691–712.

Urban, Michael. 2004. *Russia Gets the Blues: Music, Culture, and Community in Unsettled Times*. Ithaca, N.Y.: Cornell University Press.

Varfolomeyeva, Valentina. 1997. *Moskva: 850 let torgovlia i uslugi*. Moscow: Departament potrebitelskogo rinka i uslug [Department of the Consumer Market and Services].

Van Gennep, Arnold. 1960. *The Rites of Passage*. Chicago: University of Chicago Press.

Verdery, Katherine. 1996. *What Was Socialism and What Comes Next?* Princeton, N.J.: Princeton University Press.

World Association of Chefs Societies. 2008. *WACS Culinary Guideline 2008*. Available at http://www.wacs2000.org/ (accessed March 3, 2008).

Yurchak, Alexei. 1999. "Gagarin and the Rave Kids: Transforming Power, Identity, and Aesthetics in Post-Soviet Nightlife." In *Consuming Russia: Popular Culture, Sex, and Society since Gorbachev*, ed. Adele Marie Barker, pp. 76–109. Durham, N.C.: Duke University Press.

———. 2002. "Privatize Your Name: Symbolic Work in a Post-Soviet Linguistic Market." *Journal of Sociolinguistics* 4(3): 406–434.

Zavyalov, Nikolai. 2006. *Istoriia obshchestvennogo pitaniia Moskvy*. Moscow: Informatsiony Proyekt PIR.

Zimin, Alexei 2007. "*Lavry rozdany.*" *Vedomosti* 11(48), March 30.

Zukin, Sharon. 1995. *The Cultures of Cities*. Oxford: Blackwell.

SEVEN

The Social and Gendered Lives of Vodka in Rural Siberia

KATHERINE METZO

When I first met Soelma[1] she was a vibrant woman in her thirties, passionate about her job in the cultural sector, and a loving and attentive mother and wife.[2] A year later, when I returned to the village of Shonokhoi, friends told me that Soelma had died, apparently from alcohol poisoning. I use Soelma's story to structure my discussion of the social and gendered lives of vodka in rural Siberia. I am not suggesting that all drinking ends in tragedy; rather, I hope to show how the social and gendered aspects of drinking keeps women from receiving help with their problem drinking. Women, I assert, are silent victims of vodka.

Vodka—and alcohol more generally—is an index of social relationships, hospitality, ritual, honor, and disgrace. The perception of drunkenness is rooted in social relations and varies from culture to culture

(Gefou-Madianou 1992). In Russia drunkenness and disgrace are rarely discussed in reference to women, but not because women do not drink or because there are no female alcoholics; instead, women are thought to be in control of the many situations in which vodka is used and to be responsible for the successful, and unsuccessful, outcomes of those events. Women themselves are portrayed as more sensible, more temperate, in their drinking. This attitude even extends to stereotypes about drinking preferences. The perception of women's temperance and responsibility is so deeply engrained that rather than responding when a woman's behavior crosses into socially unacceptable excessive drinking, it is met with silence.

My goal in this essay is not to interpret the material socioeconomic consequences of drinking in Russia or to take a moral position on the subject. Although alcohol-related deaths were increasing in the 1990s and have been correlated to the devastating economic conditions of post-socialism, I argue that the reality of vodka is far more complex. One acquaintance repeatedly told me, "We're not always like this," explaining her drinking binges by saying, "it's just that this is such a difficult time and there is so little happiness." On a number of occasions, this same acquaintance invoked a cultural rationale to entice others to share a bottle. Thus the reasons given for drinking vary based on context. At the same time, however, I do not engage in the kind of "problem deflation" of which anthropologists have been accused (Dietler 2006; Gefou-Madianou 1992). That Russians like their vodka is no secret, and the rise in alcohol-related deaths in the early 1990s negates the argument that there is no problem (Nemtsov 1997; Cockerham 1997).

I use Soelma's tragic story to highlight how tightly vodka is woven into the social fabric of contemporary Russian villages and how this affects women. Discussions of women in relation to vodka are often limited to physical abuse, the psychological impact on the family, or advice to women seeking to "cure" an alcoholic husband. The first two, though important health and human rights interventions, tend to place the emphasis on men's drinking. The third is more germane to the current discussion, because this advice tends to identify men as the victims while blaming women for their husbands' decline into alcoholism. I emphasize women's drinking and female alcoholism to underscore the depth in which social norms and expectations about drinking are embedded. I suggest that these social norms, through their silence about women's alcohol abuse, create a form of symbolic violence.

Meeting Soelma

⚓

Soelma and Volodya were clearly in love. It was apparent in the way they held hands, and when they sat beside each other at the table, Volodya frequently reached around Soelma's shoulders to hug her or sneak a quick kiss on the cheek. They enjoyed spending time with friends, celebrating birthdays, holidays, or visits from friends and relatives, which is how I first met them. I was visiting Tanya, a friend in the village of Shonokhoi, when Soelma came by to celebrate payday. The presence of an American visitor created an even better occasion to celebrate. Soelma had already invited some girlfriends to join her at Tanya's, for all agreed that Tanya's flat was the best gathering spot for a "girls' night out" as she was a single mother.

Several friends residing in the same part of town eventually joined us, as Tanya, Soelma, and I prepared a small meal of fried potatoes and traditional Russian salads. At first the group included only women, but soon Volodya and a male friend joined us. The evening turned out to be festive, with toasts made to friendship between nations, to acquaintanceship (Rus. *znakomstvo*), and to love, and was typical of the type of socializing to which I had become accustomed among young people in rural Siberia. I note here that Soelma, Tanya, and their friends are all ethnically Buriat or of mixed Buriat-Russian descent. With a few minor exceptions, which I discuss below, the drinking practices of Buriats in social gatherings match the drinking culture I have observed in Russian homes in Buriatia and elsewhere.

Occasions for Drinking and Hospitality

My first encounter with Soelma and Volodya was quite normal in terms of the culture of drinking in rural Russia. One normally does not drink with the express intention of getting drunk. There must be an occasion for drinking. The occasion may be a significant event such as an anniversary, birthday, or promotion, but even small events warrant celebration if the "lucky person" is willing to purchase drinks for his or her colleagues (Timofeyev 2006). Payday is often a sufficient occasion for celebration (Connor 1971), particularly in communities where unemployment is around 30 percent, and even those with jobs are paid two months or more behind schedule (Metzo 2001).

Drinking culture in Russia is first and foremost a communal activity. The solitary drinker is by definition a problem drinker.[3] One reason drinking cannot be done alone is because it is highly ritualized. Pesman (2000:171) notes that "drinking time was different from other time," and that the social time marked by drinking tea or "something stronger" made real time stand still. Drinking together and the concomitant cessation of real time create social bonds that allow people to share heartfelt or soulful (Rus. sing. *dushevnyi*) thoughts. The separation from real time is marked by the consumption of the first two drinks, which follow in rapid succession and identify the occasion to which the evening is dedicated—in my case, *znakomstvo* and international friendship. Koester (2003:1) points out that drinking practices in Russia disturb notions of the everyday, "precisely because the power of drinking plays upon the boundaries between the special occasion and everyday life." Thus a routine day can be transformed into a special occasion through the initiation of drinking.

Drinking occasions abound and mostly take place within the home, especially the kitchen. Location is linked to another important aspect of drinking culture—the need to consume food while drinking alcohol (Pokhlebkin 1992; Pesman 2000). For some, *zakuski*, or hors d'oeuvres, are as critical as drinking.[4] The mechanics of drinking in Siberia that I observed are virtually identical to Pesman's description (2000:171): one would "exhale, drink, and then, before one could smell the alcohol, wash it down with a sip of brine from a pickle or tomato jar, fruit juice, or diluted jam; or snack on appetizers," including sniffing a slice of black bread.

The social and culinary aspects of Russian drinking culture are in turn related to Russian ideas about hospitality. Hospitality, according to Pesman (2000), is about creating a home for one's soul. The host must work to anticipate and take care of a guest's needs, urging one to eat even after the requisite polite refusals, preparing food and placing it on a plate in front of a guest rather than inviting a guest to "help him/herself." The lavish tables to which visitors to Russia have become accustomed are based on the desire to share everything with one's guests, to not hold back. Ethnic stereotypes about hospitality and generosity also abound. Like the residents of Omsk, the Siberians I knew, both urban and rural, on trains and in homes, remarked that Siberians share everything with their guests, contrasting this with the rigidity and stinginess of Muscovites (Pesman 2000:151).

Hospitality imposes on the host an obligation to share everything, but Koester, invoking Marcel Mauss's (1990) famous analysis of gifting practices, notes the guests' equally important obligation to receive. Although it is polite to refuse offerings of food, the hospitality of the person offering a drink must be acknowledged. By setting a bottle on the table, the host creates an obligation shared by those present as guests to "receive" until all bottles on the table are emptied. What one might perceive as aggressiveness is actually interpreted by Russians as the "height of generosity. All those bottles must appear on the table and each must be drained completely" (Segal 1990:17), or else either guest or host would be insulted.

As I discuss below, women have a more defining role in terms of hospitality, one of nurturing as well as responsibility. The way in which a woman provides food to her guests is often taken by the outside world to represent how well she provides for her family. Most women also work outside the home, but much of their status remains linked to their subsistence activities and cooking abilities.

In Buriatia, traditionally a nomadic culture in which dairy products play a key role in subsistence, the customary greeting to a first-time guest in one's home is to offer a glass of milk. Milk is a sacred food, a "white food" (Bur. *sagaan edin*), which symbolizes the central role of cattle within the traditional household economy of this formerly nomadic pastoral group. Although this convention is no longer widely practiced, women in some villages continue the custom. The glass should be full, signifying the bounty of the household, but the guest need only take a sip or two to be simultaneously fed and blessed by the host. In many Buriat households, dairy products are the most important dishes to have on the table, whereas Russian families emphasize salads, such as the traditional *vinegret*. Most households proudly offer both.

The Breakup

During a visit to Shonokhoi several months after meeting Soelma and Volodya, I learned that Volodya had walked out on Soelma after a fight. According to the other women in this circle of friends, the argument circulated around accusations of infidelity and impropriety during work-related travel. Both Soelma and Volodya traveled as part of their jobs and were sometimes gone for up to a week at a time. According to statements that each made to me at different times, neither Soelma nor Volodya had had an affair, but the fight was dramatic enough that Volodya moved out temporarily and stayed at the house of his ex-wife, with whom he had remained friends over the years, a factor contributing to Soelma's jealousy. Soelma became depressed after Volodya left, and, to drown her sorrows, she began drinking a bottle of vodka every day. While Tanya was filling me in on the situation, Soelma, who lived only a few houses away, stopped by in her house slippers, pajamas, and coat. She wore no makeup and her hair was disheveled. I could smell alcohol on her breath. She had come to borrow money from Tanya for a bottle of vodka. Because it was not yet payday, her friends could gently refuse her request by saying they also had no money. But as a foreigner I clearly had money, and so she appealed to me.

Gendered Stereotypes: Responsibility and Appropriate versus Inappropriate Drinking

For men in Russia, the ability to drink is a sign of their character or soul, and drinking is associated with valor (Segal 1990) or goodwill (Phillips 2000). Even as women have been "liberated" by socialism, men are pressured to continue fulfilling the more traditional role of "breadwinner." Thus they also drink as a form of escape (Conner 1971) or as a way to "manoeuvre between [society's] conflicting claims" (Sokolov 2006:x).

Men's excessive drinking is tolerated, even expected and accepted. Indeed, a man who refuses to drink or displays a low tolerance for alcohol is ridiculed (Segal 1990; Conner 1971). Temperance and restraint, on the other hand, are associated with women.

Even alcohol preferences are gendered, with vodka and beer perceived as predominantly male drinks and wine as mainly a female drink, although champagne is associated with particular types of celebrations (Timofeyev 2000).[5] In mixed company, as I have described, women prepare the table while men open bottles and pour, taking care to top off glasses after each toast. Although women are welcome to make toasts, this is also a male domain. Within this division of labor, there is tension between the male and female stereotypes. Men use toasting to set the drinking pace for all guests, ensuring the collective intoxication of the group. The men present are thus able to display their masculinity to the group, and women, perhaps, are liberated from the constraints of responsibility. On the other hand, women can slow the drinking tempo with good food and multiple dishes, insisting that a particular guest either has not had enough to eat or has bypassed a particular dish.

I have focused on drinking in mixed company, but studies of Russia largely center on drinking as a male activity (Connor 1971; Ries 1997; Pokhlebkin 1992; Segal 1990). Empirical studies support the stereotype that men are far more likely to drink than women (Stack and Bankowski 1994). Being less likely to drink, however, does not exclude women from the drinking culture, from drinking, or from becoming alcoholics. As Pesmen observes, "the fact that it is statistically 'male' is much less important than that it is in or informed by a voice labeled 'male,' a voice fully available to be fluently spoken in by others" (Pesman 2000:178). I agree with Pesman, but I push her critique further by arguing that precisely because the voice of drinking is male, attention to the consequences of drinking focuses predominantly, even exclusively, on men, ignoring the potential dangers facing women who drink.

If heavy drinking is a sign of valor, when does one cross the line to become an alcoholic or a drunk (Rus. *alkogolik, pianets*)? Drinking alone or drinking without an occasion are certainly signs of a problem, but based on my observations in Russia, I contend that they are necessary but not sufficient conditions for labeling someone an alcoholic. Men are generally not considered to have a problem with vodka unless they fail to take care of financial obligations to their families. At the same time, it is fairly common for a woman to go to her husband's workplace on payday to collect his salary before he starts to spend it on vodka. In postrevolutionary Russia, women went to factories to collect their husband's salary as a strategy "to limit the impact that expenditures on alcohol had on their own family's economic well-being" (Phillips 2000:96). This behavior, I observed, is equally prevalent in post-Soviet Russia.

Because women's status in rural areas largely derives from activities within the home, and because a woman with a drinking problem is more likely to drink in private, alcoholism among women is more remote from public view than among men. Drinking in private, though harder to see, is also a clear sign of a problem. The fuzziness of the boundary between suitable and inappropriate drinking for men is part of the draw (Koester 2003), and men are more likely than women to find drinking companions, thus deflecting some of the criticism. To find a drinking buddy, men can create occasions for drinking such as a forgotten holiday or birthday or even a much-needed rainy day in an agricultural community. Because women *are* statistically less likely to drink, they tend to lack these kinds of opportunities.

Laura Phillips (2000) describes the gendered aspects of alcohol consumption in Russia during the early part of the twentieth century, quoting an expression that reflects the different expectations for women and men: "when a husband drinks, the floor of the home rots, but when a woman drinks, the whole home rots" (103). Women's greatest concern in those earlier days, as today, was to maintain a stable household economy and, as such, it is "a mundane, personal fight" (109). Women are reserved in their own drinking, because they are responsible for the material and moral success of the household.

The perception of women as more responsible extends to women being held accountable for their husband's drinking. Thus men are seen as victims, while women are blamed for shortcomings that drive men to violate the social rules of drinking. In 2000, while Soelma's story was unfolding, an article under the rubric "School for Survival" ("Shkola vyzhivaniia") appeared in a regional newspaper. The reporter set out to respond to the following claim: "I have come to hear from foreign guests that 'Russian men drink a lot only because Russian women allow it.' I was very surprised. Could this really be the case?" (Izvekova 2000). The reporter's initial surprise suggests that she may take a more Western feminist or individualist stance. Instead, she advises women:

1. Learn to cook well. A satisfied (man) is not drawn into hard drinking.
2. Don't encourage drinking at every occasion.
3. Listen to your husband! It's better for him to share his problems and troubles with you than in other company with a bottle.
4. Don't shame him when he's drunk. Wait until morning.
5. Don't blackmail him with sex.
6. Be happy with any hobby he picks up, even if it seems stupid to you. (Izvekova 2000:20)

This advice reifies traditional gender expectations that women feed their families and maintain moral order. In supporting the stereotype, the author blames women for unacceptable patterns of male drinking. At the same time as these recommendations are supposed to aid women in combating excessive drinking, they imply that women themselves are responsible for the underlying cultural practices that are the foundation for excessive drinking.

Women are not only responsible for ensuring that their male partners drink within measure, they are also charged with the task of recognizing and treating alcoholism when it does occur. In the 1920s anti-drinking powders were marketed to women to sprinkle on their husbands' food to keep them from drinking (Phillips 2000:113–114). Today pamphlets on intervention, such as "99 Ways to Stop Alcoholism" are marketed to women. A television advertisement from 2007 illustrates this continued bias not only that men alone experience drinking problems but that women are the ones to fix it. The advertisement begins with the camera slightly out of focus but centered on a man walking down a set of steps. The steps are filled with empty, unlabeled glass bottles, in the shapes and sizes of standard half-liter beer bottles and vodka bottles. With each step the man takes, bottles crack. He is not knocking them down; they simply shatter as he walks past them. As a hand reaches out to the man and stops him, a male voice-over says, "Help him quit" (Rus. *Pomogi emu ostanovit'*). The camera then comes into clearer focus and the colors are perceptibly sharper. The commercial cuts to an image of the new anti-alcohol medicine that is the subject of the advertisement, provides details on the preparation, and then returns to the image of the man and the woman whose hand stops his literal descent down the stairs and his figurative descent into alcoholism. In the last shot the woman is hugging the man and looking into the camera as the voice-over returns and repeats, "Help him quit." Throughout the commercial the viewer never sees the man's face. The appeal is clearly to women as the protectors of male sobriety.

Soelma's Growing Dependence on Alcohol

I did not want to give Soelma money for vodka. I told her that I did not have enough cash with me, only enough to get back to the city. She persisted, and I said I would take a look. Tanya and I insisted that she eat something, since she had been asleep for more than twelve hours. Tanya told her to run home to retrieve something she had borrowed that we would need to prepare food. Her departure gave us time to discuss the situation. Tanya immediately told me not to worry about giving Soelma money, that Soelma would scrape together the ten rubles necessary to buy a bottle. She had seen that I was uncomfortable lending the money for alcohol. I replied that ten rubles was enough for *spirt* (ethanol) but not for a bottle of genuine vodka. We then weighed the potential outcomes of giving Soelma the money versus denying her the money. The forty rubles required for a full-size bottle of vodka was an inconsequential amount of money to me (approximately U.S.$1.30), and even twenty rubles would buy a 200-ml bottle from a store. We both acknowledged that Soelma would not quit drinking anytime soon unless her life changed dramatically. In reality, buying a bottle would grant her one more day of drinking untainted vodka that is dangerous only when consumed in large quantities rather than dangerous simply because it is consumed. Tanya assured me that no one expected me to give Soelma money for alcohol, nor would anyone think less of me for giving her the money. When Soelma returned, I told her I was very worried about her drinking, but I gave her twenty rubles, emphasizing that I was only giving her money because I knew she would find a drink somewhere and I wanted to be sure she was not drinking machine alcohol (*mekhanicheski spirt*). I told her that Tanya would buy her a bottle of real vodka, and when that bottle was empty I wanted her to get ready for work on Monday and to stay sober so Volodya would talk to her. Soelma continued to drink for several weeks before she managed to bring her life back into her pre-binge routine.

Alcohol Poisonings and Deaths

When money is tight or alcohol is hard to acquire, Russians have sought out existing alternatives or have produced their own homemade vodka (*samogon*). Throughout the first half of the twentieth century, in rural areas, approximately 80 percent of the per capita consumption of alcohol came from *samogon*. In the early part of this century, approximately 50 percent of alcohol consumed was either industrial alcohol or *samogon* (Zhelnorova 2000). In my experience it was often the former.

In many villages the consumption of *spirt*, a generic term for ethanol from various sources including the grain alcohol used to clean factory machinery, is a deliberate choice. It is cheap and as widely available as vodka. In 2000 those looking for an inexpensive way to get drunk could purchase 200 ml of *spirt* for about ten rubles (roughly thirty cents at the time) as opposed to a bottle of vodka for forty-five to sixty rubles (a dollar and a half to two dollars). *Spirt* and vodka were often used as payment for physical labor (Metzo 2001). Since imperial times, vodka production was managed as a state monopoly and became, particularly during post-Soviet financial crises, an important currency of exchange (Hivon 1994; Pesman 2000). Hivon (1994) asserts that the value of vodka comes from its stability as a form of payment—in contrast to the fluctuating value of the ruble—and its flexible use—it is consumed daily.

At the same time, however, the lower-quality vodka, *samogon*, and *spirt* have profound health consequences. In a small, local Siberian newspaper, one author warns readers, "The market is flooded with alcoholic beverages, whose quality doesn't meet standards, and rather frequently threatens people's health and lives. Drinking a single bottle of 'false' vodka means a person takes two swallows of acetone" (Yudina 2000). In the Soviet era, statistics on mortality and morbidity, and on health and demographics more generally, were either repressed or grossly inaccurate. According to one author's calculations, statistics on per capita annual alcohol consumption in Russia between 1981 and 1993 were off by as little as 50 percent but by nearly 300 percent when one accounted for *samogon* (Nemtsov 1997:114). Despite the unreliability of Soviet-era statistics, Treml (1982:487) notes that the increase in female alcoholism under socialism is an important contributor to higher infant mortality.

According to Treml's (1983:488) numbers, more than half the deaths due to poisoning were the result of alcohol poisoning, and the numbers increased steadily between 1968 and 1976. He explains the increase as associated with "the general increase in per capita consumption of alcohol, increase in consumption of toxic home-distilled *samogon,* and in the deterioration of the quality of state produced alcoholic beverages" (Treml 1983:490). Nemtsov (1997:116) calculates that the percentage of accidental deaths in 1984 at least partly attributable to alcohol are, for males and females, respectively, 65.5 percent and 49.7 percent, and that the percentages for all types of deaths in which alcohol played some role (including cirrhosis, heart disease, or lung disease) are, respectively, 23.9 percent and 15 percent. Nemtsov's calculations are based on the fact that any association with alcohol is often left out of official statistical reporting.[6] His findings are supported by a recent study that argues that an unhealthy lifestyle (including alcohol consumption) is the main determinant of decreasing life expectancies in Russia (Cockerham 1997). Alcohol has also been linked to marital breakdown (White 1996; Stack and Bankowski 1994).

Soelma's Intervention

In an effort to combat her depression and reduce her increasing reliance on vodka to get through the day, Soelma traveled to her natal village and visited a shaman from her lineage.[7] She did not go to the shaman to treat her growing dependence on alcohol. Instead, she was seeking a solution to her fractured relationship, although, in a way, this could be seen as treating the root cause of her drinking problem. Indeed, during my visits to Shonokhoi in the months of Soelma's heavy drinking, none of her friends referred to her as an alcoholic. Everyone seemed to be treating her drinking as a symptom rather than as a problem in and of itself.

A traditional offering that Soelma would have taken with her on this trip to the shaman was a bottle of vodka. The shaman would have blessed the vodka with smoke from a juniper branch and used it to make offerings to master spirits. I saw Soelma after she returned from the trip. She was still quiet, probably sad or depressed, but she no longer seemed tired and, for the time being, at least, had stopped drinking.

Ritual and Intervention

Among indigenous peoples in Siberia vodka has a complex relationship to culture. Social drinking differs little from Russian drinking, as this is one area in which indigenous Buriats have acculturated. Specific to Buriatia is that vodka is among the liquids used in ritual offerings—one of the "white foods." When asked, Buriats will respond that they practice shamanism, Buddhism,⁹ or nothing, but most Buriats and even many Russians carry out certain rituals. For example, when opening a bottle of vodka, Buriats will be sure to cut the metal band off the neck of the bottle before pouring and will offer the first drops of vodka from the bottle to the local master spirits, a ritual always performed by the eldest male present. Each person present, upon receiving a glass of vodka, also offers these same spirits the first drops from his or her glass.

In the morning Buriat women traditionally make an offering of a sacred liquid to the master spirits of the place where they live. Women stand in their courtyard spraying a small amount of milk, milky tea, or vodka toward the sky in each of the four cardinal directions, turning clockwise. I have been told that this offering was originally done with milk, *tarasun* (milk brandy made from cow or horse milk) or *arkhi* (distilled milk vodka). Much later, after Russians appeared, vodka replaced these traditional beverages as the sacred liquid of choice. Vodka, like these traditional fermented and distilled dairy beverages, was transparent and thus fell under the classification of "white foods." Some have noted that vodka replaced the distilled dairy beverages simply because households stopped preparing these beverages. Others claim that because the alcohol content of vodka is higher, it is seen as a stronger beverage and, by extension, a superior ritual offering.

The perception that vodka is stronger or more appropriate as an offering is one that many are trying to combat in contemporary Buriatia. One reporter implores readers: "The Mongols, including Buriats, never had such a tradition of pouring out vodka at every ritual. Ask a lama which is better—milk, vodka, or arkhi? There's no difference. Milk is even better. The Buriats' gods are drunk [enough] as it is, he will answer" (*Buriaad Unen* 1999). One lama with whom I spoke suggested a logic by which milk is the better ritual beverage. Given that milk is produced within the home, greater benefits accrue to household members when it is used in a ritual.

To some extent this campaign is also a strategy to make vodka less ubiquitous and reduce the number of occasions for drinking. Drinking at a sacred site or at a temple or arriving in a drunken state can produce negative consequences for the individual as well as for others who live near the site and are considered to be under the protection of the master spirits of that place.

Soelma's Story Ends

For several weeks after her visit to the shaman, Soelma ceased drinking and life appeared to return to normal. Volodya again spent time with her and the children but had not yet moved back into the house. It was during these weeks that I left again, only to return one year later to learn that Soelma had died. Shocked, I asked Tanya how it happened. Had she purchased *spirt* as I feared or had something else occurred? Tanya recounted that no one had seen Soelma for several days when her daughter came to tell Tanya that she thought her mother was dead. No autopsy was done, and I never learned the official cause of death.

Alcohol, Women, and Silence

My retelling of Soelma's story has many holes, for I had not set out to conduct research on alcohol; indeed, one of the challenges during my fieldwork was to avoid occasions to drink, as I often visited people in their homes and they were keen to demonstrate their hospitality. A more critical reason for gaps in the story is that I was not present for many key events. In fact, I was not in the village of Shonokhoi at all when key events transpired. Also, because much of Soelma's story took place in private, it was impossible to document through observations or interviews. When Soelma was around, even after becoming sober, she was reluctant to speak about drinking. Soelma's story is an example of how anthropological methods are better suited to "measuring the pleasures" rather than the problems of drinking (Room 1984:172). At the same time these gaps in the narrative are precisely what makes Soelma's story important to share. When I visited Shonokhoi in 2001, Tanya's very first words to me were that Soelma had died. Her manner was calm and reserved, and she provided little detail. Tanya was the only person who ever mentioned Soelma's death, and after this initial conversation nothing more was said. The silence surrounding Soelma's death contrasts sharply to the American experience in which I was raised.

Social science literature on gender and drinking in Western societies focuses on women's vulnerability in the realm of drinking (Robbins 1989). Women are viewed as biologically more vulnerable because of body weight and composition, but also more vulnerable psychologically because of the social norms attached to men's drinking versus women's drinking. Several authors have noted that women's drinking, whether binge drinking or addiction, carries a greater social stigma. "It is felt that she has trespassed on territory beyond her proper sphere, that she has degraded herself in a particularly odious, even unnatural manner" (Sandmaier, in Robbins 1989:118). Because women are seen as the keepers of sexual virtue and as nurturers, both at home and at work, transgressing that boundary is, by implication, a sign of loose morals. Simply put, women who drink become the subject of conversation and gossip.

Russian cultural norms, on the other hand, make it possible to evade criticism regarding individual drinking practices. As Sokolov writes, "In Russian culture, intoxication is seen as a state that temporarily places individuals outside the moral boundaries of the community—and then admits them back in without the fatal damage to their moral status that would otherwise have been inevitable" (Sokolov 2006:18). Thus silence about drinking may be a way for individuals to "save face" when on a drinking binge, and this seems to hold true for men more than women. Drinking alone is another level of silence, perhaps more accessible to women than the liminality of intoxication. Pesman (2000:187) suggests that drinking transforms time and unites "people and domains felt to be fractured by life." The solidarity of drinking with her girlfriends following Volodya's departure stopped time for Soelma. Her solitary drinking, perhaps, was a way to keep time at a standstill as she awaited Volodya's return. As reflected in these cultural norms, silence may even be seen as a positive value.

The gendered stereotypes about morality, hospitality, and responsibility primarily inform the silence about women's drinking in Russia. Silence replaces that which need not be said, namely, that men have drinking problems and women prefer sweet, light drinks. In this silence women are only the victims of vodka, as when their husbands drink too much and beat them or fail to support their families financially. Soelma's story is profound, and unusual, in its tragedy, but the silence about her drinking and about her death is a symptom of a symbolic violence against women. Many women embrace certain aspects of gendered drinking norms— refusing additional drinks because they are "light drinkers," insisting on the most basic of meals to accompany drinking even when the goal of the evening is intoxication. The problem lies in the stereotypes of men as drinkers and women as teetotalers, which compels women to drink in isolation or downplay the degree to which drinking is affecting their daily lives. Rates of alcohol poisoning are on the rise in Buriatia, and although the rates are higher among men, the rates among women are keeping pace (*Goskomstat* 2000).

Although I had not developed a close friendship with Soelma, I quite liked her irreverent and passionate attitude toward life and I was sad to see her life change so dramatically. Sharing her story is an attempt to make sense of her death within the context of cultural norms about men and women, drinking and drunkenness, hospitality and responsibility. Drinking in Russia is a special domain, a space in which time stands still. It is also a male domain in which women are only thought to visit. While sharing in the communal aspects of drinking, women must ensure that guests are properly taken care of and that drinking does not cross into drunkenness. Drinking in Russia is also a dangerous realm because of the prevalence of poor-quality alcohol that contributes to alcohol poisoning. For women, the danger of drinking is also linked to the silence they face when drinking moves from a social activity to one that disrupts their lives. This problem will continue to grow until people finally deal with the reality of drinking in Russia.

ACKNOWLEDGMENTS

Most of the research for this paper came after Soelma's death. I want to thank Lissa Caldwell for her encouragement and support for this project as well as her incredible patience in seeing it through to reality. I have worked to preserve the anonymity and confidentiality of those involved in the events described in this essay, but I must also thank the women of Shonokhoi for allowing me to share in their lives and I dedicate this article to them and to their daughters and to all the daughters of Russia.

NOTES

1. All names, including the name of the town, have been changed and certain details of Soelma's story have been omitted to respect her anonymity and the anonymity of her children and her friends.

2. Although not legally married, they were culturally recognized as married because they had lived together for several years and used the terms "husband" and "wife" when referring to each other.

3. I routinely found that people whom we would label "alcoholic" in the United States were regularly excused by those around them; only those who fit the most extreme stereotype of a "homeless bum," doing manual labor in order to be paid in liquid currency, were properly considered alcoholics.

4. Pokhlebkin's *History of Vodka* (1992) argues against Gorbachev's anti-alcohol campaign. Pokhlebkin asserts that, rather than a wholesale prohibition of alcohol, Russians need the highest quality of vodka and also the education on how to drink it properly.

5. Although there is some foundation for this stereotype in statistics on drinking in Russia, it appears that, over time, drinking habits continue to converge with the stereotype (Timofeyev 2006:3).

6. An acquaintance who worked in the emergency medical service in the village of Kyren told me that supervisors there encouraged medical workers to find a category other than alcoholism within which to report accidental deaths whenever possible and, in those cases, to leave out information about alcohol.

7. Soelma could have gone to a shaman in Shonokhoi, but it is always best to return to one's natal home to find a shaman of one's lineage.

8. Buddhism was brought to Buriatia from Tibet via Mongolia.

REFERENCES CITED

Buriaad Unen. 1999. "Mongolia Has Quit Drinking. What about Us?" *Buriaad Unen,* November 11, 1999, No 125:2.

Cockerham, William. 1997. "The Social Determinants of the Decline in Life Expectancy in Russia and East Europe: A Lifestyle Explanation." *Journal of Health and Social Behavior* 38(2): 117–130.

Connor, Walter D. 1971. "Alcohol and Soviet Society." *Slavic Review* 30(3): 570–588.

Dietler, Michael. 2006. "Alcohol: Anthropological/Archaeological Perspectives." *Annual Review of Anthropology* 35:229–249.

Gefou-Madianou, Dimitra. 2007. *Alcohol, Gender, and Culture.* London: Taylor and Francis.

Goskomstat Rossii, Goskomstat Respublika Buriatiia [*Goskomstat*]. 2000. Mortality of the Population in the Republic of Buriatiia. Publication No. 04-40. Ulan Ude.

Hivon, Myriam. 1994. "Vodka: the 'Spirit' of Exchange." *Cambridge Anthropology* 17(3): 1–18.

Izvekova, Olga. 2000. "Russia." *Argumenty i fakty*, No. 15:20.

Koester, David. 2003. "Drink, Drank, Drunk: A Social-Political Grammar of Russian Drinking Practices in a Colonial Context." *Anthropology of East Europe Review* 21(2): 41–47.

Mauss, Marcel. 1990. *The Gift: The Form and Reason for Exchange in Archaic Societies*. Translated by W. D. Halls. London: Routledge.

Metzo, Katherine R. 2001. "Adapting Capitalism: Household Plots, Forest Resources, and Moonlighting in Post-Soviet Siberia." *GeoJournal* 55:549–556.

Nemtsov, Aleksandr V. 1997. "Alcohol Use and Death in Russia." *Sotsiologicheskie issledovaniia* 9:113–117.

Pesman, Dale. 2000. *Russia and Soul: An Exploration*. Ithaca, N.Y.: Cornell University Press.

Phillips, Laura. 2000. *Bolsheviks and the Bottle: Drink and Worker Culture in St. Petersburg, 1900–1929*. DeKalb: Northern Illinois University Press.

Pokhlebkin, William. 1992. *A History of Vodka*. London: Verso.

Ries, Nancy. 1997. *Russian Talk: Culture and Conversation during Perestroika*. Ithaca, N.Y.: Cornell University Press.

Room, Robin. 1984. "Alcohol and Ethnography: A Case of Problem Deflation?" *Current Anthropology* 25(2): 169–191.

Segal, Boris M. 1990. *The Drunken Society: Alcohol Abuse and Alcoholism in the Soviet Union: A Comparative Study*. New York: Hippocrene Books.

Sokolov, Mikhail. 2006. "Cruelty, Sex and Pedagogical Authority: On Some Functions of Alcohol in Contemporary Russian Culture." *Kultura* (7–8): 17–19.

Stack, Steven, and Elena Bankowski. 1994. "Divorce and Drinking: An Analysis of Russian Data." *Journal of Marriage and the Family* 56:805–812.

Timofeyev, Mikhael. 2006. " 'No Reason Not to Drink': Alcohol Drinking Patterns in Contemporary Russia." *Kultura* (7–8): 3–7.

Treml, Vladimir G. 1975. "Alcohol in the USSR: A Fiscal Dilemma." *Soviet Studies* 27(2): 161–177.

———. 1982. "Death from Alcohol Poisoning in the USSR." *Soviet Studies* 34(4): 487–505.

White, Stephen. 1996. *Russia Goes Dry: Alcohol, State and Society*. Cambridge: Cambridge University Press.

Yarmoliuk, E. D. 2004. *The Market for Alcohol Production of the Siberian Federal Okrug in 2003*. Abakan: TsIIU Khakasstata.

Yudina, N. 2000. "Shield of Imitation Vodka." *Saiany*, July 22, 2000, No 29 (9048): 1.

Zhelnorova, Natalya. 2000. "Do We Know How to Vacation?" *Argumenty i fakty v Buriatii* 36, no. 123 (September 2000): 3.

Turnips and Mangos

Power and the Edible State in Eastern Europe

ELIZABETH CULLEN DUNN

> The use and application of power frequently enter into changes
> in a society's food consumption habits. Where this power originates;
> how it is applied and to what ends; and in what manner people
> undertake to deal with it are all part of what happens when food habits
> change. We do not understand these processes at all well, even though
> they are of enormous importance to the world's future.
>
> —*Sidney Mintz,* Tasting Food, Tasting Freedom

The anthropology of food is a quirky topic, particularly when the focus is on Eastern Europe. If it is the food you like—pillowy dumplings, boiled potatoes, a steady diet of pork and beets leavened occasionally by pickled herring or a good goulash—wonderful cookbooks abound. If, on the other hand, you are really interested in understanding the momentous social and economic changes that have occurred over the last twenty years, why not read the political scientists or the economists? With their ideal-typical models and macro-level studies to tell you either what has happened or what should, they make far stronger claims to generalizability than anthropologists do. So what insights can a small group of anthropologists add to the study of the momentous changes that began twenty years ago, and why would analyzing a few ingredients and a dish or two, rather than reams of statistical data, help them say anything important?

The answer, as the collection of essays in this volume shows, is that anthropology has a surprising facility for showing how power really operates. As a discipline, anthropology's relentless focus on the lived experience of everyday life has challenged dominant narratives of the "transition" in Eastern Europe that assumed that removing the heavy political and economic hand of state socialism would automatically lead to "freedom." Instead, the ethnographies in this volume use the production of food as a lens to show the changing structures of constraint and opportunity that have changed the life chances of people in different social groups in Eastern Europe. This focus on food offers a slantwise perspective on the relationships of those who make and consume food that puts aside standard presuppositions about rational action, markets, and democracy, and provides a steady look at new social relationships without merely judging how far they diverge from some ideal-typical model of what "market democracy" is supposed to be like. The study of food is a way to access how people genuinely live and to uncover their thoughts on abstract issues in tangible contexts. This alone makes the anthropology of food diverge radically from the slew of studies—most of them more prescriptive than descriptive—written by economists and political scientists with little familiarity with everyday life in the region.

In most of the essays in this book the relationships revealed through an examination of milk or coffee or sausages turn out to be unequal affairs. The authors explore this inequality from both ends of the socioeconomic spectrum: some concentrate on the practices of new elites using coffeehouses as public spaces or seeking professionalized "cuisine" in upscale restaurants; many others use the study of food to explore how people marginalized and excluded from the region's great economic boom are making do, an approach more significant, perhaps, for Eastern European than for Western readers. In much of the region the experiences of people who have been disadvantaged by postsocialist class formation are seldom discussed in the media or in political debates, and few outside their own neighbors know the consequences of postsocialist transformation on poor, disadvantaged, or elderly people. The study of food has the remarkable ability to portray these people's lives in images and language that opens up the discussion of social and political equality without threatening listeners' post-Marxist sensibilities. Whereas an extended discussion of class may attract no listeners, a discussion of organic milk with a subtext of social inequality might. Food studies make these sensitive topics more engaging and less intimidating—in short, more palatable.

This consistent focus on big issues differentiates the anthropology of food from mere "food porn," or glossy studies of culinary pleasure. Certainly the essays here take the experience of cooking and eating seriously —just look at Stas Schectman's investigation in this volume of Food Network-style cooking competitions in Moscow. And, of course, the work here strongly considers food quality as well as the plethora of symbols people use to express it by associating these matters to different places and historical epochs; Neringa Klumbytė's careful study of Lithuanian sausage brands in chapter 5, for example, looks at what Sid Mintz (1996) called "inside meanings," or the culturally constructed symbols that make food meaningful to consumers. But what makes the anthropology of food important is that it constantly connects immediate sensory experience and "inside meanings" to what Mintz called "outside meanings": the political and economic systems that create inequality at the same time they make food. Food studies is a way of understanding those political and economic systems and how they come to be experienced in the travails of daily life, how those systems are made concrete through quotidian acts of production and consumption, and how they are literally embodied. This matters because food is the most important and frequently encountered material object that translates regulatory regimes and power relationships into lived experience. Thus food has the almost magical property of jumping scale: as it moves, it links the global economy and household economies, political bodies and the bodies of individuals, the world and the self.

To study food, then, is to study power. The study of food in Eastern Europe provides a useful and novel means of studying the new architectures of power that have emerged after socialism, precisely because the study of food makes it possible to integrate the operations of power at multiple scales. This has traditionally been done in food studies with Marxian-inspired political economy (e.g., Watts and Little 1987; Marsden et. al. 1996; Fine 1994; Mintz 1981), but, as the essays in this book show, there is more than one way to investigate changing structures of power. Here the operations of power are not seen as premised on class alone or exercised purely through the exploitation of labor; rather, they are viewed as regulatory regimes that shape, but do not dictate, the contours of social life. This focus on regulation—in both its cultural and informal as well as its codified and formal sense—animates this new perspective on social change in Eastern Europe.

Food Regimes: Regulation in the Socialist System

To understand the novelty of the regulatory approach most contributors to this volume take requires contrasting this approach to previous studies of Soviet agriculture. Like most food and agriculture studies from the 1950s to the 1980s, economic analysts who looked at Soviet production emphasized the problem of quantity (see, for example, Nove 1988). The creation of a highly industrialized food system was a priority from the beginning for the Soviets, who struggled to achieve full collectivization of agriculture, food processing, and even dining (Scott 1998; Fitzpatrick 1994; Hessler 2004). The goal was to eliminate waste and dramatically improve the quantity of food moving through the system to reach the urban proletariat, supposedly the vanguard of the revolution. This system's early failure is, of course, legendary: nearly nine million people died of famine during the collectivization process in the 1930s.

Less noted, however, are the socialist regime's successes in improving food quantity after World War II. Although the food systems of the Eastern bloc were never fully nationalized and always relied on private production by the peasantry, the majority of food in Eastern Europeans' diets after World War II was made up of food grown on large industrial collective or cooperative farms (Wegren 2005:26). Much of that food was further processed in state-owned factories, which produced limited ranges of standardized food commodities for sale at artificially low prices. There were many technical and logistical advantages to highly processed food in a socialist system: more durable food could better withstand the vagaries of the Soviet boom-and-bust production cycle, and it could more easily be hoarded for reallocation later, when it might be traded for other goods or swapped for political favors. As Smith (2008:146) points out, "It was both easier and ideologically more desirable for the Soviet food industry to create processed foods than it was to distribute high-quality fresh ingredients."

The advantages of industrial food production, however, were not limited to improving quantity. Industrial food was the material vehicle for a regulatory project that was as much a political and symbolic project as it was utilitarian. In the first place, the increase in industrial food production was one of the key elements of empire (see Caldwell's introduction to this volume). By processing food from one region and then circulating it in semi-durable form to other parts of the empire, the Soviet system was able to standardize, at least partially, diets once dependent on local produce and regional cuisines (Dunn 2008). There were canned Bulgarian-style red tomatoes that replaced some of Georgia's pickled green tomatoes (Dunn 2008), generic European-style lagers that edged out "dark, thick, sweet" Khevsur beers "prone to giving powerful headaches, like an evil version of Guinness" (Manning 2007), and standardized nationally distributed hams, like Poland's canned Krakus hams that replaced locally smoked specialties.[1]

These foods were not standardized because the factories that produced them created their own standards or because retailers demanded products that met certain specifications (cf. Friedberg 2004 on the UK and France). Rather, they were standardized because of active state intervention in the food system—state regulation that was a key goal of the system, not just a by-product (see Jung, this volume). State ministries set out standards that not only specified food safety procedures but spelled out obligatory product ranges, mandated ingredients and amounts, and specified preparation techniques in minute detail. In the USSR, regulations for industrially prepared food were laid out in *Sovstandardy*, the Soviet Food Code. Bulgaria, as Jung (this volume) tells us, had a similar food code. Standards in the USSR even extended as far as restaurant food, which, as Stas Shectman (this volume) explains, had to be prepared to the specifications laid down in the *sbornik retseptur*, a legally mandated set of recipes for use in public catering. These codes wove bureaucrats, public health officials, managers, workers, and consumers together into a net of power that allowed the state to control people's working lives and enter into the micro-spaces of domestic life.

The point was primarily to make people rely increasingly on the state sector for their daily diets and thus bind them more tightly to the political realm. This was never fully accomplished, of course: chronic shortage meant that home plots and the gray market in agricultural goods were necessary to feed the population. But highly processed "state food" became a regular staple in people's diets, and a Soviet cuisine played an important role in the lifestyle of *Homo Sovieticus*. The value of this food was often as symbolic as it was nutritive. Jenny Smith (2008) uses the case of Soviet ice cream to show how standardized individually wrapped frozen treats came to symbolize the socialist state's care for its population. Providing ice cream to the Eastern bloc was no mean feat: at the end of World War II there was not a single commercial ice cream freezer in the USSR and probably very few in the satellite states. Building the production infrastructure necessary to make and distribute ice cream commercially was enormous. It required not only giant industrial freezers but also freezer trucks, small retail freezers in local grocery shops, and dry-ice–cooled pushcart freezers for sales on the street. But by 1970 a delimited range of mass-produced ice creams was available in every town and village in the Eastern bloc—an amazing accomplishment achieved mostly through Soviet science rather than imported technology (Smith 2008:151). The reason for this massive investment in what might otherwise be seen as a frivolous item was political: in a system with few luxuries, ice cream bars were presented as a preview of the more joyful, more comfortable, and sweeter life that state socialism was building. It was a blatant concession to a population dissatisfied by chronic shortage of other retail goods. Ice cream marked the socialist allocation of fun. It was a standardized, industrialized, mass-produced kind of fun, but by making this icy pleasure available to almost every citizen in the region, socialist states attempted to forge a relationship between state and citizen based not only on coercion but on persuasion, care, and pleasure. As Smith (2008: 148) writes, "In the postwar Soviet Union the state wagered that its political legitimacy and social stability would derive at least in part from access it could provide for its citizens to everyday luxuries such as ice cream."

All sorts of luxury-branded consumer products—most important among them food and beverages—forged new links between the state and its worker/consumer/citizens as socialism went on. True, in the early years of state socialism, particularly in the USSR, many food products were sold as unbranded commodities, valuable only as a utilitarian means of delivering nutrition. Bread, cheese, milk, eggs, flour, and so on, were often sold as pure use values, without brand names, fancy labels, or advertising images (Manning 2007), because official Soviet ideology saw branding and advertising as a way to dupe consumers and create desires for items people did not need (Kessler 2000·195). But as early as the 1950s, luxury food and beverage items with brands linking them to local place names and heroic historical personages were rolling out of state socialist factories (Yurchak 2006). In the USSR cigarettes, chocolates, cognacs, and vodka were given brand names such as *Kazbek* (the name of a mountain), *Kosmos* (a reference to the Soviet space program), and *Stiuardessa*. There was Krakus ham (a figure from a Polish folktale), BoboFrut juice, Szeged paprika (a place name), and Pick salami. In each case the brand name marked the product as a "common luxury" (Gronow 2003) and set it apart from the domain of basic needs. Following Hessler (2004), Yurchak argues that these common luxuries were tied to the notion of *kul'turnost'*, or culturedness, which was part of the state campaign to colonize and reform everyday life. Through brands and their relationship to *kul'turnost'*, the state could make demands on citizens' public comportment and private habits (Manning 2007); it could arrange potentially rebellious consumers into stable orders of value in which, by being "cultured," for example, or having fun in an un-fun regime by consuming state-produced ice cream, consumers could express their distinctiveness from the proletariat without actually threatening the state.

Thus food was a primary means through which socialist states regulated the citizenry. Yet for all the rigors of central plans and socialist standards, the state's control was always only partial. Peasants were notorious for evading state quotas and for hiding crops and animals to consume themselves or sell on gray markets. (As one Georgian farmer told me, "We had two kinds of sheep here: private sheep, and state sheep. But oddly enough the wolves only ever ate the state sheep.") Although the state standards on the books would appear to dictate fully which goods were produced and how, chronic shortages meant that ingredients were often substituted, amounts called for in recipes were shorted, and production methods were changed to cope with broken machinery and the inevitable need to "storm," or work furiously once all the inputs had finally been gathered (Dunn 2004; cf. Burawoy and Lukaćs 1994). Workers stole time from regimes of factory discipline and materials from the shop floor. Retail clerks hid goods for special customers and slacked off while customers were waiting. Customers responded by engaging in complex interpersonal relationships to jump queues, by buying products directly from peasant producers on gray markets, and by smuggling valued Western products. For all its draconian appearance, state control of the population via the food system was punctured by holes that allowed some measure of individual freedom and ingenuity, even if the necessity of these workarounds was annoying and labor-intensive.

As patchy as it was, state control of the food system was meaningful regulatory power. Whether allocating the right or duty to make food through collectivization, moving peasants into new regional centers to work in food-processing factories, allocating food to consumers through ration tickets, holding people in long lines to buy food (Verdery 1996), or placating the population with everyday luxuries, the food system was a primary nexus through which state policy and state power were translated into everyday experiences and people's bodies. Food was the medium through which differential relationships to the state—inequalities of class, gender, and ethnicity—were most commonly articulated, as some people got more and better food than others. Food and state power were intimately entwined, not only at the point of production but through the regulation of consumption practices and habits. The socialist "parent state," as Verdery (1996) has called it, built its relationship to its citizen-children as many parents do: by feeding them.

Alimentary Forms of Social Life: Regulation after Socialism

The essays in this volume use Eastern Europe's history of alimentary relationships between states and citizens as an important backdrop to the studies of food in postsocialism. Because food was a primary means for the state to regulate peasants, industry, and consumers in the socialist period, the essays here track transformations in food systems to portray the ways in which these groups are regulated today. This means, necessarily, rejecting simplistic assumptions about how market democracies free producers from constraints or free consumers to choose from a world of goods. Instead, the volume authors ask, "How were these people regulated before, and how are they regulated differently today?" They answer these questions by focusing on people embedded in particular agroindustrial sectors.

Since 1989 new commodity chains have been launched, and Eastern Europeans now have regular access to fresh fruits, vegetables, and other products nonexistent in socialist times, from avocados to arugula. Food processors are incorporating new flavors into packaged foods, and Eastern European firms now make juices, candies, and ice creams in flavors such as kiwi, guava, and passion fruit. As Eastern European consumers buy microwaves and freezers and build kitchens with more storage space, the market for processed food has exploded. Between 2000 and 2006 alone, the Eastern European market for frozen food grew 38.4 percent—an astronomical rate of growth for any product category (Research and Markets 2007). Eastern Europe is the fastest growing beverage market in the world, with the consumption of alcoholic and nonalcoholic drinks combined now almost 45 liters per person per year (*Entrepreneur* 2007). There has been an explosion of restaurants offering foreign cuisines in almost every town across the region. In the early 1990s ethnic restaurants were so unprecedented that when the first Taco Bell opened in Warsaw, the restaurant glossed burritos as *naleśniki meksykańskie,* or Mexican blini. Today consumers in Warsaw, Moscow, Prague, and other Eastern European cities have a plethora of Italian, Indian, Chinese, and other restaurants from which to choose, including one called Qchnia Artystyczna in Warsaw, which offers "postmodern cuisine," a Polish version of molecular gastronomy.

This wealth of new eating opportunities comes from a radically transformed infrastructure. The European Bank for Reconstruction and Development, the development agency most active in European agribusiness, has invested millions of Euros in updating socialist-era firms such as Poland's Hortex, which received U.S.$53 million and is now one of the top three beverage producers in the region, or Serbia's Soko Šark, a chocolatier that received U.S.$10 million. Multinational firms such as America's Smithfield, the world's largest producer of pork (Dunn 2005) or France's Groupe Danone have updated Eastern European factories with new capital, new machinery, and new product lines. Managers in these firms have also been provided with intellectual capital, including knowledge of logistics, processing technologies, and methods of packaging that make them equals of their Western counterparts.

What does this mean for people's relationship to new forms of power and regulation? First and foremost, new forms of food production link the people who make food to both state and non-state forms of regulation in surprisingly restrictive ways. As Zsuzsa Gille shows in this volume, new forms of standardization such as the EU-mandated Hazards Analysis of Critical Control Points (HACCP) programs, increased the costs of production and transformed the ways in which people performed everyday jobs in the food business (see also Dunn 2005). Where many workers assumed that privatization and the demise of the Soviet-era food ministries would have made enterprises less regulated, to their surprise regulation was even tighter than before. The reason was a transformation in the nature of the state in Eastern Europe from one rooted in the Party and in ministerial institutions to a composite state made up not only of government offices but also of firms, NGOs, and supranational institutions including the European Union and the World Health Organization (see Li 2005). Gille's essay in this volume on Hungarian paprika demonstrates dramatically the operations of this new, neoliberal form of governance. Whereas once the Hungarian state would have enforced phytosanitary laws to eliminate aflatoxins and ochratoxins in Hungarian paprika, today the healthfulness and sanitation of the product depends far more on a combination of EU regulations and changes in tariffs and trade barriers—which, paradoxically, makes the product less safe. The desire for quality and standardization that EU membership evoked in consumers leads producers to import more colorful paprika from Brazil and Spain, and label it as a Hungarian product. But the Brazilian and Spanish peppers are laden with carcinogens, thus making the more standardized, "higher-quality" product a greater health hazard than paprika produced under state socialism. As Gille persuasively argues, the dispersion of regulatory authority from the nation state to supranational and subnational entities —a combination of the EU's Food Safety Commission and the firms themselves—led, in effect, to looser norms and hazardous food.

The paprika case shows that stricter regulation does not always lead to improved outcomes in health, product quality, or the taste of the product. Although consumers are not always directly aware of the structural reasons why this is so, clearly many of them have an inchoate sense of that paradox. Neringa Klumbytė's investigation of the surprising success of "Soviet"-brand sausages plainly shows that some consumers perceive unmistakably the irony of the negative effects of neoliberal regulation. Although during the Cold War "Europe" and "the West" meant high-quality products and "Soviet" and "the East" were codes for "low-quality trash," Klumbytė found that consumers of meat products now held the "Soviet" brand in much higher esteem. One firm's attempts to use the brand name "Euro" to indicate high technology, innovation, trust, and value failed, whereas their competitors' "Soviet"-brand sausages were associated with natural, tasty, high quality meat free of cheap additives and fillers. This rosy image probably overstates the actual quality and safety of meat produced during the Soviet era. Nonetheless, it functions as an effective critique of the new modes of power that shape not only food but the people who make it and eat it.

As strongly as this newfound neoliberal "freedom" regulates food producers and consumers, the people outside the regulatory system face an even grimmer situation. Mincyte's essay (this volume) on farmers who produce and distribute raw milk in Lithuania is a case in point. Raw milk is a symbol that flouts every bureaucratic and technical method the EU uses to regulate food safety and quality. The EU depends on farm-to-table tracking, pasteurization, microbial testing, and extensive paper records on every producer and lot, whereas the raw milk distributed by rural farmers in urban parking lots is uncertified, unpasteurized, untested, and undocumented. Customers who buy this milk consider it more natural and more healthful precisely because it comes from a distribution system that relies on face-to-face interaction and trust between producers and consumers rather than on standards and auditing. These consumers see raw milk as the tangible result of peasant *metis* rather than bureaucratic *techne* (see Friedberg 2004 for a parallel case in Africa). Providing this milk, as Mincyte argues, gives the women who make it a sense of autonomy and power. They gain independence both from patriarchal structures of power and from the EU's bureaucratic regulation. Mincyte's milk producers are not alone in seeking black markets in agricultural goods as a way to evade state-sponsored regulatory systems: in Poland, EU health and safety regulations have forced small-scale village slaughterhouses to close, leading small-holder farmers to butcher their hogs outside any system of formal regulation and sell the meat from their cars, much as Mincyte's milk producers do. In Georgia, makers of smoked whitefish seek to evade both taxation and government regulations on production, and so choose to sell their products in illicit markets—a practice contributing to the widespread incidence of botulism (Varma et al. 2004).

This points to a key insight expressed by the essays in this volume: that the new regulatory regimes in Eastern Europe are spatially uneven. The EU, for example, may posit the idea that its regulations blanket the new accession states as well as any of the nearby countries seeking to export to the EU's lucrative markets. In doing so, regulators claim to be creating a new "technological zone," or a zone of qualification in which technical standards are harmonized in order to let goods and people flow easily across space (Barry 2006). The ethnographies in this book, however, challenge the notion that neoliberal regulation covers all social space evenly. As Gille and Mincyte show by examining the ways that food is actually produced and consumed, neoliberal power is as patchy as was its state socialist predecessor. Just as they did under state socialism, people exploit this unevenness to eke out a living and also to gain the social and psychological rewards that accrue from outfoxing the rules.

New Forms of Inequality: Turnips and Mangos; or, the Chinese in Every Hungaricum

A most significant aspect that the anthropology of food reveals about the new Eastern Europe is the multiplicity of ways that inequality is produced. The grades and standards and regulations that create the rough network of power engage producers and consumers in markedly different ways, which often ranks them in a hierarchy of value (Goldman, n.d.; Friedberg 2004). At the largest scale this is a geographically variable ranking, with producers and consumers from one place considered more valuable than producers and consumers in another. The EUROP system of meat grading, for example, classes pork products in a supposedly objective manner, with "E" signifying the highest grade of meat and "P" the lowest. However, these grades are almost immediately overlaid onto geography, as "E" grade meat is shipped to lucrative markets in Germany and "P" grade meat is sent to economically poorer Ukraine. The implication is clear: German consumers are more worthy of higher-quality products than are their Ukrainian counterparts. As Klumbytė points out in this volume, these kinds of food-related grading practices are parts of a "geo-politics of taste." By reading how institutions and consumers rate different food products, and by understanding their systems of preference, we can read the geographical, political, and gustatory orders in which the people who make and consume food are embedded (see, for example, how Jung, in this book's first essay, does so for Bulgarian consumers of industrially produced canned goods). Some consumers, however, contest mappings that make Eastern Europeans into second-rate consumer/citizens. They reverse the implicit hierarchy, as do the consumers Klumbytė says prefer "Soviet" over "Euro" sausages. Alternatively, as Gille shows, Eastern Euro-peans create new spatial hierarchies of value in which they and their products are given symbolic value by being contrasted to Others who are seen as even less valuable. Hungarian producers, for example, extend the hierarchies of geography outside Europe and constitute a symbolic value for "Hungarian" products by contrasting them to cheap mass-produced "Chinese" products destined for consumers who are less discerning and less wealthy. These hierarchies are only intelligible as defined by mutually constituting Others: as Gille says, every Hungaricum must have a trace of Chinese in it. These symbolic representations of the geopolitics of taste, then, are a means of working out not only new culinary statuses but new global cultural orders of power and value extending far beyond food.

Similarly new agro-culinary orders reflect and produce domestic social hierarchies. The most striking one, of course, is class. Class poses a par-ticular conundrum in Eastern Europe, because so much of the language of class and inequality has been made illegitimate by the collapse of Com-munism. Food, however, provides a way of both marking the existence of class and contesting it. Klumbytė's example of the so-called turnips is a case in point. New elites in Lithuania try to label working-class opponents of Europeanization as "turnips," the quintessential root vegetable of state socialism. These "turnips" are the same class of people that Mincyte describes as the producers and consumers of milk made outside the EU's systems of regulation: the rural, the poor, and the elderly. The new elites accuse the "turnips" not only of embracing a backward-looking populism but of being stumbling blocks themselves to a new European modernity. We might think of the "turnips" not just as objectively existing social classes—which they certainly are—but also as exaggerated caricatures that new elites draw as their own antitheses. I have suggested, jokingly, that we refer to Eastern European nouveaux riches as "mangos." The mango was unavailable under socialism, is a key flavor in many of the fashionable foods and drinks developed in the postsocialist period, is overvalued precisely because it must be imported, and is sold at a cost dramatically higher than that of fresher, healthier local foods like black currants or gooseberries even though it tastes worse. Though a bit spiteful, the joke points out how dichotomizing discourses about class have become, and, as Caldwell and Shectman (this volume) both point out, how much they are mobilized through discourses of distinction, taste, and culinary choice in the postsocialist context.

Yet as hard as the mangos try to portray themselves as European, forward-looking, and modern by contrasting themselves to the turnips, the dichotomy does not hold. The mangos may wish to portray food produced to EU standards as legible, transparent, trustworthy, and modern compared to the food made under state socialism, which they see as backward because its production process was unknown and its producers untrustworthy (Jung, this volume). But that polarization is being increasingly disturbed by revelations about un-transparent and unhealthy practices in the new capitalist food sector. The food scares plaguing Europe, including Mad Cow Disease, tainted Coca-Cola, fears of GMOs, and a German meat merchant who distributed 120 tons of tainted meat, have led Eastern Europeans to question their food supply in the same ways that Western Europeans now do. Suddenly the "transparency" of capitalism is thrown into question, and the much more immediately visible labor processes of state socialism are revalued as being more transparent and more accountable, and hence more likely to have produced healthy and safe food than new elites portrayed them to be (see also Burawoy 1992 on the transparency of labor in socialism). Whether this leads to a concomitant revaluing of the *people* still associated with state socialism, the "turnips," is an open question. But the debate shows that questions of what constitutes modernity, which of us are modern, and what the correct path to modernity is remains unresolved.

Conclusion

What does anthropology ultimately offer to the study of Eastern Europe? Why study food, in particular? The essays in this volume answer these questions by fundamentally disrupting the narratives of triumphalist modernity that once animated discussions of the "transition" in Eastern Europe. Rather than assuming that only one path to modernity is possible, a path dictated by the European Union, the essays here show the multitude of ways that Eastern Europeans are forging new and unique politics, economies, and societies that make use of their own histories and cultural schemas as well as imported ones. Food is key in making these new social and economic formations. As a nexus between tradition and modernity, rural producers and urban consumers, pastoral landscapes and industrial-processing facilities, food has become a substance in which people can hold contradictions simultaneously without deciding in favor of either side of the dichotomy. Through the materiality of food, Eastern Europeans can localize and domesticate international standards for food production; they can reactivate aspects of socialist modernity that seem to echo European or global standards and, in so doing, refute the simple narratives of historical progression that animate neoliberal development plans; and, finally, they can make localized forms of globalized goods or globalized means of making local goods.

These macro-level changes are echoed in people's daily lives and their beliefs about themselves. As Jung tells us in her essay:

> *Standardization itself is acquiring different meanings based on changing ideas of the effects of control and reliability on quality. It is not simply the state or even the system [e.g., the capitalist system based on market competition] that acts as the agent of control and the object of reliability. The agent of control is more ambiguous. . . . [consumers] recognize their own ability to choose certain brands that produce reliable and affordable products that taste good without necessarily associating these brands with certain interests. As consumers, they execute their own control over food consumption.*

This sentiment is echoed by those who declare, "I am my own government," and who believe in their own capacities as producers and consumers to regulate the food they make and eat (see Mincyte, this volume). Although these consumers perhaps overstate their own regulatory powers, they make larger claims about their countries' abilities to regulate and control their own food systems in ways that fit local values and historical experiences.

In sum, the anthropology of food shows how Eastern Europeans are using food to create new modernities. As the age of postsocialism passes, and as Eastern European countries continue to forge new relationships with global markets and institutions, they will become increasingly defined by the varying contours of the new modernity they create rather than by their shared socialist past. By using the study of food in everyday life as a lens, anthropologists are well poised to see this new modernity by tracing new hybrids that extend well beyond the socialist/capitalist dichotomy.

NOTE

1. My thanks to Ewa Hauser for her memories of Krakus hams and to Katherine Verdery for her recollections of Sibiu salami.

REFERENCES CITED

Barry, Andrew. 2006. "Technological Zones." *European Journal of Social Theory* 9(2): 239–253.

Burawoy, Michael, and Janoś Lukaćs. 1994. *The Radiant Past: Ideology and Reality in Hungary's Road to Capitalism.* Chicago: University of Chicago Press.

Dunn, Elizabeth Cullen. 2005. "Standards and Person Making in East Central Europe." In *Global Anthropologies: Governmentality, Technology, Ethics,* ed. Aihwa Ong and Stephen Collier, pp. 173–193. London: Blackwell.

———. 2008. "Postsocialist Spores: Disease, Bodies and the State in the Republic of Georgia." *American Ethnologist* 35 (2): 243–258.

Entrepreneur. 2007. "Eastern European Beverage Sales Rise." Available at http://www.entrepreneur.com/tradejournals/article/111747319.html (accessed November 3, 2008).

Fine, Ben. 1994. "Towards A Political Economy of Food." *International Political Review* 1:519–545.

Fitzpatrick, Sheila. 1994. *Stalin's Peasants: Resistance and Survival in the Russian Village after Collectivization.* Oxford: Oxford University Press.

Friedberg, Susanne. 2004. *French Beans and Food Scares: Culture and Commerce in an Anxious Age.* Oxford: Oxford University Press.

Gille, Zsuzsa. 2003. "The Pig That Died for Europe: Making Hungarians into Europeans." Paper presented at EUtopias conference, University of Illinois, Urbana-Champaign.

Goldman, Julie. n.d. "The World According to Fruit." Unpublished manuscript.

Gronow, Jukka. 2003. *Caviar with Champagne: Common Luxury and the Ideals of the Good Life in Stalin's Russia.* Oxford: Berg.

Hessler, Julie. 2004. *A Social History of Soviet Trade: Trade Policy, Retail Practice, and Consumption, 1917–1953.* Princeton, N.J.: Princeton University Press.

Li, Tania Murray. 2005. "Beyond 'the State' and Failed Schemes." *American Anthropologist* 107 (3): 383–394.

Manning, Paul. 2007. "'Our Beer': Ethnographic Brands in Postsocialist Georgia." *American Anthropologist* 109(4): 626–641.

Marsden, Terry, Richard Munton, Neil Ward, and Sarah Whatmore. 1996. "Agricultural Geography and the Political Economy Approach: A Review." *Economic Geography* 72(4): 361–375.

Mintz, Sidney. 1981. *Sweetness and Power: The Place of Sugar in Modern History.* London: Penguin.

——. 1996. *Tasting Food, Tasting Freedom: Excursions into Eating, Culture and the Past.* Boston: Beacon.

Nove, Alec. 1988. "Soviet Agriculture: The Brezhnev Legacy and Gorbachev's Cure." RAND Corporation Occasional Papers. Available at http://www.rand.org/pubs/joint_reports-soviet/JRS03/ (accessed November 11, 2008).

Research and Markets. 2007. "Frozen Food in Eastern Europe to 2011." Available at http://www.researchandmarkets.com/reports/c88772 (accessed November 3, 2008).

Scott, James C. 1998. *Seeing Like a State: How Certain Schemes to Improve the Human Condition Have Failed.* New Haven, Conn.: Yale University Press.

Smith, Jenny Leigh. 2008. "Empire of Ice Cream: How Life Got Sweeter in the Postwar Soviet Union." In *Food Chains: from Farmyard to Shopping Cart,* ed. Warren Belasco and Roger Horowitz, pp. 142–157. Philadelphia: University of Pennsylvania Press.

Varma, J. K., G. Katsitadze, M. Moiscrafishvili, T. Zardiashvili, M. Chokheli, N. Tarkhashvili, et al. 2004. "Foodborne Botulism in the Republic of Georgia." Emerging Infectious Diseases. Available at http://www.cdc.gov/ncidod/EID/vol10no9/03-0806.htm (accessed March 15, 2009).

Verdery, Katherine. 1996. *What Was Socialism and What Comes Next?* Princeton, N.J.: Princeton University Press.

Watts, Michael, and Peter Little, eds. 1997. *Globalizing Agro-Food.* London: Routledge.

Wegren, Stephen K. 2005. *Russia's Food Policies and Globalization.* Lanham, Md.: Lexington Books.

Yurchak, Alexei. 2006. *Everything Was Forever, Until It Was No More: The Last Soviet Generation.* Berkeley: University of California Press.

CONTRIBUTORS

MELISSA L. CALDWELL is Associate Professor of Anthropology at the University of California, Santa Cruz. Her research focuses on changing economic conditions in Russia, with particular attention to food systems. She has written on such topics as fast food and globalization, food nationalism, culinary tourism, natural foods, food insecurity, and food-relief programs. She is the author of *Not by Bread Alone: Social Support in the New Russia* and editor, with James L. Watson, of *The Cultural Politics of Food and Eating*. Her articles have appeared in *Ethnos; Journal of Consumer Culture;* and *Food, Culture & Society*. She has just completed a book on *dacha* life in contemporary Russia.

ELIZABETH CULLEN DUNN is Associate Professor of Geography and International Affairs at the University of Colorado, Boulder. She has worked on food and power since 1993, when she spent sixteen months making baby food in one of the first factories privatized after the fall of the Berlin Wall. Her book on food, class, and neoliberal regulation, *Privatizing Poland,* won the 2005 Ed A. Hewett Award for the political economy of Eastern Europe—the first time a non-economist has ever won that prize. Dunn has also worked on food and industrial consolidation in the Polish pork industry, and on the economic origins of foodborne illness in the Republic of Georgia. She is currently researching how development agencies attempt to create value chains for dairy products in the Republic of Georgia, and how this transforms (or fails to transform) farmers' beliefs about the economy. Of all the foods of Eastern Europe, she likes *khinkali* the best.

ZSUZSA GILLE is Associate Professor of Sociology at the University of Illinois at Urbana-Champaign. She is the author of *From the Cult of Waste to the Trash Heap of History: The Politics of Waste in Socialist and Postsocialist Hungary* (Indiana University Press, 2007); co-author of *Global Ethnography: Forces, Connections and Imaginations in a Postmodern World*; and editor (with Maria Todorova) of *Postcommunist Nostalgia*. She is also the guest editor of the *Slavic Review*'s thematic cluster on Nature, Culture, and Power In Eastern Europe, Russia and Eurasia (March 2009). She is presently working on the manuscript "Paprika, Pigs, and Predestination in Hungary: The Cultural Politics of the Eastern Enlargement of the European Union."

YUSON JUNG is a research associate at the Center for East European, Russian/Eurasian Studies, University of Chicago, and teaches as a lecturer in the Department of Anthropology, Harvard University. Her research and teaching interests focus on consumption, globalization, postsocialism, and the anthropology of the state. She has been conducting ethnographic research in Bulgaria since 1999 and is currently working on her book manuscript "Balkan Blues: The Poverty of the State."

NERINGA KLUMBYTĖ is Assistant Professor of Anthropology at Miami University. Her research interests lie at the intersection of political and economic anthropology, postsocialism and postcolonialism, and Eurasian and European Union studies. She has published on issues of identity and politics, nostalgia, consumption and food, morality and citizenship, as well as nationalism and integration into the European Union.

KATHERINE METZO is Assistant Professor of Anthropology at the University of North Carolina at Charlotte. Her research centers on the transformation and informal transmission of local sacred ecological knowledge and how this knowledge impacts institutionalized histories and heritage conservation in the Lake Baikal World Heritage Site.

DIANA MINCYTE is a sociologist and visiting assistant professor in the Department of Advertising at the University of Illinois, Urbana-Champaign. Her research focuses on land-use politics, environmental health, social inequalities, informal economies, and gender politics, all in the context of globalization. Her work has been published in *Slavic Review; Cultural Studies—Critical Methodologies;* the *Journal of Sports and Social Issues;* and several edited volumes.

MARION NESTLE is the Paulette Goddard Professor in the Department of Nutrition, Food Studies, and Public Health at New York University, which she chaired from 1988 to 2003. She also holds appointments as Professor of Sociology at NYU and Visiting Professor of Nutritional Sciences at Cornell University. Her degrees include a Ph.D. in molecular biology and an M.P.H. in public health nutrition, both from the University of California, Berkeley. She has held faculty positions at Brandeis University and the UCSF School of Medicine. From 1986 to 1988, she was the senior nutrition policy advisor in the Department of Health and Human Services and managing editor of the *1988 Surgeon General's Report on Nutrition and Health.* Her research examines scientific, economic, and social influences on food choice. She is the author of three prize-winning books: *Food Politics: How the Food Industry Influences Nutrition and Health; Safe Food: Bacteria, Biotechnology, and Bioterrorism;* and *What to Eat.* Her latest book is *Pet Food Politics: The Chihuahua in the Coal Mine.* Her web site is www.foodpolitics.com. She writes the "Food Matters" column for the *San Francisco Chronicle.*

STAS SHECTMAN is a Ph.D. candidate in visual anthropology at Temple University, where he is currently writing his dissertation on professional cooks, the food-service industry, and culinary culture in the context of globalization and social, cultural, and economic change in post-Soviet Moscow. In addition to his ethnographic research in Moscow, his interests focus on the anthropology of consumption, media, performance, and globalization. He has been published in *American Anthropologist.* As a freelance writer and journalist, his work has been published in various magazines and newspapers, including *The Moscow Times* and *Russia!*

INDEX

Milton Keynes UK
Ingram Content Group UK Ltd.
UKHW020946110724
445408UK00005B/213